# Jefferson's Western Explorations

## Discoveries made in exploring
## the Missouri, Red River and Washita
## 1806

To our friend Elliott
all our best,

*Doug Erickson*

*Murray Shor*

*Paul Merchant*

*(clockwise, from top left)*
William Clark, Dr. John Sibley, Meriwether Lewis, William Dunbar.
*Images courtesy of Lewis & Clark College Special Collections.*

# Jefferson's Western Explorations

Discoveries made in exploring the
Missouri, Red River and Washita

by Captains Lewis and Clark,
Doctor Sibley, and William Dunbar,
and compiled by Thomas Jefferson.

THE NATCHEZ EDITION, 1806

A facsimile, edited with an introduction by
DOUG ERICKSON, JEREMY SKINNER,
AND PAUL MERCHANT

THE ARTHUR H. CLARK COMPANY
Spokane, Washington
2004

THE ARTHUR H. CLARK COMPANY
P.O. Box 14707
Spokane, WA 99214

ISBN 0-87062-335-4

Library of Congress Cataloging-in-Publication Data
United States. President (1801-1809 : Jefferson)
 [Message from the President of the United States]
 Jefferson's western explorations : discoveries made in exploring the
Missouri, Red River and Washita by Captains Lewis and Clark, Doc-
tor Sibley, and William Dunbar, and compiled by Thomas Jefferson ;
the Natchez edition, 1806 ; a facsimile / edited with an introduction by
Doug Erickson, Jeremy Skinner, and Paul Merchant.— 1st ed.
     p. cm.
 Includes bibliographical references and index.
 Originally published: Natchez, Miss. : Andrew Marschalk, 1806.
 ISBN 0-87062-335-4 (alk. paper)
 1. Lewis and Clark Expedition (1804-1806) 2. West (U.S.)—Discovery and exploration. I. Jefferson, Thomas, 1743–1826. II. Lewis, Meriwether, 1774–1809. III. Clark, William, 1770–1838. IV. Sibley, John,
1757–1837. V. Dunbar, William, 1749–1810. VI. Erickson, D. M. (Doug
M.) VII. Skinner, Jeremy. VIII. Merchant, Paul. IX. Title.
 F592.3 2004
 917.804'2—dc22
                                    2004023507

# Contents

# ❧ Illustrations and Maps

## *Maps*
### (*in pocket at rear*)

To ROGER WENDLICK,
IRVING ANDERSON,
ELDON CHUINARD,
and GEORGE TWENEY,
who all dreamed of possessing
the original of this rare text.

# ❧ Acknowledgments

Special thanks are due to George A. Miles, Curator, Yale Collection of Western Americana, The Beinecke Rare Book and Manuscript Collection, Yale University Library and his staff, for generous hospitality and assistance in the preparation of this volume, and in particular for permission to reproduce in facsimile one of the Library's three copies of the 1806 Natchez printing of *Discoveries Made in Exploring the Missouri, Red River, and Washita.* Thanks also to the staff of the British Library for their prompt supply of a reproduction of their copy, to Christine Campbell of the British Library Picture Library for her kind permission to reproduce a small number of pages, and to R. J. Goulden of the British and Early Printed Collections for a detailed description of the volume. We are grateful also to the staff of the New York Public Library's Rare Book Room and H. George Fletcher, Director of Special Collections, for explanation of the provenance marks on their copy. The staff of the Library of Congress were most helpful in supplying images of the maps in their possession. We are most grateful also to Elizabeth Freebairn, Reference Librarian, The Roger & Julia Baskes Department of Special Collections, The Newberry Library, Chicago; Anne Salsich, Reference Division, Western Reserve Historical Library and Archives, Cleveland; Jack Robertson, Director, and Bryan Craig, at The Jefferson Library at Monticello; Wendy Richter, Head of Special Collections at Ouachita Baptist University, Arkansas; Kristina Gray Perez, Archivist, Missouri Historical Society; and the library staff at Lindenwood College, Missouri, who all responded generously to provenance and condition inquiries and supplied materials. We are greatly indebted to these special collections librarians for their expertise and assistance. Our own staff at the Watzek Library of Lewis & Clark College, in particular James J. Kopp, Director; Roger Wendlick, Collector in Residence; and staff members Laura Ayling, Jenny Bornstein, Deborah Bosket, Linda Dunne, and Jeremy McWilliams, have all been supportive.

The following scholars have responded generously to inquiries: Tom Edwards, Professor Emeritus, Whitman College; Dan Flores, University of Montana, Missoula; James Fox, Head of Special Collections, University of Oregon; Tami Goldman, The Missouri Historical Society; Fred Gowans, Professor Emeritus, Brigham Young University; John Hawk, Head of Special Collections, University of San Francisco; Normandy Helmer, University of Oregon; Candace Lein-Hayes, National Archives, Pacific Northwest Region; Robert Cox, Keeper of Manuscripts, and Martin Levitt, Librarian, The American Philosophical Society, Philadelphia; Rick McCourt, Curator of Botany, The Academy of Sciences, Philadelphia; Carla Rickerson, Head of Manuscripts, Special Collections, University of Washington, Seattle; Patricia Schechter, Portland State University; and Richard Smith, National Archives, College Park, Maryland.

Many members of the bibliographic community have kindly supported the project, offered general advice and answers to specific questions, and supplied books and materials. These include: Dr. James Kidd, Portland, Oregon; Justin Phillips, Bloomsury Book Auctions, London; William Reese, William Reese Company, New Haven. Special thanks to Roger and Ilse Roberts, Hawthorne Boulevard Books, Portland, for suggesting that we submit this volume to the Arthur H. Clark Company. Their friendship and encouragement have sustained us over many years.

Warm thanks are also due to Charles Seluzicki, Portland; Nils Thingvall, Denver; Dr. Jim Walker, Eugene, Oregon; Mark Wessel and Michael Lieberman, Wessel and Lieberman Booksellers, Seattle; and Vic Zoschak, Tavistock Books, Alameda, California.

We acknowledge the help of Elizabeth Palmer and Adam Seluzicki in the preparation of research materials, and of Phoebe Skinner in the digital editing of facsimiles. Finally, grateful thanks to Robert A. Clark, president of the Arthur H. Clark Company, for his initial enthusiasm for this facsimile edition and meticulous care in its production, and to editor Ariane C. Smith for her expert skills in bringing this complicated volume to print.

DOUG ERICKSON
JEREMY SKINNER
PAUL MERCHANT

# ❧ Preface

The information age is a descriptor most often viewed as applying to the rise of computer technology and the development of the internet in the late twentieth century. As apt as that designation is, the roots of the information age can be traced to another historical era, commonly known as the Enlightenment. It was during this age that the United States itself was formed in concept and in reality, and information and its dissemination were key aspects of these developments. As the United States matured, the quest for information was critical to the continuing political, economic, and cultural evolvement of the young nation. With the arrival of the nineteenth century and the presidency of Thomas Jefferson, this quest for information reached new frontiers, literally and metaphorically, and the Lewis and Clark Expedition was the epitome of this quest. From Jefferson's letter of instructions to Meriwether Lewis in 1803 to the official publication of the journals of the expedition in 1814, the importance of the information gathering and dissemination of this monumental event is apparent.

Similarly, with the arrival of the bicentennial observation of the Lewis and Clark Expedition, the quest for information on the Corps of Discovery and its impacts and influences has again reached new levels of interest and enthusiasm. Assisted by the tools of the current information age, more data are regularly becoming available to scholars, students, and anyone with an interest to explore a wide range of details about the expedition. Much of this information, however, still centers on the writings of Lewis, Clark, and a few other members of the Corps of Discovery, as well as reports, official and not, that were made of these adventures. Of major importance in making that information available has been the quest of such individuals as Eldon Chuinard, George Tweney, Irving Anderson, and Roger Wendlick, who compiled some of the finest collections of printed materials on the Lewis and Clark Expedition. Through these endeavors, in turn, it has been possible to pull together a broad reflection on the information output of and about the expedition, recently compiled as *The Literature of the Lewis and Clark Expedition: A Bibliography and Essays* (Lewis & Clark College, 2003), with informative essays by Stephen Dow Beckham and an extensive bibliography compiled by the authors of the book in hand—Doug Erickson, Jeremy Skinner, and Paul Merchant. *The Literature of the Lewis and Clark Expedition* provides a sweeping overview of the information gathered and disseminated regarding the Corps of Discovery.

Yet as exhaustive as this compilation is, and as diligent as the efforts of Chuinard, Tweney, Anderson, Wendlick, and others were in collecting the sources related to the expedition, one substantial document eluded these collectors and serves as the prize gem of the literature of the expedition. This rare and highly sought-after item is the 1806 reprint of the *Message from the President*, published in Natchez, Mississippi, in which Thomas Jefferson provided the U.S. Congress, the American people, and interested parties throughout the world with a summary not only of the Lewis and Clark Expedition but of other expeditions of the time, as well as scientific data not found in earlier printings of the *Message*. The document's value is not just in its rarity but in the wealth of information it provided—to individuals in the first decade of the nineteenth century regarding the then-unknown wildernesses, and also to those examining it two hundred years later (and beyond). The publication of this facsimile of the 1806 Natchez reprint of Jefferson's

*Message,* along with a detailed analysis of its historical and bibliographical significance, is an important contribution to the examination of not just the Lewis and Clark Expedition but the broader quest for information taking place at this time.

In many respects the 1806 *Message from the President* is a more complete glimpse through the window into the Jeffersonian view of the importance of information-gathering as the nation sought to increase its understanding about the lands recently acquired and into which it would eventually expand. The recent emphasis on the Lewis and Clark Expedition, as major as it was, overshadows other important contributions of William Dunbar, George Hunter, and John Sibley, who are included in Jefferson's report, as he viewed the territories in the southwest of importance also. The Natchez reprint of the *Message,* appearing after versions published in Washington and New York, includes extracts from Dunbar's journal not included in the earlier editions (although it omits one of the tables from these other editions). In addition, the Natchez edition includes significant botanical observations not printed in the Washington or New York editions. As such, the Natchez reprint is distinctly valuable in providing this unique information and a printed facsimile of this item is long overdue.

The value of this facsimile is enhanced because, in addition to providing the text of the Natchez edition, the authors present a historical and bibliographical analysis of the 1806 *Message from the President of the United States* and place the document in the context of Jefferson's interest in exploration of the West. They offer comparisons between the expeditions included in the *Message* and discuss the sources that assisted the leaders of these endeavors. A textual introduction follows this background information, along with an informative assessment of the location and provenance of known copies of the Natchez edition. Two valuable appendices follow the text of the *Message* itself, supplying pages from the Washington edition that were omitted in the Natchez edition and a survey of correspondence of John Sibley available at the Library of Congress. All of this provides for a complement to the document itself and further exemplifies its importance as a central element in the literature of the Lewis and Clark Expedition, as well as other explorations pivotal to the early history of the United States.

That Thomas Jefferson's *Message* serves as a cornerstone in the foundation of the early "information age" in America should be no surprise. It was during Jefferson's presidency that the Library of Congress took shape (in fact, the first books for the library arrived in Washington just weeks after his inauguration in 1801) and, after much of the original collection of the library was destroyed by the British in the War of 1812, it was Jefferson's own library that was the basis for the rebuilding of that collection. In a similar way, his 1806 *Message from the President of the United States Communicating Discoveries Made in Exploring the Missouri, Red River and Washita* can be viewed as reflecting the quest for information that served as the basis for other quests in American history.

JAMES J. KOPP
Director, Watzek Library
Lewis & Clark College

# Jefferson
## and the
## 1806 *Message* to Congress

### THE JEFFERSONIAN EXPLORATIONS

#### *Jefferson as Expedition Instigator*

Thomas Jefferson's only monograph published under his name (*Notes on the State of Virginia*, 1782)[1] set a high standard of reporting on the geography, geology, and natural history of the newly independent nation. Described as "the most knowledgeable person of his time on the geography of the western part of America,"[2] he would have been an ideal editor of a volume covering the North American continent. That book never materialized, but Jefferson's 1806 *Message from the President* brought together the most authoritative accounts of the recently acquired Louisiana Purchase, combining information from the explorations of Lewis and Clark on the Missouri, William Dunbar and George Hunter on the Ouachita,[3] and Dr. John Sibley's researches on the Red River territory into one report, introduced by Jefferson himself. As the organizational genius behind these western explorations, Jefferson was eager to publish the expedition journals.

The volume presented here in facsimile, the 1806 Natchez reprint of the *Message,* has its own important place in the publishing record. It is known as one of the rarest of all Lewis and Clark Expedition imprints, but it is unique in that it presents a revised appendix of trans-Mississippi

[1]Published in France in 1785. Surviving Jefferson texts of a more occasional character include numerous reports to Congress, published letters, and other printed materials.

[2]Benson *et al.*, 43.

[3]The modern spelling of the Ouachita is used throughout this text, except when quoting from the original *Message to Congress,* where the spelling "Washita" occurs. Neither of these spellings should be confused with the Washita River in present-day Oklahoma.

botany, developed apparently in association with Benjamin Smith Barton, but too late to be included in the *Message*'s initial Washington printing, which contained a single-page listing of plants.[4] After the return of Lewis and Clark, Barton was chosen to write a scientific overview as the third volume of the Expedition's official history, edited by Nicholas Biddle and seen through the press by Paul Allen in 1814. Barton was plagued by chronic ill health, and the third volume never appeared. The appendix in the Natchez reprint of the *Message* presents a fragment of Barton's response to the plants of Louisiana, a memorial to a pioneering American scientist who might have been the Linnæus of the American frontier. In the end his assistant Frederick Pursh published—in England—the first taxonomy of the plants of the whole continent also in 1814.[5]

Even before his presidency, Thomas Jefferson had argued strongly for exploring the western and northern boundaries of the United States where they met the lands governed by Britain, France, and Spain. In 1783 he had thought of commissioning George Rogers Clark, William's older brother, on a westward expedition, and five years later he was in discussion with André Michaux about making a transcontinental survey. One of these early journeys almost took place. In 1787 Jefferson had encouraged John Ledyard, a veteran of Cook's third voyage, who intended to walk the whole width of Russia to its Siberian coast, and then cross North America from Nootka Sound to the East Coast. The grand design came to nothing when Ledyard was arrested in Irkutsk by orders of Catherine the Great and was expelled from Russia, but its impact on Jefferson's thought is well expressed in the first biography of Ledyard:

> To a statesman like Mr Jefferson it was evident, that a large portion of that immense country, separated from the United States by no barrier of nature, would eventually be embraced in their territory. He was convinced of the propriety, therefore, of its being explored by a citizen of the United States, and regretted the fail-

[4]Benjamin Smith Barton (1766–1815) was a professor at the University of Pennsylvania and author of the first botany text published in America, *Elements of Botany* (1803).

[5]*Flora Americae Septentrionalis* by Frederick Pursh (1774–1820) describes more than three thousand species in almost five hundred genera, including over one hundred collected by Lewis and Clark, among them the genera *Lewisia* and *Clarkia*.

ure of Ledyard's attempts in his own country to engage in a voyage before the same thing had been meditated anywhere else. These views were deeply impressed on the mind of Mr Jefferson, and in them originated the journey of Lewis and Clark over land to the Pacific Ocean, twenty years afterwards, which was projected by him, and prosecuted under his auspices.[6]

Jefferson had already dispatched Lewis and Clark on their journey when Napoleon's surprising offer of the Louisiana Territory at the end of 1803 gave fresh impetus to the expedition. Uncharted and ill defined at its borders, the territory of Louisiana was understood to extend to the sources of the Mississippi's tributary rivers. Meanwhile, in southwest Louisiana Territory, there was particular interest in the large Mississippi tributary, Red River, and its watershed, including the Ouachita. Lewis and Clark were in winter quarters at the mouth of the Missouri when the Louisiana Purchase was negotiated and finalized, so that both commanders were at St. Louis in mid-March to witness the formal transfer of Louisiana to the United States. Lewis signed the official document of cession on March 9, 1804.[7] The purchase gave new meaning to the Corps of Discovery's exploration of the Missouri to its source, and to their hopes for a water route to the Pacific—the continuation of the long search for a Northwest Passage.

### Parallels Between the Jefferson Expeditions

The methodical Jefferson gave similar instructions to the leaders of all of his expeditions, ensuring as far as possible a high degree of uniformity and success in the patterns of exploration and reportage. The expeditions were all riverborne, in small boats rowed by soldiers under military command. All shared the same rigorous scientific principles, expressed in the daily logs of scientific data and the detailed journals kept by more than one member of each party. Each expedition also carried a traveling library of research materials.

[6] Jared Sparks, *The Life of John Ledyard, the American Traveller.* Cambridge: Hilliard and Brown, 1828, p. 154.

[7] See illustration in Gilman, 80.

In the famous letter of June 20, 1803, to Meriwether Lewis on the mission of the Corps of Discovery, particularly regarding the native peoples of the Mississippi and Missouri watersheds, Jefferson wrote,

> The commerce which may be carried on with the people inhabiting the line you will pursue, renders a knolege of those people important. You will therefore endeavor to make yourself acquainted, as far as a diligent pursuit of your journey shall admit, with the names of the nations & their numbers; the extent & limits of their possessions; their relations with other tribes or nations; their language, traditions, monuments; their ordinary occupations in agriculture, fishing, hunting, war, arts, & the implements for these; their food, clothing, & domestic accomodations; the diseases prevalent among them, & the remedies they use; moral & physical circumstances which distinguish them from the tribes we know; peculiarities in their laws, customs & dispositions; and articles of commerce they may need or furnish, & to what extent. And, considering the interest which every nation has in extending & strengthening the authority of reason & justice among the people around them, it will be useful to acquire what knolege you can of the state of morality, religion, & information among them; as it may better enable those who may endeavor to civilize & instruct them, to adapt their measures to the existing notions & practices of those on whom they are to operate.[8]

That Jefferson emphasized the native peoples is reflected in his 1803 Confidential Message to Congress requesting funds for commerce with the Indians,[9] and in the single sentence describing the purposes of the expedition, in the opening paragraph of the 1806 *Message*: "They were to enter into conference with the Indian nations on their route, with a view to the establishment of commerce with them." The system developed to present the new research was influenced by Antoine-Simon Le Page du Pratz's 1763 *History of Louisiana*, with its descriptions of the native inhabitants, and by Alexander Mackenzie's 1801 *Voyages*, which contained Knistenaux, Algonquin, and Chipeweyan vocabularies while surveying (in the words of its title page) the

[8] Jackson, *Letters*, item 47. The letter is reprinted in the Biddle-Allen *History of the Expedition* (1814), pp. xiii–xxi, and in the Coues reprint of that edition, pp. xxiii–xxxiii. Flores reprints (pp. 319–25) Jefferson's very similar letter of instructions to Thomas Freeman.

[9] January 18, 1803, first printed in 1828 in the *Executive Journal* for 1803, pp. 437–39; original draft transcribed in Jackson, *Letters*, item 8.

"present state of the fur trade" of North America. Benjamin Smith Barton also published vocabularies in his 1797 *New Views of the Origin of the Tribes and Nations of America*, and Jefferson supplied blank vocabulary lists to Lewis for the Missouri tribes and later to John Sibley for tribes of the early southwest.[10] The Philadelphia physician Benjamin Rush, another associate of Jefferson, Lewis, and Dunbar, had long been interested in the health of Native Americans, and supplied the Lewis and Clark Expedition with a questionnaire on the health, morals, and religion of the tribes encountered.[11]

We see a similar methodical inquiry in Jefferson's letter to Dunbar immediately following France's cession of Louisiana:

> . . . it is very important for the happiness of the country that [Congress] should possess all the information which can be obtained respecting [Louisiana], that they should make the best arrangement possible for its good government. . . . I have, therefore, sent some queries to Mr. [Daniel] Clark, of New Orleans, to be answered by such person as he shall think best qualified, and to be returned to me before the meeting of Congress; and knowing that you have turned your attention to many of the subjects, I enclose you a copy of them. . . . My wish is to have every thing, compare all together, and to do what, on the whole, I conscientiously think for the best.[12]

It was this wish to act only on the fullest intelligence that led to the systematized reports of Indian nations in William Clark's "Statistical View" and Sibley's "Historical Sketches."

The questions posed to the influential merchant Daniel Clark in New Orleans and to Dunbar in Natchez can be substantially reconstructed from the letters of response from Dunbar, on August 19 and September 29, 1803,[13] and Clark on August 18.[14] Dunbar's August reply left questions on "the population & geography of the Province" to be answered by Clark, and focused instead on the line of

[10] An early Jefferson blank vocabulary, from 1790–1792, is illustrated in Gilman, p. 217 and note, p. 379. See also Thwaites, Vol. VII (ii): following p. 409.

[11] His 1791 questionnaire to Pickering is in Rush, *Letters*, pp. 580 ff., and that of 1803 to Lewis in Jackson, *Letters*, item 38 and footnote. Another member of the American Philosophical Society (APS) interested in Indian languages was William Dunbar, who in 1809 published in the Society's *Transactions* (vol. 6, pp. 1–3) an essay "On the Language of Signs among Certain North American Indians."

[12] *A Letter from Mr. Jefferson to Mr Dunbar. Relative to the Cession of Louisiana* [July 17, 1803]. Printed with *Letter of the Hon. John Quincy Adams in Reply to a Letter of the Hon. Alexander Smyth.* Washington, D.C.: Gales & Seaton, 1828, 15–16.

[13] Rowland, 122–23, 124–25.

[14] Library of Congress, Papers of Thomas Jefferson, Jefferson to Daniel Clark, July 17, 1803, and the reply of August 18, 1803.

demarcation between Spanish and French territories. Daniel Clark's August letter promised that he

> shall by each successive Post forward such information as it is possible to procure, in obtaining which I rely greatly on the friendly dispensations of the Officers of the Spanish Government. I have by this post forwarded to the Secretary of State as exact a Manuscript map as could be procured of this Country, on which the different Posts or Settlements are delineated and numbered, and hope to have a more perfect one completed, in time to be of Service. I have joined to it some Memorandums respecting the Country hastily put together long before the news of the Cession reached us, and am happy to have so far anticipated your wishes in this particular.

The "Memorandums" may be the three-page notes on "The interior Provinces of the Kingdom of New Spain,"[15] still located among the Jefferson Papers. Finally, Dunbar's September letter dealt with the number of militia in Louisiana, the extent of Louisiana's sea coast, and the boundary line between Louisiana and Texas, still left undefined, as Dunbar notes, by the Treaty of Cession from Spain to France. The president was gathering from many sources the most accurate estimates of the boundaries, inhabitants, indigenous populations, and military strengths of the new territories, while at the same time evaluating their commercial potential and trading capacities.[16]

A similar set of objectives can be seen in Jefferson's letter of instructions to Thomas Freeman on April 14, 1804, as the Red River expedition was in its planning stages.[17] The native peoples were to be assured that "henceforth we become their fathers and friends that our first wish will be to be neighborly, friendly and useful to them and especially to carry on commerce with them on terms more reasonable and advantageous for them than any other nation ever did."[18] Most of the instructions to Freeman, especially those on topographical and natural history research, were repeated almost verbatim from those offered to Lewis:

[15] Library of Congress, Jefferson Papers, Daniel Clark's "Notes on Population of Mexico" (1803).

[16] Much of this material was included in [Sibley], *An Account of Louisiana* (1803).

[17] Jefferson to Freeman, April 14, 1804, in Flores, pp. 319–25. Compare the almost identical instructions from Jefferson to Lewis of June 20, 1803, in Jackson, *Letters*, item 47.

[18] Flores, 322.

The following objects in the Country adjacent to the rivers along which you will pass will be worthy of notice. The soil and face of the Country, the growth and vegetable productions expecially those not of the maritime states. the animals of the Country generally and especially those not known in the maritime states. the names and accounts of any which may be deemed extinct. the mineral productions most worth notice but more particularly metals limestone, gypsum pitcoal, saltpetre, rock salt and salt springs and mineral waters, noting the temperature of the last and such circumstance as may indicate their characters. Volcanic appearances. Climate, as characterized by the thermometer by the proportion of rainy cloudy and clear days, by lightning hail snow ice, by the access and recess of frost by the winds prevailing at different seasons the dates at which different plants put forth or loose their flower or leaf times of appearances of different birds, reptiles or insects. Most of these articles may be entered in a callendar or table so as to take little room or time in entering.[19]

We recognize here the impetus behind Lewis and Clark's weather journals, the meteorological tables of Sibley and Dunbar/Hunter, the meticulous description of the mineral waters at the Arkansas Hot Springs, and the extended appendix of vegetable productions of the Ouachita country and the medical properties of the Hot Springs, at the close of the Natchez reprint. Dunbar's detailed instructions to Freeman on April 28, 1806, simply reiterated the survey methods familiar from Andrew Ellicott's Mississippi, Lewis's Missouri, and his own Ouachita: ". . . the depth of the river may be sounded every evening & the temperature of the water taken every morning by the Thermometer." The letter continued with advice on taking latitudes and longitudes, the measurement of temperatures and rainfall, and made suggestions for geological and botanical research.[20]

### The Traveling Libraries

To carry out Jefferson's demanding instructions, each of the expeditions was outfitted with a traveling library of the

[19]Flores, 321–22.
[20]Rowland, 339–40.

most contemporary scientific publications relevant to their survey work. The contents of the library carried by Lewis and Clark have been described by Donald Jackson in a landmark article.[21] Lewis was sent for training with five of the major scientists of the day: botanist and Native American researcher Benjamin Smith Barton, astronomer and surveyor Andrew Ellicott, mathematician Robert Patterson, physician Benjamin Rush, and anatomist and paleontologist Caspar Wistar. All five men were members of the American Philosophical Society in Philadelphia, whose meetings and published *Transactions* hosted the latest research in every scientific field. While training Lewis, these men recommended to him those books that would be most useful on the expedition, confining themselves to works written in English.

Among books and manuscript materials on Louisiana, the expedition made use of Antoine-Simon Le Page du Pratz's *History of Louisiana* (1774 edition), Alexander Mackenzie's *Voyages* (1802), and the journals of frontiersmen Jean Baptiste Truteau (in Jefferson's translation), John Evans, and James Mackay. Lewis and Clark could find more general information, particularly on botany and zoology, in a four-volume dictionary of arts and sciences (1754–55). For plant identifications they used John Miller's English *Linnæus* (two volumes, 1779 and 1789) and Barton's *Elements of Botany* (1803). They took the standard text on minerals, Richard Kirwan's *Elements of Mineralogy* (second edition, 1794). In the all-important task of surveying, for which daily astronomical measurements were suggested, they were guided by Ellicott's *Journal* (1803), Patrick Kelly's *Introduction to Spherics and Nautical Astronomy* (1796 and 1801), Nevil Maskelyne's astronomical *Tables Requisite* (1766–1802 and updated annually), the *Nautical Ephemeris* for 1804–6, and Patterson's manuscript astronomy notebook. Questions of health and discipline were governed by Rush's *Directions for Preserving the Health of Soldiers* (1778)

[21]Jackson, "Some Books Carried." Jackson's findings are analyzed and extended in *Literature*, 25–63. The traveling library's main texts were assembled over two decades by collector Roger Wendlick, creator of a fine collection of Expedition publications housed, with those of Irving Anderson, Eldon Chuinard, M.D., and George Tweney, in Special Collections at Lewis & Clark College in Portland, Oregon.

and the *Articles of War*, reissued annually. The party consulted at least two printed maps, du Pratz's "Louisiana" and
Arrowsmith's enormous "New Discoveries" (1802), carried
folded or in sections. As they journeyed, Clark was also
developing manuscript maps. In this he was aided by
Nicholas King's "blank" manuscript chart of 1803, which
incorporated elements from early American maps by Guil-
laume de l'Isle (1718), James Cook (1784), George Vancouver
(1798), Alexander Mackenzie (1801), and Ellicott (1803).
They also carried copies of maps by Evans, Mackay, and
Antoine Soulard. Armed with this impressive stock of
instructional materials, the Corps of Discovery was able to
cross the Plains and Rockies, and return to St. Louis carrying an enormous amount of new information, with the loss
of only one man.[22]

We have no comparable list of sources for John Sibley, or
Dunbar and Hunter. All three were masters of the scientific literature, and needed no special training. Having been a
newspaper owner, and trained as a physician, Sibley would
have known the value of published research. It is a curious
fact, and perhaps an indication of his desire to be the sole
authority on Louisiana, that his printed papers and correspondence contain no reference to earlier sources, apart
from a reference to a piece on Louisiana in the Charter City
*Gazette* of Freneau & Williams, attributed by Sibley to
Judge Bay.[23] We can be sure, however, that Sibley was
dependent on many published accounts, including *Louisiana* by du Pratz, in addition to his word-of-mouth inform-
ants, who are mostly identified by name.

As a member of the American Philosophical Society and
contributor of papers to its learned journal, Dunbar was an
associate of the scholars who had trained Lewis. His traveling library contained some of the same texts, though unlike
Lewis, he would also have been able to make use of texts in
Latin, as did Freeman and Custis. His letters are scholarly
in tone, and frequently acknowledge his sources. In his

[22] Of the authors listed here, Linnæus, Kirwan, and Maskelyne
were also corresponding members
of the American Philosophical
Society.

[23] Sibley, letter to Governor Claiborne, October 10, 1803. Library
of Congress, Thomas Jefferson
Papers. See Appendix B1, paragraph five.

[24]Dunbar, *Journal* (ed. 1904), Journal, 8; Geometrical Survey, 7. Ferrer, a corresponding member of the APS, delivered to the Society a list of "Astronomical Observations . . . for the Purpose of determining the Geographical Position of various Places in the United States," taken in May and June 1801. *Transactions*, 6 (1809): XXIX, pp. 158–64, one of eight astronomical and surveying papers by Ferrer in the volume.

[25]Dunbar, *Journal* (ed. 1904), 16, 111.

[26]Dunbar, *Journal* (ed. 1904), 36, 70.

[27]Dunbar, *Journal* (ed. 1904), Geometrical Survey, 4. Nevil Maskelyne, *Tables Requisite*, London, 1766–1802; Tobias Mayer, *Tabulae Motuum Solis et Lunae* (ed. Maskelyne), London, 1770, or its English translation, *New and Correct Tables of the Motions of the Sun and Moon*, London, 1770.

[28]"Bruce and his Abyssinians," Dunbar, *Journal* (ed. 1904), 54.

[29]Dunbar, *Journal* (ed. 1904), 104.

[30]The first two papers in the APS *Transactions* volume 4 (1799), and the first six of volume 5 (1802) were delivered to the Society by Priestley between 1796 and 1800.

[31]Flores, 64–66.

[32]Presumably John Garnett's New Brunswick reprint of this formerly British publication. See *Literature,* items 1a.8 and 1a.9.

report to Jefferson on the Ouachita expedition, Dunbar twice mentioned the work of his contemporary José Joaquín de Ferrer of Cadiz,[24] who established the longitude of Havana and was Dunbar's authority for the longitude of the mouth of the Red River. Also mentioned twice was William Bartram,[25] son of John Bartram, founder of America's first botanical garden, in Philadelphia, and charter member of the American Philosophical Society. William, whom Dunbar knew personally, was perhaps even more celebrated than his father, as the author of *Travels through North and South Carolina, Georgia, East & West Florida* (1791), a masterpiece of reporting on the natural history and native inhabitants of the southeast. Richard Kirwan also received two mentions in Dunbar's journal, along with "other Chemists."[26] Another familiar traveling library name mentioned was that of "Mr Maskelyne astronomer royal," who "has long since observed that the Sun's diameter as taken from Mayer's tables is 3″ too much, I observe that this error is corrected in the almanac for 1805."[27] Finally, two other British luminaries were named: James Bruce,[28] Scottish explorer and author of *Travels to Discover the Source of the Nile* (1790), and Dr. Joseph Priestley,[29] associate of Benjamin Franklin in the study of electricity, discoverer of many gases, including oxygen and carbon monoxide, and a 1794 emigrant to the United States, who had died recently in Pennsylvania.[30] George Hunter, another distinguished chemist in Pennsylvania, would also have had access to the latest research, though he identifies no sources in his Ouachita journals.

In the standard account of the Jeffersonian expeditions in the southwest, Dan L. Flores has surveyed the known items of the Freeman and Custis traveling library,[31] some of them reminiscent of Lewis's materials. Freeman was a skilled surveyor, and produced accurate latitudes and longitudes with the use of the *Nautical Almanac* for 1806.[32] Custis, a trained naturalist, carried J. A. Murray's condensation of Linnæus,

*Systema Vegetabilium* (1784 or 1786), and knew also Humphrey Marshall's *Arbustrum Americanum* (1785), Thomas Walter's *Flora Caroliniana* (1778), and Linnæus's *Systema Naturae* (1789, ed. J. F. Gmelin). Like all the explorers, he had consulted du Pratz's *History of Louisiana,* and Flores also records use of Jefferson's *Notes on the State of Virginia* and Bartram's *Travels* (1791). Further resources included a copy of an unpublished map by von Humboldt, Sibley's Red River report, and issues of the major scientific journals of the day. Except that a number of these sources were in Latin, this traveling library has much in common with the one assembled by Lewis in 1803.

### The Search for Leaders of a Southwest Expedition

Lewis and Clark were ideally matched, bringing two very different temperaments to the tasks of leadership—Lewis was mercurial and often solitary, spending much of the journey on shore, gathering botanical samples and assessing the territory, while the more methodical Clark carried the main burden of day-to-day organization and command. In 1804, Jefferson was eager to find a pair of equally well-matched leaders for the expedition to the source of the Red River. To this end, he had been in frequent communication with William Dunbar, a successful Scots-born Natchez plantation owner and probably the most able scientist in the southern states. Born in 1749 and educated in Glasgow and London, Dunbar had sailed to Philadelphia in 1771 with a stock of goods intended for his entry to the fur trade. By 1773 he was able, in partnership with John Ross, to establish a plantation near Baton Rouge, worked by African slaves purchased in Jamaica. In 1792 the partnership founded The Forest, a plantation southeast of Natchez, where Dunbar made a fortune in cotton and indigo. Among his contributions to the improved manufacture of cotton, he is remembered as introducing the square bale for more efficient storage.

Working as a surveyor for the Spanish territorial government, he became surveyor general of Spanish West Florida in 1798, and assisted Andrew Ellicott in establishing the boundary with the United States. In September 1800, introducing his preliminary report, Ellicott spoke of Dunbar with particular appreciation:

> To William Dunbar, Esq. of the Mississippi Territory I feel myself under the greatest obligations, for his assistance during the short time he was with us; his extensive scientific acquirements, added to a singular facility in making mathematical calculations, would have reduced my labour, to a mere amusement, if he had continued.[33]

After taking American citizenship, Dunbar was elected in 1800 to the American Philosophical Society, and between 1800 and 1808 contributed twelve articles on scientific topics to its *Transactions*. His scientific interests were similar in many respects to those of Philosophical Society fellows Benjamin Rush, Caspar Wistar, and Thomas Jefferson. They included fossil bones, inoculation against smallpox, and Indian sign languages, in addition to astronomical studies. His observatory at The Forest near Natchez was the best equipped in the southern states. Dunbar died at his plantation in 1810.[34]

In 1804, at the age of fifty-five and in poor health, Dunbar was reluctant to undertake the journey proposed by Jefferson, as far as today's western border of Texas. Other candidates actively considered over a number of months included George Hunter, John Sibley, and Thomas Freeman. Dr. George Hunter, who was to receive the accolade "the renowned *Man* of Jefferson" from Audubon, was born in Edinburgh in 1755, and served his apprenticeship with Edinburgh and Philadelphia druggists. After three years in the army and three more in the navy, in 1783 he began in a series of partnerships, first as a distiller in New Jersey and then in the contrasting activities of drug production and coach manufacture in Philadelphia. He eventually settled for a

[33]Ellicott, *Journal*, Appendix of Thermometrical Observations, 42.
[34]Webb, "William Dunbar."

career as a pharmacist in 1792. In 1818 he was reported as having moved to New Orleans. Hunter made two journeys into Kentucky, in 1796 and 1802, before sharing in Dunbar's Ouachita River expedition. He died in New Orleans in 1823, leaving a library of 251 volumes, including 64 on chemistry and mineralogy, and 6 maps.[35] While planning for the projected Red River expedition in April 1804, Jefferson introduced Hunter to Dunbar with a shrewd sense of the potential distractions in an expedition of this sort:

> You will percieve by the instructions that a Doct. George Hunter of Philadelphia is appointed to do as a coadjutor & successor in case of accident to the principal; his fort is chemistry; in the practical part of that branch of science he has probably no equal in the U.S. and he is understood to be qualified to take the necessary astronomical observations. The thing to be guarded against is that an indulgence to his principal qualifications may not lead to a diversion of our mission to a march for gold and silver mines. These are but an incidental object, to be noted if found in their way, as salt or coal or lime would, but not to be sought after.[36]

Although Dr. John Sibley never led a Jeffersonian expedition, he played an important role in the survey of the Louisiana Territory. As a resident of Natchitoches, Louisiana, on the Red River, Sibley compiled multiple reports and communications to the U.S. government regarding the Red River region, partly based on second-hand information, but also including some personal observations. Sibley was not chosen to explore the river, possibly because of rumors questioning his character. However, Jefferson valued his reports on the Red River enough to incorporate them in government publications, including his compilation *An Account of Louisiana* (1803) and his *Message from the President* (1806).

The third candidate for leadership of a Red River expedition, Thomas Freeman, came to America from Ireland in 1784, and worked for President Washington on the survey of the capital, which may have brought him to Jefferson's attention. In 1797 he joined Ellicott's boundary survey team

[35]McDermott, 5–18.

[36]Jefferson to Dunbar, April 15, 1804. Jefferson Papers, Library of Congress, part quoted by McDermott, p. 6, fn 8. Text from Rowland, 194, where, however, it is dated "April 16[?], 1806."

in Natchez, where he would have worked with William Dunbar. Offended by his behavior, apparently with justice, Freeman criticized Ellicott, who became vituperative and embittered, allowing Freeman no mention in his *Journal*. Freeman found a better friend in General James Wilkinson, a secret agent for Spain while leading the U.S. army. While on Wilkinson's staff, Freeman came to share an active interest in the Spanish Southwest, and in November 1805 was asked by Jefferson to lead a new expedition to the source of the Red River.[37]

The man first chosen in 1804 to lead the Red River exploration had been George Hunter, but the Spanish government's opposition caused those plans to be abandoned. Hunter's preparations for the Red were put almost immediately to use when attention shifted from the Red to the Ouachita, and Hunter himself proved an effective counterpart to Dunbar, adding depth to the scientific investigations, particularly at the Hot Springs. In preparation for the Red River expedition, Hunter had designed a "chinese" boat with a square sail,[38] which was built to his specifications in Pennsylvania in May 1804 and brought down the Ohio and Mississippi rivers to Natchez for use on the Ouachita.

> Whilst at Pittsburg I was employed in superintending the building of a boat to carry us to Natchez. . . . The boat is over fifty feet long on deck, 30 feet straight Keell, flat bottom somewhat resembling a long Scow in use to fery over waggons &c. It is 6 ft. 2 Inches broad at the bottom at its extreme breadth which is about ¼ from the bow & runs taper to the stern where it is 5 feet broad. . . . The Rudder is large & extends below the bottom of the boat, to help to keep the boat to windward. . . . She is covered with light boards from the Stern 32 feet foret [forward], so as to give good accomodations to the passengers & firnished with a Stout mast 36 feet long [&] a Sail 24 feet by 27. in the Chinese stile, fastened to a yard 24 feet & a boom 29 feet, & spread by 5 sprits the whole width of the boom. Has 2 large Sculls 50 feet long each, fixed in the chinese way, 6 seting poles & 2 side oars.[39]

[37]Flores, 49–52.
[38]A drawing of the boat, in Hunter's hand, is illustrated in McDermott, 57, and Flores, 43.
[39]McDermott, 57–58.

The boat left Pittsburgh on the June 15 without three of its crew, who were reluctant to trust themselves to the vessel, and after six troublesome days on the Ohio Hunter left the craft in the charge of Captain George Carmichael, to journey by land to Louisville, rejoining the boat there in July 1. They descended the Mississippi to Natchez, arriving there on July 24, with the loss of one passenger from a delirium that led to an accidental drowning. When put into use on the Ouachita Expedition, Hunter's "chinese" boat, like Lewis's iron-frame pirogue, also built in Pittsburgh, proved unsatisfactory, and was replaced at Fort Miro (modern Monroe, Louisiana) by a craft more suitable to the Ouachita's shallow water and riffles.

Meanwhile, between June 9 and 14, 1804, still committed to the Red River Expedition, Dunbar sent out a series of letters.[40] The first was to Jefferson with ideas for the exploration of the Red and Ouachita rivers; the second to Peter Walker, a translator from Spanish and draughtsman in 1805 of two manuscript maps of the Southwest,[41] with questions about the Red River; and the third to Thomas Freeman, ordering boats and soldiers for an exploration of the Red. All of these preparations would bear fruit, though not immediately.

## JEFFERSON'S 1806 *Message* TO CONGRESS

### The Fort Mandan Materials

Materials arriving in Washington from west of the Mississippi were edited under the president's supervision and published rapidly to satisfy readers eager for news of the territory. One of the earliest reports was Jefferson's compilation from materials largely supplied by John Sibley, *An Account of Louisiana*, published in multiple editions in 1803 and 1804.[42] A note in the Beinecke Library's copy of the first edition identifies Jefferson's editor as "Mr. Wagner, chief-clerk in the office of Mr. Madison Secretary of State; the materials

[40]Rowland, 133–38.
[41]Flores, 40; Wheat I, 131.
[42]Wagner-Camp-Becker 2b:1–14.

were collected by the President of the U. S. (Mr. Jefferson) who received them in answer to certain interrogatories put by him to discreet and intelligent men in Louisiana." This publication received an extended review in Samuel L. Mitchill's *Medical Repository,* vol. 7 (1804), 390–402, with excerpts or summaries relating to every section of the text. More recent scholarship has established that some of the information gathered was simply fanciful: "It is ironic that the acquisition of this vast region . . . should have been heralded by this tattered, badly printed, credulous synthesis of hazy fact and ill-founded rumor."[43] While the president placed enough confidence in the publication to send it to Meriwether Lewis at Cahokia on November 16, 1803, he may have wanted future compilations to be more accurate and more carefully edited.[44] The Lewis and Clark materials sent from Fort Mandan were rather scrupulously prepared for publication, as can be seen from their manuscript originals, transcribed in the Thwaites and Moulton editions of the expedition journals.[45] It is not known who was the editor of these materials, but it is likely that Jefferson entrusted them to Nicholas King, who was well acquainted with the Corps of Discovery's aims, having researched the available maps of the Missouri and compiled them into a "blank" chart taken on the expedition.[46]

As the largely invisible editor of much, if not all, of the *Message,* King may deserve most credit for the clarity and economy of its presentation.[47] He certainly shaped the discursive Ouachita journals of Dunbar and Hunter into a readable narrative, was later the editor both of the Pike and of the Freeman and Custis expedition reports, and drew all three pioneering maps presented in this volume, of the Missouri, Red, and Ouachita Rivers.[48] Jefferson's choice of individuals to carry out his designs now seems inspired, and his choice of Nicholas King was no exception. Though he is generally regarded as merely a surveyor or cartographer,[49] King had more than a passing interest in the details of

[43]Wagner-Camp-Becker, pp. 14–15, fn. The copy referenced here is that believed to be the first edition of 1803, published by J. Conrad in Philadelphia.

[44]Jackson, *Letters,* item 94.

[45]Thwaites 6: 80–113; Moulton 3: 386–445

[46]Jackson, *Letters,* item 21. See also *Literature,* 57, and Moulton, Atlas, map 2.

[47]Nicholas King, who immigrated to America from Britain in 1796, was surveyor of the city of Washington from 1803 to 1812. He was known to Meriwether Lewis, who left a recipe for making wine obtained from "Mr. King of Washington" among his papers (Jackson, *Letters,* item 21, fn 3). When, on August 7, 1805, a Board of Trustees was formed for a Permanent Institution for Education of Youth in the city of Washington, its president was Jefferson, and King its secretary (*National Intelligencer,* same date).

[48]See Flores, 91–92, where King is described as "the forerunner of Nicholas Biddle in the field of western exploration." See also note 119.

[49]Over fifty of his maps are housed at the Library of Congress, among them a handful of important expedition charts; most of the remainder are surveys of the city of Washington.

exploration. In 1799, for example, he had published in the *Transactions* of the American Philosophical Society[50] an article on boats for river navigation that would have caught the eye of the Society's president, Thomas Jefferson, if he were not already aware of King's potential as an organizer as well as a mapmaker.

Jefferson reported to his secretary of war, General Dearborn, on July 14, 1805, that he had commissioned King to compile a map from the twenty-nine-sheet map sent back with the other documents from Fort Mandan.[51] In his *Message* to Congress, Jefferson described this new Missouri River map, promising copies to accompany the report to Congress. No surviving copy of the report contains this map. Gary Moulton has carefully considered the question.[52] Clark had actually created and delivered two maps, described separately in the president's preface as "the Missouri, according to courses and distance" (a map on twenty-nine sheets, of the Missouri from Camp Dubois to Fort Mandan), and "a general map of the country between the Mississippi and the Pacific" (known as Clark's map of 1805, or the Fort Mandan map). These distinctions are also preserved in Jefferson's summary to Dunbar on January 12, 1806: "We have Capt. Lewis' notes of the Missouri to his watering place at Fort Mandan, and a map of the whole country watered by the Missouri and Columbia composed by himself last winter on a very extensive information from Indians & traders, in which he expresses a great deal of confidence."[53] If King completed an engraving from the twenty-nine sheet map, no trace of it (or the original sheets) has survived. On the other hand, King's engraving from Clark's Fort Mandan map survives in three versions, reproduced as items 32a–c in Moulton's Atlas volume.[54] The final paragraph of the president's *Message* promised a second map, of the Ouachita as explored by Dunbar and Hunter. This map, also prepared by Nicholas King, is found in some copies of the Washington edition of *Message*, though no

[50] "An Improvement in Boats, for River-Navigation, described in a Letter to Mr. Robert Patterson, by Nicholas King." Letter of September 28, 1797, in *Transactions* 4 (1799): 298–302. Illustration facing page 354 not included in reprint.

[51] Jackson, *Letters,* item 159.

[52] Moulton 1 (Atlas volume): 8–9.

[53] Rowland, 188–89.

[54] See also Wheat II, 12, and II, 32–38.

surviving copy of the Natchez edition contains the printed version. This Ouachita River map is discussed below, and is reproduced in this volume.

### Lewis's Fort Mandan Letter

On April 7, 1805, Lewis wrote a progress report to the president from Fort Mandan, expressing confidence in the expedition's eventual success and predicting with remarkable accuracy a return date of September 1806. The original text of the letter was transcribed by Jackson.[55] The letter was lightly edited and abbreviated by Jefferson, Nicholas King, or another amanuensis, and this text was sent to newspapers, as the first report by Lewis to be published. It appeared on Wednesday, July 17, in *The National Intelligencer and Washington Advertiser*[56] and on Tuesday, August 13, in the Hudson, New York, paper *The Balance, and Columbian Repository*.[57] Both newspapers gave the correct dateline of April 7. The same edited text was also provided to A. & G. Way for printing with the 1806 *Message* to Congress. This printing, closer in a number of instances to the original, was clearly derived from an edited manuscript copy rather than one of the newspaper printings, but was unfortunately provided a dateline of April 17, 1805, a mistake followed by all subsequent printings of the letter. The public was evidently eager to hear more about the expedition. The *National Intelligencer* published two more reports in the same month, describing the prairie dog sent back to Jefferson[58] and printing Clark's April letter to Governor Harrison.[59] But the impressive Lewis letter, a model of intelligence and modest assurance, was Jefferson's choice to lead off the 1806 *Message*.

### A Statistical View

Authorship of "A Statistical View" is unclear. This compilation of ethnographic data is unsigned. In his preface to the *Message*, Jefferson gave credit to Lewis for "a statistical

[55]Jackson, *Letters,* item 149.

[56]Vol. V, No. DCCXLIV.

[57]Vol. IV, No. 33. No doubt other newspapers picked up the report around this time.

[58]July 22, Vol. V, No. DCCXLVI.

[59]July 26, Vol. V, No. DCCXLVIII.

view, procured and forwarded by him." Actual authorship was presumably shared between the two commanders. The final sentence of the preliminary essay "The Indian Trade," reading "These establishments are not mentioned as being thought important at present in a governmental point of view," has something of the feel of Lewis's comment on "A Statistical View" in his Fort Mandan letter: "a view of the Indian nations, containing information relative to them, on those points with which I conceived it important that the government should be informed." It is likely that the task of assembling information at Fort Mandan was a joint venture. In this volume, the document is assigned to Clark, but only in the sense that he was its literal compiler and scribe.

The published text offers no explanation for the absence from all surviving copies of the 1806 *Message* of the Missouri River engraving promised in Jefferson's preface. William Clark's manuscript notes from Fort Mandan, however, were included. The manuscript copy now at the American Philosophical Society, a huge document pasted together from seven large sheets of paper, is around three feet wide and two feet tall, and has the title "A List of the Names of the different Nations & Tribes of Indians Inhabiting the Countrey on the Missourie and its Waters." Perhaps the earliest spreadsheet in American history, it provides information in multiple categories, for all the nations known to the explorers at Fort Mandan. Sent to "To Genl. Jno Clark Kentucky," Clark's brother, it was deposited with the APS in 1818 by Nicholas Biddle, who had been editing the Lewis and Clark journals for publication. The copy sent to General Dearborn, now lost, contained even more information, according to Clark's notation on the back of the copy that survives at APS. The extra categories were summarized by Clark as follows:

> additional Remarks made on the Copy Sent to the Secretary at War
>
> 1st the boundaries of the Countrey which they claim—the quantity of land & face of the Countrey

2d their Ancient residence if Known.

3 the State of their Trade whether it Can be expected to increase and in what proportion.

4th their Trafick with other Indian nations, in what it Consists, and where Carried on

5th their Disposition towards the whites, and their conduct to their Traders

6 to what place they might be prevailed on to remove to make room for other nations

7 whether they cultivate or not

8 whether Stationary or roveing

9 whether the nations is increasing or Demenishing

Genl. remarks on the Trade & remittances and amt. Esimtated # of Establishments in a Govtmt pt. of view—Notations on Indian Names Sub Divisions of the Sioux Bands & names of the principal Chiefs.[60]

This additional information was carried over (either verbatim or more likely in a rendering by Nicholas King), mostly into the large final category "S" in "A Statistical View." King was almost certainly responsible for recasting the material into a lettered list, and is likely to have created the table of pronunciation notations, presumably guided by the "Notations on Indian Names" among the "Genl. remarks." The introductory paragraphs "The Indian Trade." also appear to derive from the "Genl. remarks."

For most of "A Statistical View" the printed text is longer than the surviving Clark notes, the difference being supplied from the extra material, now lost. For a number of pages following the "Sioux Proper" folding table, however, the printed text is markedly more elliptical than Clark's manuscript. The listings (from the Kiowas to the Crow, pages 37–41) are more abbreviated and repetitive, as if in those sections King was working under time constraints and took the opportunity to repeat similar materials.

King's other editorial interventions included choosing between alternative estimates provided by Clark, showing a conservative approach in always selecting the lower of two numbers. He also combined related materials into single

[60]Moulton, 3: 386–87.

categories, moved information from one category to another, clarifying the document throughout and reworking Clark's notes into continuous prose. The shoulder notes for "A Statistical View" show a small number of cases where the printed text differs in detail from the surviving Clark manuscript, but in general King appears to have been a conscientious editor who turned a chart of mostly raw data into a readable narrative.

### Sibley's Two Reports to Dearborn

Dr. John Sibley (1757–1837), who had originally been considered as a possible leader of the projected Red River expedition, was a Massachusetts-born physician, who moved from that state to Fayetteville, North Carolina, in 1784 to found the Fayetteville *Gazette*, leaving his wife and two small sons to join him later.[61] He was married a second time, a year after his first wife's death in 1790, but in 1802, after the failure of the *Gazette*, he moved again, to New Orleans, once more leaving a family now increased by a daughter and a third son.[62] His letters to his sons in North Carolina, encouraging them to give support to their stepmother,[63] and his August 1808 letter,[64] mentioning plans to bring his family to Louisiana, indicate an awareness of his obligations, and the charges of abandonment brought by his enemies seem to have been overlooked by Jefferson, Governor Claiborne, and General Dearborn in their assessments of his value.

Sibley's importance as a reporter on Louisiana stems from his journey of March 5, 1803, up the Red River from Natchez to Natchitoches, during which he kept a detailed journal, published in the *Message* to Congress as a letter "To General Henry Dearborn, Secretary of War." Although his initial impression of the settlement was not favorable (in the *Message* he describes it as "a small, irregular, and meanly built village") he reported that the "southern and eastern

[61]Tregle, "John Sibley."
[62]Brandt, 367.
[63]Abel, referenced in White, *News of the Plains and Rockies* sources, page 27.
[64]Brandt, 367.

prospects from it are very beautiful." He settled there, purchasing valuable property at Grand Ecore, further up the river, to the west of the town. Here he developed a cotton plantation to which he eventually retired. He married for the third time in 1813, two years after the death of his second wife, and continued in his varied career as army surgeon, Indian agent, an officer in Colonel Long's 1819 raid into Texas, and territorial judge and state legislator. He played an important role in preserving good relations with the Indians of Upper Louisiana before the independence of Texas, and ended his days in prosperity as a cotton farmer, salt manufacturer, and cattle rancher.[65]

Apparently the standard catalogs are correct in identifying Sibley as the key supplier of information to Jefferson's 1803 compilation *An Account of Louisiana.* It was a remarkable store of data. Its sheer quantity probably attests to his wide range of contacts, especially among those traders and native leaders who would seek out a frontier town's best-trained physician. Sibley's contribution to the 1803 *Louisiana* is most evident in the description of New Orleans: "The houses in front of the town, and for a square or two backwards, are mostly of brick, covered with slate or tile, and mainly of two stories. The remainder are of wood, covered with shingles. The streets cross each other at right angles, and are 32 French feet wide."[66] This may be compared with Sibley's letter of December 13, 1803, to J. Gales, a North Carolina printer: "The town is regularly laid off; the streets are 50 feet wide, and intersected at right angles; the houses are principally of brick, some two, some three stories high, many of them elegant with flat roofs."[67] Sibley's authorship is apparent in the brief sketches of the native tribes in the 1803 compilation and in the more substantial "Historical Sketches of the Several Tribes in Louisiana" sent to Dearborn on April 5, 1805, and published in the 1806 *Message.*

Unfortunately, it is likely that many of the weaknesses of the 1803 publication must also be assigned to Sibley, in par-

[65]Tregle, "John Sibley."
[66] [Sibley], *An Account of Louisiana* (J. Conrad edition, 1803), 18.
[67]Sibley, *Letter to J. Gales,* 2.

ticular the claims of rich silver mines in Louisiana and word of a mountain of salt along the Missouri River. The reference to the silver mines begins with caution: "It is pretended that Upper Louisiana contains in its bowels many silver and copper mines, and various specimens of both are exhibited. Several trials have been made to ascertain the fact; but the want of skill in the artists has hitherto left the object undecided."[68] The source of this story is revealed in the letter to J. Gales:

> I am well acquainted with an elderly French gentleman of very large fortune, and strict veracity, who was born there, and who went there a few years ago, and brought away the Burr mill-stones which were left there by the French. From him I have had an accurate description of this country. He says there are, to his certain knowledge, three silver mines, as rich as any in Mexico, from which he has taken ore, and had it proved.[69]

The elderly French gentleman is identified in the *Message* to Congress[70] as [François] Grappe, born at the site of the old French fort and flour mill near today's Texarkana.[71] By 1805 Grappe's fabrication, which probably originated with Le Page du Pratz,[72] had been distanced a little further:

> . . . we arrive at a river that falls in on the right side, which is called by the Indians *Kiomitchie*, and by the French *La Riviere la Mine*, or Mine river, which is about 150 yards wide, the water clear and good, and is boatable about 60 miles to the silver mine, which is on the bank of the river, and the ore appears in large quantities, but the richness of it is not known.[73]

At about the time he delivered this report to General Dearborn, Sibley showed enough confidence in Grappe to repeat his story in similar terms, but with additional particulars, in a letter to William Dunbar:

> . . . thick cane again on both sides for 25 miles to the mouth of the River Hiomitchie as the Indians call it, and the French call it Riviere la Mine. The water is clear and good, the river is about 150 yards wide and may be ascended by boats for about sixty miles by water to the Silver mine, which is by Land 36 from its mouth, the mine is in the Bank of the River and the Oar is in large quantities,

[68][Sibley], *An Account of Louisiana*, 11.

[69]Sibley, *Letter to Gales*, 6.

[70]*Message*, 108; *Discoveries*, 105.

[71]*News of the Plains and Rockies*, 27. Grappe was Sibley's interpreter (*Message*, 87; *Discoveries*, 84).

[72]Both maps in the 1763 edition of du Pratz show a "Silver Mine of Duplessis" just west of Natchitoches. The second volume contains a two-page appendix on the silver mines of Louisiana. This was the edition owned by Jefferson, and the basis for all contemporary knowledge of the territory. Lewis and Clark carried Barton's copy of the same set. See *Literature*, items 1a.2 and 1b.1.

[73]*Message*, 106; *Discoveries*, 103.

but the Richness of it is not well known. The Indians say they found another about a year ago in a creek that empties into the Hiomitchie about three miles from its mouth the Oar of which they say resembles the other.[74]

If Grappe was an unreliable source, in 1803 Sibley was told an even more heady mixture of truth and fantasy by another Frenchman, Jean Brevel, who claimed to have traveled over the mountains to a point where the streams ran to the West. The tallest of his tales repeated in *Louisiana* was that of the salt mountain:

> One extraordinary fact relative to salt must not be omitted. There exists about 1000 miles up the Missouri, and not far from that river, *a Salt Mountain!* The existence of such a mountain might well be questioned, were it not for the testimony of several respectable and enterprising traders, who have visited it, and who have exhibited several bushels of the salt to the curiosity of the people of St. Louis, where some of it still remains. A specimen of the same salt has been sent to Marietta. This mountain is said to be 180 miles long, and 45 in width, composed of solid rock salt, without any trees, or even shrubs on it. Salt springs are very numerous beneath the surface of the mountain, and they flow through the fissures and cavities of it.[75]

In the letter to Dunbar of two years later, this tale is presented as part of Brevel's reported narrative:

> . . . they steering northwesterly, 'till the River divided into innumerable small branches that issued from amongst these hills and mountains all of which they found bare of trees, but a light covering of grass, as they pass'd from the top of one hill to the top of another, & then another etc. for several days interspers'd with deep ravines in which they sometimes found water, they saw large quantities of Salt Rock in the sides of the Mountains, and plenty of an Oar that the Indians told him was his (meaning the white peoples) treasure, . . . after traveling over this broken elivated country they at length found the waters running toward the Setting Sun, the country declining, . . .[76]

In the version supplied at the same time to Dearborn, the speaker is Brevel:

[74]Sibley, letter to Dunbar of April 2, 1805, in Rowland, 168.

[75][Sibley], *An Account of Louisiana,* 12.

[76]Sibley to Dunbar, letter of April 2, 1805, in Rowland, 171. This important long letter is not included in the Appendix, since it is available in transcription in Rowland, pp. 162–74.

After traveling for several days over a country of this description, the country became more broken, the hills rising into mountains, amongst which we saw a great deal of rock salt, and an ore the Indians said was my (meaning the white people's) treasure, which I afterwards learned was silver. . . . We traveled on from the top of one mountain to the top of another, in hopes the one we were ascending was always the last, till the small streams we met with ran the contrary way, towards the setting sun, and the lands declining that way.[77]

This story by Brevel, touched with fantasy as it was, nevertheless represented a cautionary tale about the breadth and ruggedness of the barren Rocky Mountain chain ("in hopes the one we were ascending was always the last") that might have been useful to Lewis and Clark in their preparations, if it could have been believed. But by the time it reached Dearborn in the spring of 1805 the Corps of Discovery would already have left Fort Mandan. Salt was, of course, a valuable commodity, and Sibley lived comfortably in his later years on its manufacture from the plentiful salines near his plantation.

Between 1803 and 1805 Sibley worked hard to become the government's primary informant on trade and political developments in this territory. After providing information to the 1803 *Account of Louisiana*, in December of the same year he submitted for publication the report quoted earlier, to the North Carolina printer Gales. The following March he wrote to Jefferson, formally introducing himself and sending some dye specimens derived from the bark of the "bois d'arc" (Osage orange).[78] A very similar letter, addressed to Calvin Jones, M.D., containing a brief topographical account of the Natchitoches area, a description of the Osage orange dyes, and news of a mammoth skeleton near Quelqueshoe Lake, was sent for publication in July.[79] Sibley was again in communication with Jefferson in September 1804, this time on local political conditions in Louisiana, in particular the relationship between the Spanish

[77] *Message*, 109–10; *Discoveries*, 106.
[78] Sibley, letter to Jefferson of March 20, 1804. Library of Congress, Thomas Jefferson Papers. The letter is transcribed as Appendix B2.
[79] Sibley, letter of July 10, 1804, to Calvin Jones, *Medical Repository* 9 (1806): 425–27. This letter is listed in some bibliographies under the name of [Dr. Samuel L.] Mitchill, editor of the journal.

and the native populations.[80] He was to become increasingly useful in maintaining good relations with the native tribes, to the irritation of the Spanish authorities,[81] and would provide valuable evidence on rival French and Spanish claims to territory in the southwest.[82]

By April 1805 Sibley sent detailed notes to Dearborn and Dunbar on the native tribes of Louisiana,[83] the Red River as far as Santa Fe,[84] and a general description of the country between the Mississippi and the Rio Bravo (Grande).[85] The first two of these documents were published in expanded form in the *Message* and its Natchez reprint. The notes for all three documents are printed here in Appendix B. On May 27, showing his confidence in Sibley's scholarship, Jefferson sent him a packet of blank vocabularies, requesting him to complete and return them.[86] Replying on August 9, acknowledging receipt of the (water-damaged) vocabularies two days earlier—an indication both of the slow pace and uncertain safety of the mails to this remote American outpost—Sibley promised to collect the word lists, and offered to send through Secretary of State Madison a copy of a French manuscript in the possession of the Messier family. This was sent to Madison the following day.[87]

The father of the Messier family had been governor of Texas at San Antonio, but at his death the family moved back to their former home in Natchitoches, where Dr. Sibley was their family doctor. Messier's widow was a daughter of the duc d'Orléans, of French royal blood. The children (two sisters, of excellent qualities, and three brothers, of which Sibley singled out the oldest, the county treasurer, for praise), were "all strong republicans" and "highly pleased with the cession of Louisiana to the United States."[88] Though Sibley's covering letter to Madison was almost as mysterious on this subject as the letter to Gales, it does at least make clear that he is enclosing (at Governor Claiborne's suggestion) a copy of a French manuscript inherited by the oldest son. Nothing is said about the contents of the

[80]Sibley, letter to Jefferson of September 2, 1804. Library of Congress, Thomas Jefferson Papers.
[81]Brandt, 370.
[82]Andrew Marschalk's *Mississippi Herald* for Friday, December 20, 1805, prints depositions taken by Sibley as justice of the peace from inhabitants familiar with early French and native settlements, including Grappe family members. François Grappe's affidavit is among those printed in Senate and House documents of December 1805 (Streeter, III: 1, p. 1805).
[83]"Sibley's acct of the Indians," Library of Congress, Thomas Jefferson Papers. See Appendix B3.
[84]"Sibley's account of Red river," Library of Congress, Thomas Jefferson Papers. See Appendix B5.
[85]"Sibley, on the country between Misipi & Rio Bravo," Library of Congress, Thomas Jefferson Papers. See Appendix B4.
[86]Jefferson, letter to Sibley of May 27, 1805. Printed in *The Writings of Thomas Jefferson*. Washington, D.C.: The Thomas Jefferson Memorial Association, 1903, volume XI, pp. 79–81. See Appendix B6.
[87]Sibley, letters to Jefferson, August 9, 1805, and James Madison, August 10, 1805. Library of Congress, Thomas Jefferson Papers.

"large folio bound volume," which contained enough material to justify copying expenses of eighty-five dollars.[89] It may have been merely of antiquarian interest, but it seems more likely that a manuscript belonging to these surprisingly republican blue-bloods may have contained French claims to territories in the southwest, and would thus have been of value to Madison during negotiations of the Purchase.

Before the end of 1805 Sibley had sent Jefferson two completed Indian vocabularies, of the Caddos and Natchitoches,[90] and he continued to provide information. "A Report from Natchitoches in 1807," introduced by Annie Heloise Abel, is valuable for its first-hand descriptions of meetings with important tribal figures. Penny Brandt's edition of a letter of August 6 in the same year from Sibley to Governor Claiborne shows an alert political and social observer, writing with considerable verve about frontier history in the making. Sibley's two contributions to the president's *Message* were the work of an energetic (if occasionally uncritical) researcher and reporter. He was careful to update his information, so that the estimates of tribal populations are revised between 1803 and 1805, in every case showing drastic reductions, including the extinction of what had been sixty Avoyals and the same number of Humas, two nations close to the Mississippi. His work on the anthropology and geography of the unexplored southwest is impressive.

## The Dunbar and Hunter Journals

By the middle of 1804 Spanish opposition had made the Red River expedition impossible.[91] Disappointed in their initial plans, Dunbar and Hunter decided on a more modest exploration—of the Ouachita River to its source in the Hot Springs—to be led by Dunbar as geographer and Hunter as chemist. On August 18, Dunbar wrote to Jefferson agreeing to the suspension of the Red River expedition, and transferring attention to the Ouachita:

[88] Sibley, *Letter to J. Gales*, 7–8, where the reason for mentioning the family at all is left unexplained.

[89] Sibley, letter of August 10, 1805, to Secretary of State James Madison. Library of Congress, Thomas Jefferson Papers.

[90] Sibley, letters to Jefferson of August 27, 1805, and December 14, 1805, Library of Congress, Thomas Jefferson Papers.

[91] The eventual exploration, planned by Dunbar and carried out by Freeman and Custis in 1806, was allowed only as far as the present Oklahoma border, where it was confronted by a Spanish force and turned back.

In consequence of the permission you are pleased to grant me, I have determined to make an excursion up the Washita river & to the hot springs, this interesting part of Louisiana cannot be seen by the party in the Spring. I therefore give it a preference; immediately on the receipt of your letter I wrote to Col. Freeman to suspend preparations for the principal expedition, & in lieu of the larger boat to provide only a good strong flat bottomed broad & safe canoe fitted up in the plainest manner, & such as may be impelled rapidly against the stream by six oars & which I have requested him to dispatch with all convenient speed manned by a discreet non com. officer & private with 3 months rations.[92]

On October 14 and 15, Dunbar sent last-minute reports to Jefferson.[93] On October 16 he set out from St. Catherine's Landing at Natchez with Dr. Hunter and thirteen soldiers (a sergeant and twelve men)[94] of the New Orleans garrison. After renting a flat-bottomed barge to replace Hunter's "Chinese" boat[95] at Fort Miro on November 10, the expedition completed its mission, arriving at the Arkansas Hot Springs in early December and researching the area until early January 1805, before returning in the same month to Natchez and New Orleans. This journey of less than three months, of relatively minor historical importance, was carried out with commendable diligence and analytical rigor. It provided the first description of a natural wonder (the Hot Springs) in the newly-acquired Louisiana Territory, using the most recent tools of measurement and research. As a contribution to science, the Dunbar/Hunter account offered additional justification for the Louisiana Purchase. In the minds of the reading public it will have been a preparation for a more ambitious project: the three-volume presentation of Lewis and Clark's journals.[96]

The final section of the president's *Message* to Congress, the Ouachita expedition of Dunbar and Hunter, was eventually prepared for the printers by Nicholas King, who also drew the one map to accompany that publication. Like the six published journal-writers of the Corps of Discovery, William Dunbar and George Hunter both kept detailed

[92]Rowland, 139–40.

[93]Rowland, 140–41, 160–62.

[94]Sergeant Bundy, Peter Bowers, John White, Robert Wilson, Mathew Boon, William Court, Edward Rylet, Jerimiah Loper, William Skinner, William Little, William Tutle, Manus McDonald, and Jeremia Smith. Also in the party were Hunter's son George, the guide Samual Blazier, and Dunbar's slave. McDermott, 65.

[95]Dunbar, *Journal* (ed. 1904), 43; McDermott, 88.

[96]*History of the Expedition Under the Command of Captains Lewis and Clark.* Nicholas Biddle and Paul Allen, editors. New York: Bradford and Inskeep, 1814. Two volumes only, lacking the intended scientific volume assigned to Benjamin Smith Barton. See *Literature*, item 5a.1.

A View on the Washita

This woodcut, depicting an imagined scene along the Ouachita River explored by William Dunbar, is from the first illustrated printing of the report to Congress, *An Interesting Account of the Voyages and Travels of Captains Lewis and Clarke, in the Years 1804–5 & 6 . . . published by P. Mauro in Baltimore, 1813.*

journals of the Ouachita Expedition. Indeed, like Lewis and Clark, both kept a double journal, comprising a record of the country explored, along with a scientific log of temperatures, distances, and astronomical measurements. Dunbar's original field notes are in Special Collections at Ouachita Baptist University, as a gift of the Dunbar family, and remain unpublished.[97]

Dunbar made at least two copies of his field notes. One of these was an official account, edited for the president. On February 2, 1805,[98] Dunbar sent Jefferson a brief preview of this account that reveals his measured assessment of their discoveries. It began with a description of the Hot Springs, noting their temperature and describing the interesting

[97] Special Collections, Riley-Hickingbotham Library, Ouachita Baptist University, Arkadelphia, Arkansas. Call number 976.703 D899w.

[98] Dunbar, letter to Jefferson of February 2, 1805. Library of Congress, Thomas Jefferson Papers. Reprinted in McDermott, 14–15.

miniature bivalve collected there. After a brief report on their journals of measurements and daily occurrences, he apologized for the scanty botanical evidence in these winter months, but claimed a new discovery, the "mountain dwarf Cabbage." His letter ended with a chemical analysis of the water at the Hot Springs. The tone is measured and balanced, one scientist addressing another. On February 13, 1805, within two weeks of returning from the expedition, Dunbar sent Jefferson sheets of his journal, "carefully compared and corrected," along with a specimen of the moss from the Arkansas Hot Springs.[99] Ten days later, on February 23, he sent two further sheets of the "continuation of the geographical Survey of the river Washita," with a list of vegetables ("Some few may be nondescripts—") together with some seeds.[100] On March 9 he again wrote, announcing the conclusion of the "journal of survey" and again supplying some vegetable specimens.[101] Finally, on March 16 he reported that his "journal of occurrences" had almost reached a conclusion, and offered "an apology for its extreme length."[102] It seems clear that the "journal of occurrences" was the main Exploration Journal as we now know it, and the "journal of survey" the shorter "Geometrical Survey."

These journals (the first of two hundred pages in manuscript, and the second of sixty-four pages) were presented by General Daniel Parker through Professor James Cutbush to the American Philosophical Society in Philadelphia on July 18, 1817, as acknowledged on the manuscript by the Society's Secretary John Vaughan.[103] They were transcribed and published in 1904.[104] The second copy of the journals is housed in the Mississippi State Archives in Jackson[105] and was transcribed by Eron Rowland in her 1931 compilation of William Dunbar papers. These two copies are almost identical, even as to punctuation, as far as December 10, 1804, the company's arrival at the Hot Springs, but differ increasingly from that point. The enforced leisure of wet and overcast weather allowed Dunbar time for "bringing up and completing" his

[99] Rowland, 143–45.

[100] Rowland, 145–46.

[101] Rowland, 146.

[102] Rowland, 147.

[103] Dunbar, "Journal of a Voyage." Daniel Parker (1782–1846) was adjutant inspector-general of the U.S. Army. James Cutbush (?–1823) was assistant apothecary-general of the Army, and rose to acting professor of chemistry and mineralogy at West Point. He was the author of three books on chemistry and pyrotechnics.

[104] Dunbar, *Journal* (ed. 1904).

[105] Mississippi Department of Archives & History, Jackson. Call number Z 0114.000 S M.

journals,[106] at which moment Dunbar may have made two almost identical copies. With the renewal of scientific duties at the Hot Springs, and on the return journey, there was probably time only for the field notes, so that copies made from the field notes after December 10 diverge into two texts: an official record for Jefferson (the APS journal), and a more discursive and personal account for Dunbar's own use (the journal at the Mississippi State Archives). A comparison of the field notes and two journals leaves no doubt that the version at the American Philosophical Society is the closest throughout to the text published in the *Message* to Congress, and is therefore likely to have been the actual manuscript used by Nicholas King for his redaction, with the addition of materials sent to him later by Dunbar, most of which were printed as footnotes in the Washington and Natchez editions. Examples of late additions are the footnotes on pages 115, 131 (first note), and 132 of the Natchez reprint. These pieces of information were not in Dunbar's or Hunter's manuscripts, and were presumably supplied to King by Dunbar after the main redaction was completed.

George Hunter's original field notes also reside in the library of the American Philosophical Society,[107] along with his official journal derived from the field notes.[108] This journal was sent by Hunter on April 20[109] to General Henry Dearborn, secretary of war, recipient of Sibley's two communications earlier in the same month. Hunter's journal, like Dunbar's, was presented to the APS by General Daniel Parker.[110] His field notes have been transcribed and expertly edited by John Francis McDermott, who also included some readings from the official journal, but omitted Hunter's scientific log, which was a close copy of Dunbar's. There are a number of passages in *Message* and its reprint *Discoveries* that clearly derive from Hunter's journal, and for which there is no corresponding material in Dunbar's journal. These include the description of embankments between Catahoola and the Black River,[111] the saline examined on

[106]Dunbar, *Journal* (ed. 1904), 106.

[107]George Hunter Journals, American Philosophical Society. Call number B H912. Available on microfilm (Film 200).

[108]George Hunter, "Manuscript Journal of George Hunter up the Red and Washita Rivers with Wm. Dunbar 1804 by order US & up to Hot Springs," American Philosophical Society. Call number 917.6 Ex7.

[109]McDermott, 16.

[110]The journal of Thomas Freeman was also in the possession of General Parker (Wagner-Camp-Becker, item 6b, footnote), but appears now to be lost.

[111]*Message*, 120, fn, *Discoveries*, 117, fn, McDermott 82–83, fn.

November 29,[112] the analysis of the Hot Springs water,[113] and the account of the separate return of the Hunter party.[114] We may presume that King used both journals, following Dunbar for his narrative and summaries of the expedition's findings, and consulting the Hunter journal for his unique observations. King also used the sketches and astronomical readings provided by Dunbar and Hunter in developing his "Map of the Washita River," as is clear from Dunbar's letter to Jefferson of March 18, 1806,[115] in which he remarks on the accuracy of the map, sent to him by the president on January 12 of the same year.[116]

### Nicholas King as Editor

The president showed characteristic forethought in May 1805, when he decided to place the redaction of the Dunbar (and Hunter) journals into the hands of Nicholas King. He informed Dunbar in a letter of May 25:

> Your several letters, with the portions of your journals, forwarded at different times have been duly received; and I am now putting the journal into the hands of a person properly qualified to extract the results of your observations, and the various interesting information contained among them, and bring them into such compass as may be communicated to the Legislature. Not knowing whether you might not intend to make a map yourself of the course of the river, he will defer that to the last part of his work, on the possibility that we may receive it from yourself.[117]

We can only presume an editorial presence for Nicholas King in the Sibley portions of the *Message*. There is no intervening manuscript between Sibley's notes[118] and the communications to Dearborn, so we cannot assess King's editorial impact, if any, on those sections.[119] In the Dunbar/Hunter section, King shows his skills as a redactor. A comparison of the 1904 transcription of Dunbar's full report to Jefferson with the final text in the *Message* and *Discoveries* reveals an editor carrying out with some subtlety the specific task assigned by the president—to extract the

[112]*Message*, 138–39, *Discoveries*, 134–35; McDermott, 98–99.

[113]*Message*, 150, *Discoveries*, 145–46; McDermott, 103.

[114]*Message*, 157–58, *Discoveries*, 152–53; McDermott, 108.

[115]Rowland, 190–92.

[116]Rowland, 188–89.

[117]Jefferson, Letter to Dunbar of May 25, 1805. Library of Congress, Thomas Jefferson Papers. Quoted by McDermott, 15, fn, and by Rowland, 174–77, from Dunbar's copy in the Mississippi State Archives.

[118]Transcribed in Appendix, B3 and B5.

[119]For a possible parallel (King as editor of Pike), see Donald Jackson's edition of Pike's journals and Wagner-Camp-Becker, entry 6a. King's redaction of the Freeman and Custis reports is now in the Peter Force Collection at the Library of Congress (Flores, 319), but Freeman's original is no longer available for comparison.

"various interesting information" and bring it "into such compass as may be communicated to the Legislature." The resulting focus and economy of the redaction is an undeniable improvement over Dunbar's discursive report. In editing Dunbar, King cut the original by at least a third, removing almost all references to the military contingent that provided the muscle-power of the expedition, and at the same time excising the numerous descriptions of problems on the journey. The reader is spared the irritations and delays caused by the design of Hunter's "chinese" boat, which was replaced by a craft of shallower draught at the first major post on the river; Hunter's unfortunate accident on November 22, when he shot himself in the hand, the bullet then singeing his brow and passing through the rim of his hat; and the entire "Journal of a Geometrical Survey," which is digested into the "Meteorological Notes" at the end of the narrative. This editing minimized the difficulties and dangers of the journey, in favor of a narrative more closely focused on scientific discovery.

In the volume as a whole, Clark's "A Statistical View," Sibley's reports to Dearborn, and the Dunbar/Hunter journals have a similarity of appearance, as if all three elements were the products of the same process. In fact, their origins were quite different: the "Statistical View" was developed during a winter of reflection at Fort Mandan, Sibley's reports grew over many months of interviews conducted from his home base in Natchitoches, and the Dunbar/Hunter narratives resulted from a complete journey of exploration.

### Mapping the Ouachita: Dunbar, Lafon, and King

Dunbar's work was far from complete in the summer of 1805. On July 6 he wrote to Jefferson[120] that he was still working on his map of the Ouachita, and in the course of this long letter discussed in some detail the problems of establishing longitude. At the same time he mentioned his

[120]Rowland, 154–56.

St. Dennie Attacking the Natchez Indians

This fanciful woodcut is from the first illustrated printing of the Report to Congress, *An Interesting Account of the Voyages and Travels of Captains Lewis and Clark, in the Years 1804–5, & 6* . . . published by P. Mauro in Baltimore, 1813. The image depicts the well-known massacre of the Natchez Indians described in the report.

correspondence with the New Orleans French engineer and geographer Barthélémy Lafon (1769–1820), who was an ideal source of information, having completed an authoritative map of present-day Louisiana and western Mississippi, to be published in Paris in 1806. Dunbar described him to the president as "Lafon the author of the map of Louisiana & the View of New orleans tho' I do not think that he is himself much of an astronomer, yet he may help to discover what we want."

Lafon's map, "Carte Générale du Territoire d'Orléans Comprenant aussi la Floride Occidentale et une Portion du Territoire du Mississipi" was published by Ch. Piquet as being "Dressée d'après les Observations les plus Récentes

Par Bmi. LAFON Ingénieur Géographe à la Nlle. Orléans."[121] The map is of particular interest in its depiction of the Ouachita as far north as the Isle of Mallet, the boundary line of Orléans Territory, today's border between Louisiana and Arkansas. Here it records (in the only English words on the map) "Island of Mallette" and "Observed an Eclipse of the Moon here Long. 6h. 6′. 29″. W. of Greenwich." Dunbar records the eclipse in his journal for Monday, January 14 (Geometrical), and Tuesday, January 15 (Exploration), but without the calculation of longitude. No mention of the eclipse appears in the *Message*, and King's engraved map, published with the *Message*, gives only a latitude for the "Isle de Mallet," though it does provide a longitude for the Hot Springs. The French map therefore presents for the first time an accurate longitude for a key location on the Ouachita, and its source is clear in the letter of Lafon to Dunbar on August 19, 1805.[122] Lafon wrote that he was sending the "course of the Ouachitat as far as the 33rd degree [the Isle of Mallet], fixed by the astronomical observations that Mr. Hunter left for me and which you have been so kind as to communicate to me." It is clear, however, from the same letter that Lafon was proving to be of equal value to Dunbar, who was still working on his map of the Ouachita:

> The pieces that I am sending you are abstracts from my general map of the territory which I have just completed on the fifteenth of the present month. I shall present you with a copy of it as soon as my present business has relaxed somewhat. I have enclosed with it Florida and part of the Mississippi territory.

Lafon appears one further time in Dunbar's correspondence, in Dunbar's letter to Jefferson of March 18, 1806.[123] Lafon later published a commercial calendar of New Orleans businesses (from Jean Renard, 1807) and a similar publication at his own expense (*Annuaire Louisianais, 1808–1809*). His only other cartographic publication was the map titled, in language not yet fully mastered, "Plan of

[121] One of the three copies in the Library of Congress Geography & Map Reading Room (call number G4010 1806. L3 Vault) may be viewed online. Streeter, III: 1, p. 1806, records advance notice in *National Intelligencer* of November 22, 1805, of Philadelphia publication of this map in May 1806. Lafon's "Map of the Louisiana Territory, 1807," possibly this map identified by a wrong date, or a later chart, was deposited with the APS Library before 1809: *Transactions* 6 (1809), xxxiii.

[122] Rowland, 179–80, translated.

[123] Rowland, 190–92. This passage is quoted in the following paragraph.

the Baton Rouge As It As Been Formerly Built."[124] He is nowhere mentioned in the *Message,* but the *Carte Générale* contains his small, almost invisible, tribute to Dunbar and Hunter.

Eventually, on November 10, 1805, Dunbar sent his completed map of the Ouachita to Jefferson,[125] but the president had meanwhile arranged for a map of that river to accompany his *Message* to Congress.[126] On January 12, 1806, he sent a copy of King's engraved map to Dunbar:

> . . . as it was material to have the map of the Washita ready drawn, engraved & struck off for Congress, we had put your notes into the hands of Mr. King, a skilful person, who had done the bu[s]iness, and I now send you one of the engraved charts. Yours will be preserved to enter into the General map of the W. which on the return of our exploring parties we shall endeavor to have composed & published.[127]

Dunbar responded on March 18 that

> I am much pleased to observe Mr. King's copy of the map of the Washita so much resembling my own that they might be taken for copies of each other; they would perhaps have been perfectly so, had I not contracted a little the scale to accommodate it to the map which is preparing by Lafon of Louisiana. Mr. Briggs has returned from the 33d degree of Latitude on the Mississippi, & he has favored me with some of his observations, but I have not yet found time to make calculations, tho I already see that we shall remove Mr Ellicotts Mississippi farther East so as to leave more space between that and the Washita. As soon as I shall ascertain the correction I will do myself the pleasure of forwarding it.[128]

By early May he had more information for the president: "Mr. Briggs' measurement accross between the Mississippi and Washita makes a very material change in the relative position of the two rivers, this appears to be 50 miles. [H]is observations for the Longitude / he informs me / will remove Mr Ellicots Mississippi farther East, but he has not completed his calculations."[129] It appears from these letters of early 1806 that Dunbar was content to accept King's map as the official chart of his expedition.

[124]WorldCat lists a photocopy at the State Library of Louisiana.

[125]Rowland, 184.

[126]The King map had been engraved in Philadelphia (by William Kneass) in time to be described in the *Medical Repository* for November/December 1805 and January 1806.

[127]Rowland, 188.

[128]Rowland, 191–92.

[129]Dunbar to Jefferson, May 6, 1806, in Rowland, 195.

### The Names in King's Map

Dunbar praised the accuracy of King's chart, "Map of the Washita River in Louisiana." McDermott has made it possible to compare the two maps, by printing the ten sheets of Dunbar's manuscript chart in his edition of the Hunter journals.[130] The reproduction is captioned as the work of Nicholas King, though in the text it is described as Dunbar's, "here published for the first time."[131] It would seem from the minor differences (particularly in some of the rubrics) between the manuscript and King's engraved map that the manuscript was Dunbar's, or a faithful copy of it. There is no way of knowing from Jefferson's January 12 letter whether King worked entirely independently on his chart, mapping only from coordinates in the Dunbar and Hunter field notes and from French and Spanish maps of the river. If that is the case, and the manuscript is Dunbar's, the closeness of the river's course in the engraving to that of the manuscript is impressive.

The following table shows the names in the engraved map (on the left) and their modern equivalents:

|  | *Modern Louisiana* |
| --- | --- |
| Confluence of Red and Mississippi | Torras |
| Large Creek | Grand Cutoff Bayou |
| "Settlement" | Mayna |
| "Settlements," opposite Bayou Tensa | Jonesville |
| Catahoola Bayou | same |
| Ha-ha Bayou | Haha Bayou |
| Barchelet | Bushley |
| Bayou St Louis | Louis Bayou opposite Harrisonburg |
| Bayou Beuf | Boeuf River |
| Praire Noyou | Sunk Lake, across from Enterprise |
| Bayou Calumet | Bayou de Chene, north of Columbia |
| Fort Miro, or Post of Washita | Monroe |
| Baron Bastrop's plantation | North Monroe |
| Bartelemi | Jones Bayou |
| Bayou Paupa | Pawpaw Bayou |
| Mercier | Cook Creek |

[130]McDermott, 72–80.
[131]McDermott, 15, fn.

### Modern Arkansas

| | |
|---|---|
| Marais de la Saline | Marais Saline |
| Great Saline Bayou | Saline River |
| Tulips hiding place | Tulip Lake and Tulip Creek |
| Pines | Pine Prairie Bay |
| Bay Morau | Moro Bay |
| Bayou de Hachis | Lewter Creek |
| Chemin Couvert | Smackover Creek north of Calion |
| Fabris Cliff | Ecore Fabri Bayou, north of Camden |
| Bayo de Cypre | Cypress Creek, at Tates Bluff |
| Cache a Macon | Casa Massa Creek |
| Bayou de l'eau froide | L'Eau Frais Creek, south of Arkadelphia |
| Saline Bayou | same, north of Arkadelphia |

### Near the Hot Springs

| | |
|---|---|
| Fourche des Cadaux | Caddo River |
| Rocky Creek | De Roche Creek |
| Isle de Millon | Friendship |
| Fourche a Tigré | Tigre Creek, north of Rockport |
| Fourch d Calfat (Caulker's creek) | Gulpha Creek |
| Bayou Mountcerne | Mazarn Creek |

It is encouraging, two hundred years after the work of Dunbar and King in mapping the Red, Black, and Ouachita rivers, to find almost all the names of the period preserved on a large-scale modern map. It should be possible to locate any of the points on Dunbar and Hunter's journey with some precision, and to compare the printed narrative with conditions on the ground today.

## Dunbar's List of Plants
### and Hunter's Meteorological Observations

Dunbar's original list of Ouachita plants was probably begun on December 18 and 19, 1804, at the Hot Springs during a period of idleness.[132] The list survives among the Hunter Papers at the American Philosophical Society.[133] It falls into two parts. The first is a simple list of the "Common Names of some of the Trees, Plants, Shrubs &cc growing in the Country adjacent to the Ouachita." The second is a more discursive description of fourteen plants, a "List of

[132]McDermott, 121, fn.
[133]It is reprinted in full by McDermott, 120–22.

Vegetables (perhaps non-descripts) from the River Washita." This second list was clearly completed some time after the return from the expeditions, since Dunbar must have planted some of the dwarf cabbage with a horseradish taste. He reports "a few of the plants are thriving in my garden." The same is true of the Cabin wood: "a few of the plants have a place in my garden." Two other plants (the osier and the grape vines) were "brought down" and "brought away" respectively. On November 27, Dunbar had recorded, in a journal entry not retained by King, "We found a considerable number of unknown (to us) plants some of them very handsome, but our very limited knowledge in practical botany, did not enable us to discover what they were, particularly as they were not in flower."[134] In creating his lists, therefore, he could only speculate whether any of their plants were previously unrecorded. King transcribed the first list verbatim for the Washington edition, omitting only the group "Persimmon, Pawpaw, Mulberry, Spicewood, wild Cherry, Sassafras" between *Magnolia accuminata* and Black Walnut, but he ignored the non-descripts.

Finally, at the close of his work for the *Message,* King appended a table of meteorological observations covering the whole Ouachita expedition. The materials for this table appear to have been derived entirely from Hunter's field notes. When the *Message* was reprinted in Natchez, Dunbar provided his publisher Andrew Marschalk with his own set of meteorological observations, with mixed results, to be described later.

## EDITIONS OF THE 1806 *Message*

### *Publications for Congress*

On February 19, 1806, the message delivered by the president to Congress announced four different expeditions: Lewis and Clark's exploration of the Missouri and the water route to the Pacific, still in progress; Sibley's journey

[134]Dunbar, *Journal* (ed. 1904), 71.

in 1803 to the westernmost American settlement on the Red River, and his reports from that outpost; Dunbar and Hunter's study of the Ouachita River and the Hot Springs; and an unnamed Red River exploration, about to be undertaken by Freeman and Custis. From the first three of these expeditions he promised immediate printed reports. The president's two-page preface was at once published by the government printers Duane and Son (1806, backdated to 1805, the start of this session of Congress), and excerpted in the second number of the Philadelphia journal *The Evening Fire-Side; or Literary Miscellany,* and probably in other eastern newspapers. Meanwhile, the three expedition reports were sent to A. & G. Way, also in Washington, for rapid promulgation to the House and Senate.

Delivery, however, was slow. On March 7, 1806, the Boston *Repertory* reported no progress beyond the news that Congress had ordered one thousand copies of the *Message* to be printed.[135] It was March 28 before Jefferson could send Dunbar a copy of the published volume, "which I thought would be immediately printed. . . . The printer, however, has taken till this time to do his duty."[136] The President's frustration is understandable. Dunbar's journals had been sent to him in March 1805, and Sibley's reports reached Dearborn early in the following month. King had been at work on journals and maps since May, and the Fort Mandan materials had arrived by mid-July. Yet on October 20 Dunbar had still not been told of any plans to print his journal. He wrote to John Swift in London, "I shall speedily prepare an abstract of my Journal up the river Washita, it does not contain any thing of much importance; . . . You shall have a more ample account hereafter."[137] By that time, all the materials for Jefferson's compilation had been in hand for some months. It is likely that the volume had been delivered to press by at least January 12, 1806, when Jefferson sent Barton's botanical notes to Dunbar, since these would otherwise have been included in the edition.

[135] *Literature,* 78.
[136] Rowland, 192.
[137] Rowland, 322.

The Washington edition by A. & G. Way (dated February 19, 1806) finally appeared in late March in two states, differing only in their title pages. One issue, intended for members of the House, had the designation "Read, and ordered to lie on the table," that is, the Speaker's table. The other issue was described as "Printed by order of the Senate." Some or all of the Senate copies were accompanied by Nicholas King's engraved "Map of the Washita River." No copy has been seen with the other map promised in the president's preface: Clark's map of the Missouri country. An account of King's manuscript redaction of this map appeared in Samuel Mitchill's *Medical Repository* of 1806:[138] "This map contains a grand display of waters and mountains heretofore very little known to geographers, and Mr. Nicholas King, the draughtsman, has performed his part with great elegance, on a scale of fifty miles to an inch." The reporter was almost certainly Mitchill himself, who on February 18, 1804, reported on the topic of Louisiana to the House Committee of Commerce and Manufactures, arguing (successfully) for funds to explore the Red and Arkansas rivers. He continued his review of "Lewis's" (i.e., Clark's) map with the comment "This map will not be engraved and offered for general use before the voyagers return from their expedition. They may then be expected to publish a narrative of their journey and discoveries." This will explain the absence of the Missouri map, promised by Jefferson for the 1806 *Message*. Instead, it was reserved for the full account, not to appear until 1814.

### The First Public Printings

By the time this government publication of the *Message* became available, at least one portion of it had already come to the public's attention. In late 1805 and early 1806, Mitchill published two reports on the Ouachita expedition in his *Medical Repository*.[139] The first, in late 1805, was a brief summary. The second was a full review of the exploration.

[138]"Lewis's Map of the Parts of North-America which lie between the 35th and 51st Degrees of North Latitude, from the Mississippi and the upper Lakes to the North Pacific Ocean," Vol. 9 (1806): 315–18. See Moulton (Atlas volume), maps 32a–c, and the facsimile in this volume.

[139]Vol. 8 (1805): 434–35 and vol. 9 (1806): 305–08.

Among other items, it quoted a substantial paragraph taken from the copy of Dunbar's journal used by A. & G. Way, or a close transcript of it. That the paragraph was placed in quotation marks presumably rules out Dunbar as the anonymous reporter. The summary also mentions the engraving of King's map, calling it "a substantial addition to American geography," words that King himself (who had been in possession of this manuscript in 1805) would hardly have used. We can presume that Mitchill himself had access, perhaps through King, to the manuscript, and produced this report, one of many commentaries on the Jeffersonian expeditions to appear in his *Medical Repository*.[140] It is a lively piece of reporting, with reference to geography, mineralogy, the creation of mist by temperature differential,[141] ethnography, cartography, settlement history, the creation of prairies by controlled burns, flooding, and the Great Raft blocking the Red River above Natchitoches.

A very similar edition of the *Message*, aimed at the general public, appeared from the publishers Hopkins and Seymour in New York. This was an almost exact reprint of A. & G. Way, but fortunately for the bibliographer it shows minor differences in spelling and punctuation that make the two texts easy to distinguish. In the preface, for example, and on pages 6 and 7, Way spells "Clarke" while Hopkins and Seymour spell "Clark." Other variants (Way listed first) are inclosed/enclosed ([5]), enterprize/enterprise (6, 8), connection/connexion (7), and Mississippi/Missisippi (11). Two other convenient points of difference are as follows: the first word of Sibley's "Historical Sketches," "CADDO-QUES," is punctuated in Way, unpunctuated in Hopkins and Seymour; and in the opening paragraphs of the Dunbar narrative the compositors consistently spell Mississippi (Way) and Missisippi (Hopkins and Seymour). No surviving copy of this edition contains either of the maps still promised in the unchanged preface. A notice appeared on July 12, 1806, in *The Evening Fire-side*,[142] reprinted from the

[140]See White, *Plains and Rockies, 1800–1865* (supplemental volume), 25–30, for a full listing.

[141]Here the reporter notes that Dunbar's findings correspond with those of Mitchill, published earlier, an observation that may point directly to that author as advance reviewer.

[142]Vol. II, no. 28.

Richmond *Enquirer*. Identifying the volume as a "pamphlet of 128 pages . . . published in New York," the review consists of two excerpts, one from Sibley's second message to Dearborn (a description of the lakes near Natchitoches), and the other from Dunbar's account of the Ouachita, a description of the "salt prairie" on the Arkansas.

### Serializations and Reprints

The text of A. & G. Way's edition was also taken up in serial form in the *Monthly Anthology and Boston Review* for 1806.[143] This printed (in its supplement "The Political Cabinet"[144]) the president's message (pp. 39–40), and Lewis's Fort Mandan letter (40–42), but omitted the "Statistical View" and the final "Meteorological Tables" from its otherwise complete reprint of A. & G. Way. The omission is explained in an editorial showing too little confidence in their readership's interest in the native peoples, and too great a trust in the Sibley and Dunbar narratives as fixing the bounds of Louisiana:

> We very much regret that it is not in our power to insert the communication from Captains LEWIS & CLARKE; it is extremely long and is quite as unintelligible without the assistance of a map: besides it would be very uninteresting to almost every reader, and therefore we shall proceed to the documents from Dr. SIBLEY and Mr. DUNBAR, which are mentioned in the President's message. These may gratify a variety of readers, besides the student of geography, and may assist the makers of maps in correcting the boundaries, divisions, &c. of the province of Louisiana.

This partial serialization was itself reprinted, following its departures from A. & G. Way, and omitting the "Statistical View," in *Omnium Gatherum*, a compilation of quirks and oddities published in twelve monthly issues between 1809 and 1810.[145] This journal published Lewis's Fort Mandan letter in its first issue, prefaced by an eccentric editorial containing some exact information,[146] but assigning Sibley, Hunter, and Dunbar to the Lewis and Clark party:

[143] *The Monthly Anthology, And Boston Review*, Vol. 3 (1806). See Wagner-Camp-Becker 5: 5 and 5b, where, however, this serialization is incorrectly described as a "full copy" of the Natchez reprint.

[144] Pp. 39–92.

[145] *Omnium Gatherum, A Monthly Magazine.* Boston: November 1809–October 1810.

[146] The date of departure and the distance traveled up the Missouri, both quoted verbatim from the president's message.

In the year 1803, the President of the United States, pursuant to a vote of Congress, appointed Capt. MERIWETHER LEWIS, with a party of men, to explore the river Missouri, from its mouth to its source, and, crossing the highlands by the shortest portage, to seek the best water communicating thence to the Pacific ocean. Lt. WILLIAM CLARKE was appointed second in command—who were assisted by Drs. SIBLEY and HUNTER, and Mr. DUNBAR— They entered the Missouri on the 14th. May, 1804, and on the 1st. of Nov. took up their winter quarters near the Mandan towns, 1609 miles above the mouth of the river, in pursuance of the objects pre-scribed them.

The full "Political Cabinet" text appeared in subsequent issues,[147] ending with issue eleven of September 1810. As public interest in the Louisiana Territory grew, the summer of 1806 saw the publication of the volume presented here in facsimile: Andrew Marschalk's reprint of the president's *Message* from Mississippi's first press at Natchez. This reprint followed A. & G. Way throughout,[148] with the omission of a folding table and a few other pages, and with the addition of a substantial scientific appendix: twenty-one pages of new or revised material. The text and printing of this edition is discussed in detail in the following chapter. Despite its distant origins, this Natchez reprint was noticed in a Boston newspaper, the *Repertory,* on October 3, in which the reporter took a skeptical line on the Purchase:

Our Government Paper at Washington, heads the title and contents of a Louisiana Geography, just published thus–
"The last paper we have received from Natchez announces the actual publication of the account of OUR NEW WESTERN TERRITORY by Messieurs *Lewis, Clarke, Sibley and Dunbar.*
"OUR" new, western country!" Yes, Mr. Smith, we have the map, and the Spaniards and the Indians have ninety-nine hundredths of the soil.[149]

In the fall of the same year, responding no doubt to particular curiosity in the Ouachita River expedition, the *National Intelligencer and Washington Advertiser* serialized the entire Dunbar/Hunter portion of A. & G. Way (omit-

[147]On pages 12–16, 51–56, 102–9, 147–54, 196–206, 245–50, 270–71 (the list of plants of the Washita, printed out of sequence), 291–98, 345–54, 387–97, 439–43, and 486–93.

[148]In every one of the points listed, Natchez follows A. & G. Way.

[149]The addressee is presumably Samuel H. Smith, proprietor of the *National Intelligencer and Washington Advertiser,* often the first to print government reports.

ting only the final meteorological tables) in five issues between October 15 and November 12,[150] apologizing in a preliminary editorial that "Owing to the mass of interesting matter, which about that time pressed for insertion in our gazettes, the interesting contents of this message did not receive the detailed notice, which otherwise would have been given them." While the fuller materials published in the Natchez reprint had been available since August, the newspaper followed the text published in Washington. Another serialization of southwestern portions of the *Message* appeared in *The American Register*. In 1807 this journal had printed a poem by Joel Barlow ("On the Discoveries of Captain Lewis"), soon parodied by John Quincy Adams in *The Monthly Anthology*.[151] In 1808 *The American Register* serialized Sibley's second communication to Dearborn (the general account of Red River),[152] and the following year reprinted the whole of the Ouachita Expedition report, including its meteorological tables.

Another partial serialization of the A. & G. Way materials occurred in an eight-page review of the volume in Mitchill's *Medical Repository*,[153] which reprinted verbatim the whole of the president's *Message* to Congress, and almost the entire text of Lewis's Fort Mandan letter, omitting only his paragraph on the rendering of his account vouchers to the secretary of war. The remainder of the review consisted of a summary of Clark's "A Statistical View," along with an extended quotation from Sibley's Red River report. Since this journal had already reported twice on the Ouachita expedition, as noted earlier, the review ended with no more than a brief mention of that part of the text. Mitchill returned to the Lewis and Clark Expedition one further time in 1807 with a report on its completion, and on the natural history samples brought back.[154] In this review he took the opportunity of correcting the earlier stories of the mountain of salt, and again discussed the Fort Mandan map, with a renewed call for its publication.

[150]In issues 937 (October 15), 942 (October 27), 944 (October 31), 948 (November 10), and 949 (November 12).

[151]Vol. 1 (1806–7), 198–99.

[152]*The American Register, or, General Repository of History, Politics, & Science*, 4:2 (1808), [49]–67.

[153]Vol. 10 (1807): 165–74.

[154]Vol. 10 (1807): 288–91.

*Foreign Printings*

Meanwhile, Jefferson's extended explorations were attracting foreign interest. The first overseas publication of the *Message* was in London (1807), once again closely following the text of A. & G. Way, as the fifth volume in an eleven-volume subscription series of "Modern and Contemporary Voyages and Travels" compiled by Sir Richard Phillips between 1804 and 1810. The long delay in publishing an edition of the Lewis and Clark journals left the door open for imaginative documentations. The first pair of these, a Philadelphia edition and its London reprint, appeared in 1809.[155] The Philadelphia compilation (by the pseudonymous Hubbard Lester) has received harsh treatment from bibliographers, as being a dishonest amalgam of accounts borrowed from earlier printed texts, including those of Jonathan Carver, Alexander Mackenzie, and Patrick Gass, together with passages of pure invention. It could equally be seen as the first clumsy attempt to present a survey of North American ethnography, from Canada to Louisiana, undertaken in an age when respect for copyright was at best irregular. From A. & G. Way the compiler borrowed Jefferson's message, omitting the final paragraphs on Sibley and Dunbar, the whole of Clark's "A Statistical View," Sibley's "Historical Sketches," and Dunbar and Hunter's "Observations." We do not know the intention of "Lester" in presenting the 1806 *Message* in the wider context of a whole continent, but one may have some sympathy for his desire to fill in an incomplete picture, while lamenting the uncritical approach and unnecessary resort to fabrication, including a deliberately misleading title page. The volume contains five crude plates of no ethnographic value, one of them a poor replica of a Seminole portrayed by William Bartram in his *Travels*. At the same time, this volume contains a map with the earliest identification of the three forks of the Missouri and Fort Clatsop.

[155] *The Travels of Capts. Lewis & Clarke, by Order of the Government of the United States, Performed in the Years 1804, 1805, & 1806. . . . Embellished with a Map of the Country inhabited by the Western tribes of Indians, and five Engravings of Indian Chiefs. Philadelphia: Published by Hubbard Lester. 1809; The Travels of Capts Lewis & Clarke, from St. Louis, by Way of the Missouri and Columbia Rivers, to the Pacific Ocean; Performed in the Years 1804, 1805, & 1806. . . . Illustrated with a Map of the Country, inhabited by the Western tribes of Indians. London: Printed for Longman, Hurst, Rees, and Orme, Paternoster Row. 1809.* See *Literature*, 133–43, for descriptions of the whole sequence of "surreptitious and apocryphal" publications.

The London edition followed Philadelphia closely, though omitting its most shameless feature, the misleading presidential "recommendation." It was very lightly edited, mostly to good effect, and omitted the plates and irrelevant final anecdotes supplied by "Lester." Needless to say, the Philadelphia compilation appears to have been popular, and was imitated in two German-American versions (Lebanon, Pennsylvania, 1811, and Frederick, Maryland, 1812), in further imitations in Philadelphia and Baltimore (1812 and 1813), and again in Baltimore (1813). One volume in this popularizing group, a German narrative published in Leipzig (1811), offered the "Results of the Journey of Captains Lewis and Clarke from the Missouri to the Southern Ocean." This text, occupying rather more than sixty pages in a collection of narratives, confines itself to a translation of two quite legitimate sections of the London edition of 1809, Clark's "A Statistical View" and Sibley's "Historical Sketches." One is inclined to believe that good judgment rather than luck led the compiler, Königsberg professor Johann Severin Vater, to choose these authentic materials for translation.[156]

### Later Editions

Jefferson's message, offered to Congress to fulfill his reporting obligation, was first reprinted in its entirety, and then borrowed piecemeal for various publications, meeting the needs of different constituencies. In retrospect, and perhaps in the president's view at the time, it stands as an interim report, with only the sketchiest hints of nations and territory beyond the Rocky Mountains. By the end of 1806, Jefferson knew that the complete account would be contained in the journals of the Corps of Discovery. In this publishing history of the *Message* to Congress, however, the longest wait was for the official documents themselves. In 1832 the government printers Gales and Seaton included the text of

[156]The contents of all the volumes inspired by the 1809 surreptitious texts are outlined in *Literature*, 135–41.

A. & G. Way in their *American State Papers, Class II, Indian Affairs, for the 9th Congress, 1st. Session, no. 113*, pp. 705–743, and after a further twenty years, in 1852, the same publishers reprinted the text in their *Annals of Congress, Appendix to 9th Congress, 2nd. Session*, columns 1036–1146.[157]

Modern editors have made available important source materials for the *Message*. At the start of the last century, Reuben Gold Thwaites became the first to edit the known journals of Lewis and Clark in their entirety. In volume six of his eight-volume work (1905), he included Clark's "Estimate of the Eastern Indians" created at Fort Mandan, together with a parallel table for the western Indians, from Fort Clatsop, in the section "Ethnology."[158] The materials relating to the eastern Indians, sent to General Dearborn, were published as "A Statistical View." At the close of the twentieth century, Gary Moulton, in his monumental edition of the journals (1983–2001), returned, like Thwaites, to the original Clark manuscript in the vaults of the American Philosophical Society in Philadelphia, transcribing it under the heading "Mandan Miscellany."[159] Sibley has received less attention from editors, but his manuscript notes for the communications to Dearborn are at the Library of Congress, where they can be read online. They are transcribed in Appendix B of this volume. Hunter's journals, including his field notes from the Ouachita River exploration, have been transcribed and thoroughly annotated by John Francis McDermott (1963). Dunbar's journal of the same expedition was edited anonymously for the American Philosophical Society in 1904, and a large number of his letters (together with another copy of his journal) were transcribed by Eron Rowland in 1930. Finally, to this list of scholars should be added the first persons to edit these materials, who did so while occupied with other weighty matters, but who brought their own values and perspectives to the task: Thomas Jefferson and his trusted editor, Nicholas King.

[157]The *Annals of Congress* text may be read online at the Library of Congress web site.

[158]Thwaites, VI (i): 80–113.

[159]Moulton, 3: 386–445.

# The Natchez Edition Textual Introduction

## *Andrew Marschalk and His Press*

Andrew Marschalk, the printer of the Natchez edition of the *Message* to Congress in 1806, was born of Dutch parentage in New York in early 1757. By the time the revolutionary war had broken out, Marschalk was attending school at Peter Van Steenburgh's seminary at the Dutch Reformed Church in New York. Some authorities believe that Marschalk "held three commissions under George Washington"[1] Others consider this improbable, given his date of birth.[2] Marschalk spent some time in England, where he probably learned the art of printing. On his return to the States he brought with him a small mahogany press, which he held for a short time before selling it to join the Army. He served in the Ohio Indian wars under General Arthur St. Clair and General Anthony Wayne, rising to the rank of captain. After the Indian campaigns, the U.S. Army returned to noncombatant status, and Marschalk was reduced to the rank of lieutenant. Once again he pursued his interest in printing. He "bought a small font of type, about thirty pounds," and regained possession of his original press.[3]

In spring of 1797 Marschalk was with General James Wilkinson in the march down the Mississippi to take over military outposts held by the Spanish. From Fort Washington they traveled to Chickasaw Bluffs, and set up establishments at Fort Adams, and at Fort Nogales, a short distance

[1]Sydnor, 49.
[2]E.g., Welsh, 5.
[3]Welsh, 6.

from the mouth of the Yazoo River. Upon arriving at Nogales, Wilkinson learned from the Spanish that they were not ready to give up possession of the fort. Under the direction of Captain Isaac Guion, the army camped outside of Natchez, and waited for the removal of the Spanish. Fort Nogales was evacuated on March 23, 1798.[4] In nearby Walnut Hills (or Fort McHenry, at Vicksburg), Marschalk printed in 1798 the first sheets to appear in the future state of Mississippi. The authoritative account of Marschalk's early years as a printer is found in his 1837 letter to L. A. Besançon, editor and sometime owner of *The Mississippi Free Trader and Natchez Weekly Gazette:*

L. A. Besançon, Esq.:

Dear Sir: The first press in Mississippi was a small mahogany one, brought by me from London, in September, 1790. It was out of my possession for six years. When ordered to this (then) territory (I was an officer in the United States army) in the year '97–'98, I regained possession of it, and obtained a small font of type—say thirty pounds—and while at the Walnut Hills, printed a ballad, "The Galley Slave." Great excitement was caused in Natchez by the knowledge of a press being in the country, and strong inducements were held out for me to remove to that place. Finally, I constructed a large press, capable of printing a foolscap sheet, and printed the territorial laws. This press was sold by me to Ben M. Stokes, and he commenced in Natchez and continued for some time in the summer of 1799, but soon failed.

About March or April, 1800, a Mr. Green, from Baltimore, brought a press to Natchez. I do not recollect the title of his paper; it ceased while I was at the north, and the press fell into the hands of James Ferrall, who, with one Moffatt, published a paper for a short time.

I arrived from Philadelphia the last of July, 1802, and commenced the Mississippi Herald, I think on the 26th July of the same year. I cannot conveniently lay my hand on the 1st volume, but send you, as a specimen of the poverty of those days, a small file of 1803 and 4. I commenced on medium, but was reduced, for want of paper, to cap.

I am yours, &c.,
Andrew Marschalk[5]

[4]Welsh, 7.

[5]Letter of Andrew Marschalk to L. A. Besançon, Washington, Mississippi, September 2, 1837, printed in *The Mississippi Free Trader and Natchez Weekly Gazette,* August 15, 1838. Reprinted by I. M. Patridge, "The Press of Mississippi," *De Bow's Review* 5: 29 (New Orleans, October 1860), 501, and by Madel J. Morgan, *The Journal of Mississippi History* 8 (July 1946), 147–48.

This letter is our only evidence that the text printed at Walnut Hills was "The Galley Slave." According to Marschalk's bibliographer, no copy of "The Galley Slave" is known to exist; he identifies the text as being from William Reeve's opera *The Purse, or Benevolent Tar.*[6] From these beginnings at the small outpost of Walnut Hills, Marschalk saw an opportunity to expand his operations by printing both for the military and for the newly-established territorial government of Mississippi. He expressed his ambition in a 1798 letter to Governor Sargent:

> Give me leave to intreat your Excellency's pardon for the appearance of inattention to your Billet of the 14th inst it has been owing entirely to an accumulated multiplicity of business.
>
> In offering the use of the press to you, Sir, it was my wish and attention to execute, myself, such printing as you might find necessary—permit me to repeat that offer—and to assure your Excellency that it will afford me real pleasure to render the press serviceable to you—
>
> It would not be in my power to give sufficient directions for the making of Ink—the process is tedious and uncertain—and in fact—altho' I have often assisted at an attempt to make it (where none was otherwise to be had) a very poor substitute was always the result of the labor—
>
> I have conversed with the Commander in Chief [General James Wilkinson] upon the subject of establishing a printing office at Natchez—he has been good enough to promise every assistance in his power—and I expect—will mention the subject to your Excellency—I have also been offered (thro' Captn Wade who was at Natchez when you passed this post) very liberal encouragement, from a number of Gentlemen at the place—I am persuaded, Sir, that, a press well conducted, will be an object of public as well as private [be]nefit—permit me to soli[cit] such encouragement from you, as the attempt may deserve.[7]

Marschalk was in business, and began to print both privately and for the government. His earliest Natchez imprint was the 1799 pamphlet *Paine Detected, or the Unreasonableness of Paine's Age of Reason,* written anonymously by John Henderson. *The Description of Texas; with Topographic Map,* by Philip Nolan, now lost, but listed as a Natchez imprint of

[6]McMurtrie, 19.

[7]Letter of Andrew Marschalk to Winthrop Sargent, Fort McHenry, September 30, 1798, in William B. Hamilton, *The Journal of Mississippi History* 2: 2 (April 1940), 92.

the same year, would also be from Marschalk's press.[8] If it existed, this small-format volume, with an inaccurate map, would be the first of its kind on Texas, but both Charles S. Sydnor and Douglas C. McMurtrie cast doubt on Bradford's listing.[9]

Marschalk began printing for the Territorial Legislature of Mississippi in the same year, with the first of nine volumes of the *Laws* of the Mississippi Territory to appear from his press between 1799 and 1808. In this volume, "from pages 3 to 63, inclusive, odd numbered pages are on the verso of the leaf. To correct this, page 64 was omitted, so that page 65 follows page 63."[10] Problems with signatures and pagination continued to plague this frontier printer, as can be seen in the facsimile reproduced in this volume. While this may have frustrated the subscribers of his press, it does leave the modern bibliographer and collector with a treasure trove of points and textual variants.

In announcing completion of the 1799 *Laws,* Marschalk offered a valuable hint as to the volume's price:

> At length the Herculean Task is accomplished—and the good people of the Mississippi Territory may have as much law as they choose to buy. . . . From the lowest calculation possible, the books cannot be sold under two dollars—each book contains 52 sheets of writing paper. . . .

Two weeks later this estimate was revised:

> The laws ought not to be sold for less than 2 dollrs. & 25 cents per copy—each copy contains 2 quires and ½ of writing paper [approximately 62 sheets]—which at Natchez will cost more than half the money—. . . the assistant I had at Natchez has occasioned a great loss of paper to me by his carelessness in the former part of the work. . . .[11]

This price of rather more than two dollars, for a 1799 volume of slightly smaller dimensions but around twenty-five more pages, would suggest a similar unit cost of around two dollars for the 1806 volume, which was indeed its price as advertised in the *Mississippi Herald* of May 27, 1806.

[8]Bradford, Thomas Lindley, *The Bibliographer's Manual of American History* III (Philadelphia: Stan V. Henkels, 1908), 197.

[9]Welsh, 18–19.

[10]McMurtrie, 22.

[11]Marschalk to John Steele and Governor Sargent, October 21 and November 3, 1799, quoted by McMurtrie, 23.

In addition to his government printing, Marschalk founded a number of Natchez newspapers published under various titles between 1802 and 1830. He also became actively involved in local and national politics, corresponding with Henry Clay, Thomas Jefferson, and Andrew Jackson. He served as justice of the peace and postmaster of Adams County. Another significant achievement was his success in gaining the freedom of an African prince, Abd al-Rahman Ibrahima, who had been sold into slavery: "Ibrahima was born in 1762 as a prince in Futa Jallon, today part of Guinea in western Africa. He was captured in battle by enemies, sold into slavery and shipped to America," where he was purchased in 1789 by Thomas Foster, who owned a plantation near Natchez.

> In 1807, John Cox, a doctor who had fallen ill in Africa in 1781 and was cared for by Ibrahima's family, traveled to Mississippi and happened to meet Ibrahima at a market north of Natchez. Cox recognized Ibrahima as the son of the king who had saved his life. Cox tried to buy Ibrahima's freedom, but Foster refused and kept Ibrahima as a slave for twenty more years.
>
> Ibrahima's story reached Andrew Marschalk, editor of the *Mississippi Statesman and Gazette* in Natchez. Marschalk pleaded Ibrahima's case to Henry Clay, who was then secretary of state. In 1828, Foster relented. Ibrahima, sixty-six, was able to buy his and his wife's freedom with the aid of the community and the American Colonization Society, an organization that sent free blacks in America to Africa.[12]

Andrew Marschalk died on August 14, 1838. He had been the first public printer in Mississippi Territory, founder of one of its first and longest-lasting newspapers, and a powerful political figure with a social agenda. He is remembered as the Benjamin Franklin of Mississippi.

### The Natchez Reprint of the Message

Between July 27, 1802, and November 19, 1808, Andrew Marschalk was occupied with his newspapers the *Mississippi Herald* and the *Natchez Gazette,* which appeared regularly

[12]From an Associated Press article in the Lafayette, Louisiana, *Advertiser* for April 13, 2003. Online at www.theadvertiser.com.

every week under those names, separately and in combination. His editorial work, which included responding to frequent libel actions, particularly from justices and other politicians whom he had attacked, would no doubt have been onerous. It was probably early in 1806 that he was approached by William Dunbar of Natchez with the request for a reprint of the president's *Message* to Congress of February 19, 1806. In agreeing, Marschalk appears to have cleared his time for this task. His earlier commission to print the volumes of Mississippi laws had already passed by 1805 into the hands of T. & S. Terrell, who remained the territory's printer through 1807, though the task reverted to Marschalk in 1808. Between September 1805, therefore, when he advertised a 25-cent religious pamphlet by Peter A. Vandorn, and September, 1807, when he announced an eighteen-page poem addressed by Mrs. E. Soniat du Fossat to General Wilkinson, Marschalk's only publications were the 1806 reprint for Dunbar and the eleven-page *Rules of Practice established by the Supreme Court of the Mississippi Territory; at their November Term, 1805*, also dated 1806.[13] Marschalk did, however, continue the laborious weekly task of editing and printing the *Mississippi Herald & Natchez Gazette* throughout 1806, and also performed the duties of City Clerk of Natchez during the year.

On February 25, 1806, Marschalk advertised in his paper for a "Journeyman Printer" at his office, which may indicate that he had already received his commission for the reprint from Dunbar. Benjamin Barton's notes on the botanical lists arrived at Natchez on or shortly before March 18. On March 28, the president sent Dunbar the Washington publication by A. & G. Way, the copy-text for the reprint:

> Your letter of Dec 17 did not get to my hands till Feb. 11. I did not answer it immediately because I was about communicating to Congress the information we had collected as to Louisiana which I thought would be immediately printed, I wished at the same time to send you a copy of it. The printer however has taken till this time to do his duty. I send you a copy & with the more justice as you have contributed so much toward it yourself.[14]

[13]McMurtrie, 44–48.

At almost the same time, on April 1, Marschalk published in his *Mississippi Herald* the volume's preface, Jefferson's February 19 *Message* to Congress.[15] Work on the reprint must have begun at his press soon afterwards. The volume was first advertised in the newspaper on May 27, under the headline "An Interesting Work." The notice continues:

> IN THE PRESS, And will be published with all possible dispatch, Discoveries Made in exploring the Missouri, Red River, and Washita, by captains Lewis and Clark, Doctor Sibley, and William Dunbar, Esq. with a Statistical Account of the countries adjacent; With an APPENDIX by Mr. Dunbar. It will be comprised in a handsome volume, octavo, about 20 pages printed on good paper, and an excellent type. Price to Subscribers, TWO DOLLARS. A List of subscribers will be prefixed. Subscription papers are lodged in the hands of several gentlemen, who patronize the work. Natchez, May 27.

This advertisement contains almost the exact text of the reprint's title page. The promised list of subscribers does not appear in the published volume, either through inadvertence, or because the names proved too few to justify a printed list. The advertisement was reprinted, in an almost identical display, on June 3, June 10, on the front page on June 17, and on June 24.

On June 20 Dunbar wrote to his friend John Swift in England that the reprint was in press, with an "appendix lately added," and promising him a copy containing a map.[16] The copy sent to Swift, with Dunbar's corrections, but (like all other surviving copies) lacking a map, is now owned by the New York Public Library. Finally, on August 5, Marschalk devoted a full outer column of the paper to a 101-line announcement, beginning "THIS DAY IS PUBLISHED, At the Herald Office, DISCOVERIES MADE IN EXPLORING. . . ." The bulk of the description is devoted to the "Contents of Capts. Lewis and Clarke's Journal," by which is meant "A Statistical View of the Indian Nations." Dr. Sibley's Historical Sketches are summarized in eight lines, with the remaining twenty-six lines given to the

[14]Rowland, 192.
[15]Taking his text presumably from a newspaper reprint of the message.
[16]Rowland, 345.

Dunbar and Hunter Observations, with particular emphasis (near the top of the advertisement, and again at the foot) on the appendix, "Never before Published." and "Not before Published." This splendid display advertisement appeared again on August 12 and is reproduced in this volume.

One week later, on August 19, under evident financial constraints, Marschalk printed a dignified and semi-humorous appeal for payment from his subscribers:

> To enable me to meet a pressing & just demand—I lately sent an intelligent lad into a neighboring county, with accounts to collect, amounting to nearly three hundred dollars—The result of his journey is—that after an absence of ten days, he returns to me fatigued, sick—with a lame horse, & not as much money as would have borne his necessary expences, . . . To be brief—if these things have not a speedy end, the "HERALD'S" trumpet will soon cease to sound, and its voice be heard no more.

A similar appeal appears on August 26, under the head "Hint 21." Here the editor thanks paid-up subscribers, but warns defaulters that if their debts are not "discharged before the first day of October, the paper will then be exposed at public sale, to close the concern—with the names annexed." The threat must have been effective, as the paper continued without interruption until November 1808. It would appear that, despite temporary financial embarrassment, Marschalk was not disadvantaged by his efforts on Dunbar's behalf, and he may even have profited by them. *Discoveries* was likely printed in a small edition, perhaps as few as fifty, to judge from the scarcity of survivors.

### Copy for the Natchez Edition

The first sixty-four pages of the text—Lewis's Fort Mandan letter, Clark's "A Statistical View of the Indian Nations," and the two following Sibley sections addressed to General Dearborn (pp. [65] to 112)—have only one immediate source, the corresponding portions of Jefferson's *Message* to

**THIS DAY IS PUBLISHED,**
*At the Herald Office,*

# DISCOVERIES

MADE

## IN EXPLORING

THE

*Missouri, Red and Washita, Rivers*

AND

### COUNTRIES ADJACENT,

BY

*Capts. Lewis and Clarke, Dr. Sibley,*
*William Dunbar, Esq and*
*Dr Hunter.*

WITH AN APPENDIX BY MR. DUNBAR,
*( Never before Published.)*

~~~~~~

*Contents of Capts Lewis and Clarke's*
*Journal.*

---

### A STATISTICAL VIEW

OF THE

### INDIAN NATIONS

INHABITING

### THE TERRITORY OF LOUISIANA

AND THE

*Countries adjacent to its Northern and Wes-*
*tern Boundaries.*

viz.

The names of the Indian nations as usually spelt and pronounced in the English
language.

Primitive Indian names of nations and
tribes, English orthography, the syllables
producing the sounds by which the Indians
themseves exprefs the name of their respective nations.

Nick-names, or thofe which have generally obtained among the Canadian traders.

Number of warriors

The probable number of souls.

The rivers on which they rove, on which
their villages are situated.

The names of the nations or companies
with whom they maintain their principal
commerce or traffic.

The place at which their traffic isiufu-
ally carried on.

The amount of merchandize neceffary
for their annual confumption, eftimated in
dollars at the St. Louis prices.

The fpecies of peltries furs and other articles which they annually fupply or furnifh.

The fpecies of peltries furs and other articles which they annually fupply or furnifh.

The fpecies of peltries, furs and other
articles which the natural productions of
their country would enable them to furnifh
provided proper encouragement were given
them.

The place at which it would be mutually advantageous to form the principal
eftablifhments in order to fupply the feveral Indian nations with merchandize :

The names of the Indian nations with
whom they are at war.

The names of the Indian nations with
whom they maintain a friendly alliance, or,
with whom they are united by intercourfe
or marriage.

Mifcellaneus remarks.

---

*Dr. Sibley's account Contains*

## HISTORICAL SKETCHES

OF THE

SEVERAL INDIAN TRIBES IN LOUISIANA,

SOUTH OF

### THE ARKANSA RIVER,

AND BETWEEN

*The Mississippi and River Grand.*

---

*Mr. Dunbar's and Dr. Hunter's Journal*
*Contains*

OBSERVATIONS Made in a voyage
commencing at St. Catharine's landing,
on the eaft bank of the Miffiffippi, proceeding downwards to the mouth of Red
river, and from thence afcending that
river, the Black river, and the Wafhita
river, as high as the Hot Springs in the
proximity of the laft mentioned river.

---

*Contents of Mr. Dunbar's Appendix,*
( Not before Publifhed.)

Lift of ftages and diftances on the Red &
Wafhita Rivers (in French computed
leagues) to the Hot Springs.

Lifts of the moft obvious vegitable productions of the *Wafhita Country,* which are
indiginious or growing without cultivation.

Notice of certain vegetables, part of
which are fuppofed to be new.

Of the medical properties of the Hot
Springs——

Meterological obfervations, (corrected
from thofe publifhed) by the addition of the
Latitude.

---

ANDREW MARSCHALK'S ANNOUNCEMENT OF THE NATCHEZ EDITION.
The advertisement ran as one full column
of his *Mississippi Herald* on August 5 and 12, 1806.

Congress in February 1806, printed in the City of Washington by A. & G. Way, Printers, 1806. The Natchez reprint closely follows the texts of Lewis and Clark and Sibley, with two major omissions. The first was Clark's folding table "Sioux Proper." following page 30 of the original, which was either missing from their copy, beyond the capacity of the press, or overlooked. Consequently, the information on the Sioux is given only in the prose summaries, omitting the ethnographic data in the table. Included in this omitted material is the table "Subdivisions of Darcotar." The second omission is pages 64 and 65 of the original, the description of the Pania Pique and Paducas, the last tribes described in "A Statistical View." These missing pages from A. & G. Way's edition are reproduced in Appendix A. The shoulder notes to the Clark and Sibley portions of the following facsimile record only those readings in the manuscripts—Lewis's Fort Mandan letter (L), Clark's draft of "A Statistical View" (C), and Sibley's notes for his two messages to Dearborn (S1 and S2)[17]—that elucidate or correct the text of A. & G. Way. They should not be taken as potential sources of the printed text.

The printing of the Dunbar segment (pp. 113–end) is more complex, as one might expect. The copy-text is A. & G. Way,[18] but throughout the reprint we see evidence of minor corrections, some of which were certainly provided by Dunbar, who would have had ready access to Marschalk's print shop. Most importantly, while the Washington printing ended with a one and a half-page list of some of the vegetation on the Washita, followed by seven unnumbered pages of meteorological tables, edited from Dunbar's "Journal of a Geometrical Survey,"[19] in the Natchez reprint this total of eight and a half pages grew to twenty-one: a five-page summary of the expedition by stages, five pages of botanical listings in small type, three pages of discussion of the medicinal properties of the Hot Springs, and a new eight-page edition of the meteorological tables. One further

[17]The reference codes are elaborated on page 93 herein.

[18]In the last two lines of page 161, Marschalk's compositor followed A. & G. Way's error of an extra parenthesis, an error found only in the printed copy, and not in Dunbar's manuscript.

[19]Dunbar, *Journal* (ed. 1904), separately numbered 1–76.

difference between Natchez and the Washington text is in the replacement of Dunbar's homeward journey (two pages in W) with a single short paragraph, perhaps to keep the material from extending into a new signature. These replaced pages are also reproduced in Appendix A.

### The Botanical Notes, the Hot Springs Analysis, and Meteorological Tables

The new botanical listings in the Natchez reprint represent a significant expansion of the list in A. & G. Way. Although the record is unclear, the new listing may have been shaped in collaboration with Benjamin Smith Barton, the country's leading botanist, a friend of Jefferson, and one of Meriwether Lewis's Philadelphia mentors. On January 12, 1806, Jefferson wrote to Dunbar enclosing "Doctr Barton's account of the Botanical specimens you sent me from the Washita,"[20] acknowledged by Dunbar on March 18: "I am greatly obliged by Doctor Barton's observations."[21] Too late to be included in the Washington publication of the *Message,* but arriving as they did in the spring of 1806, Barton's annotations would have been perfectly timed for inclusion in the Natchez reprint. At five pages of small print, the new appendix became an ideal accompaniment to the research at the Hot Springs, as an attempt at a comprehensive listing of southwestern plant species. By the time of the reprint, presumably with Barton's help, the simple list had been ordered into four categories: Forest Trees; Lesser Trees, Shrubs and Vines; Herbaceous Plants, Creepers, &c.; and Grasses. Each specimen was provided with its Linnæan classification.

The list of "non-descripts" was retitled "Notice of certain vegetables, of which a part is perhaps new." Such uncertainty would suggest that Barton was not involved in this portion of the catalog. The lengthy descriptions in the manuscript were reduced to brief notations. Exactly half of

[20]Jefferson to Dunbar, January 12, 1806, in Rowland, 188.
[21]Dunbar to Jefferson, March 18, 1806, in Rowland, 191.

the manuscript's original fourteen are described in the printed list, which also adds eight names of its own, though some of these may be the originals under new names. Clearly the list of "non-descripts" was reassessed and revised at leisure after the return home. Barton's notes may have supplied better guesses as to some of the plants described.

It should be said that while the approximately five pages of plant listings in the Natchez reprint are a considerable advance on the single page of the Washington edition, it retains a somewhat perfunctory feel, as if Barton's attention was not fully engaged in the task. The contrast with his *Elements of Botany* of 1803, with its full-page illustrations and detailed descriptions, is striking. Taken as a whole, however, the multi-page addendum of materials presented a convincingly complete survey of the Hot Springs, the expedition's equivalent of the Yellowstone River. Where Clark's and Sibley's contributions had been largely confined to an assessment of peoples and landscapes with future commercial possibilities, the Dunbar/Hunter account was a scientific document. The expedition leaders studied the tiny bivalve almost hidden in the Hot Springs' green moss with intense curiosity, and they gathered their plant materials in a spirit more of inquiry than of commerce. While their discoveries were probably fewer than they might have hoped, Dunbar seized the chance to print them in a form that could be a model for future naturalists. Others might describe greater wonders—a Grand Canyon, a Glacier Park—but Dunbar and Hunter hold a minor but honorable place among pioneering naturalists, though their findings would soon be eclipsed by the journals of Lewis and Clark and the many specimens brought back from that expedition.[22]

The final pages of the reprint, the revised meteorological tables, present a small puzzle. As noted earlier, the tables presented by Nicholas King in A. & G. Way were derived from the field notes of George Hunter. For the reprint,

[22]See Cutright, *passim.*

Dunbar provided Marschalk with tables from his own records. In one respect, these revised tables were clearly an advance on Hunter's, since Dunbar provided a latitude reading for the majority of the dates. Hunter's tables, however, gave four temperature readings for almost every day (sunrise, 3 P.M., 8 P.M., and in river water) while Dunbar provided only three (greatest, least, and in water), and more importantly, omitted the water temperatures on a number of days. Dunbar's notes on weather conditions were laconic, mostly single-word entries, while Hunter's were descriptive. Finally, a comparison of the temperature listings and wind directions in the tables also shows occasional discrepancies between the two sets of records. One must assume that Dunbar had greater confidence in his own findings, despite their occasional lacunae, and took the opportunity provided by the reprint to replace King's redaction from Hunter's notes.

### The Compositors and the Finished Book

Copy was set almost certainly by at least two compositors, one of them presumably Andrew Marschalk. The evidence for multiple compositors is based on four kinds of evidence: pagination, type, spelling, and fidelity to copy.

a) PAGINATION—There is some carelessness in pagination: page 65 is left unnumbered, as the start of a section, but this number is given to the next page, a verso, with the result that in the following pages the rectos are even-numbered. The failure to number [66] may indicate an awareness of the problem. The error might have been resolved at page 113, where the next section break is a verso, but that page is numbered and the opportunity missed. The normal habit is recovered by numbering two facing pages 127 (at the start of signature R), but confusion reappears when page 166 is followed by a sequence beginning again with (unnumbered) 159. This was not the first Marschalk volume to show an eccentric pagination. As noted earlier, almost his first piece of printing, the 1799 *Laws* of the Missisippi Territory, a 209-page volume printed in two hundred copies,[23] has odd-numbered pages on the verso of the leaf from pages 3 to 63 inclusive, a situation corrected by omitting the number 64 and numbering 65 to follow directly after 63. Marschalk complained about this edition that "the assistant I had at Natchez has occasioned a great loss of paper to me by his carelessness in the former part of the work."[24] Since two of the errors noted in the 1806 volume occur on the first page of a signature (127 and [159], the first pages of signatures R and W), this strongly suggests cast-off copy between two compositors; further evidence of cast-off copy may be the short page 39, the last of eight-page signature D, though there is some inconsistency of page length throughout the text.

A further piece of evidence is the presence of the first line of page 25 (D1) as the last line of 23 (C4). This line of type, already set as the first element in signature D, was imposed as the last line of the inner forme of C (a forme is one side of a signature), an imposition error rather than one of cast-off copy, where the line would have appeared at the end of 24 (C4 verso). The line was reset (showing a different capital 'T' and using long 's') when it was clear that material was missing between 24 and 25. It is suggestive that this error appears between two signatures showing other signs of divided composition.

b) Type—The volume was set from three cases of type, Cases 1 and 2 containing different fonts approximating in size and character to Baskerville's Pica Roman and Italic, and Case 3 (used for footnotes, one headnote, and parts of the Appendix) approximating to Baskerville's Long Primer Roman and Italic. The first two signatures of the volume are set to a measure of 9 centimeters, in a font (Case 1) with straight tail or leg on capitals Q and R, and capital J falling below the line, and with the numeral I for 1 and numerals 3,

[23]McMurtrie, item 3.
[24]McMurtrie, 23.

4, 5, 7, and 9 falling below the line. The page numbers of signatures A and B are in an anomalously large font, and these large numerals recur in signature W's part of the Appendix, most of which (W2–W4v and all of X) is also set to the same wide measure as A and B. The remainder of the volume is set to a measure of 8.5 centimeters from a case (Case 2) with curly tail/leg on Q and R, capital J sitting on the line, the numeral 1, and with 3, 4, 5, 7, 9 placed on the line. The third font used in this volume (Case 3) was the smaller type used for the footnotes and part of the Appendix. None of the type cases possessed a degree sign (°), so all listings of longitude, latitude, and temperature use letters (d, m, s) for degrees, minutes, and seconds.

The compositor using Case 1 set long 's'—both as a separate sort and in ligatures of 'si,' 'sh,' 'sk,' 'ss,' 'ssi,' and 'st'—and the ligatures 'ct' and 'fl.' This (to a contemporary eye, "old-fashioned") habit continues part way into signature D, and is also present, though not entirely consistently, in the footnotes of signatures P and R, as well as in the small-font portions of the appendix containing the botanical directory (161–166) and the note "Of the medical properties of the Hot-Springs" (166–169). Since the appendix is the only part of the volume not in A. & G. Way, and therefore not set from printed copy, it seems very likely that after signatures A and B had been set by the compositor using Cases 1 and 3, he was also asked to set the small-font and later sections (W2–X4v) of the appendix, which he set in the same measure as the first two signatures. He was then allocated signature D, but this was set to the new narrower measure established in signature C. After completing his work on D, and possibly the tables in F and G noted below, he would perhaps have been given the footnotes in P and R to set, after which he appears to have had no further part in the volume.

c) SPELLING—The division of labor between the two men suggested above is reflected also in divergent spelling patterns. The "old-fashioned" compositor (compositor 1) of signatures A and B spells rather consistently "prairies" and "racoon," while the compositor of the majority of the book (compositor 2) spells "priaries" and "rackoon." Since the "prairies" spelling is also found in tables on F3v, G2, and G3v, it seems possible that compositor 1 of signatures A and B was also assigned the tables to set.

d) FIDELITY TO COPY—One final anomaly should be noted: it will be obvious from the shoulder notes that the compositor of signature M is more free with the text than in any other signature of the volume, resulting in three substantial examples of missing text, all omitted as a result of eye-skip between identical words. This suggests either a different compositor, possibly a third worker, employed in this signature alone (using compositor 2's type-cases), or unusual pressure on compositor 2 himself, during the setting of this signature. Whatever this tells us about compositor activity, the fact that this idiosyncratic behavior is confined to one signature can be taken as further evidence of cast-off copy.

Throughout the volume there is a consistent use of extra letter-spaces before and after semicolons, after commas, and between sentences. Another typographical idiosyncrasy throughout is the purely ornamental use of an em-dash to complete a line following a period, where the first word of the new sentence would not fill the remaining space. Neither of these two habits is confined solely to one or the other compositor's work, though the space-filling em-dash occurs only once (on B2v) in compositor 1's pages, and sixteen times in those of compositor 2.

It would be tempting to suppose that the "old-fashioned" compositor 1, used for six signatures, the tables, and the footnotes, was the journeyman possibly hired in March, and that Marschalk himself set the remaining seventeen or so signatures.

A striking feature of the various surviving copies is the shifting up and down of the text block, so that frequently one page of an opening will appear as many as four lines higher than its facing page.[25] Since these patterns vary from copy to copy, it was apparent (from observation of the patterns, and experiments with a sheet folded to represent a signature) that Marschalk had no means of aligning his sheets accurately on the press while printing, some sheets being laid too high on the type, some lower. When the sheets were folded into signatures, the first fold left the tops of the imposed pages in the fold. Only then was it folded a second time, with the fold within the gutter. If the text blocks of, for example, 1v and 4 were printed lower than those of corresponding 2 and 3v, and the sheet were then folded in half, 1v (after folding and cutting) would be lower than 2, and 3v higher than 4. This somewhat elementary defect in Marschalk's book production offers a good example of either his carelessness, or (what is more likely) the limitations of the press, perhaps the original "small mahogany one," of this frontier printer.

### Authorial Corrections in
### the British Library and New York Copies

Dunbar made manuscript corrections in the president's message, in the early pages of the Ouachita section, and in the appendix, of those copies of the Natchez reprint (N) sent to Sir Joseph Banks (DBL) and to John Swift (DNY), as follows:

Page 4, line 5 *signs for degrees, minutes, and seconds added by hand,* DBL.
line 26 *signs for degrees, minutes, and seconds added by hand,* DBL.

Page 114, line 2 Chafalaya, N; Chaffalaïa DBL, DNY.
line 37 Ocatahola. N; Catahoo[la.] DBL; Catahoola. DNY.
line 40 Ocatahola, N; [Catahoola] DNY.

Page 115, line 34 secula is N; secula are DNY.
line 39 and wholesome N; and yields wholesome DNY.

[25]This feature is not reproduced in the facsimile, since it is not seen identically in any two surviving copies.

Page 116, line 40 Ocatahola, N; catahola, DNY.

Page 117, line 25 Ocatahola, N; catahola, DNY.
        line 28 from Ocatahola N; from catahola DNY.

Page 118, line 2 Priarie N; prairie DNY.
        line 6 Beauf, N; Boeuf, DNY.
        line 7 Noyu N; Noyee DNY.
        line 25 Ocatahola, and Tensaw, N; catahola, and Tensaw, DNY.
        line 27 Tensaw and Ocatahola N; Tensaw and catahola DNY.
        line 31 Ocatahola, N; catahola, DNY.

## *Authorial Corrections in the Appendix*

Page 161, line 40 Tanthoxylum N; Zanthoxylum DBL. DNY.

Page 162, line 12 accriculata, N; auriculata, DBL, DNY.
        line 33 Gledisia, N; Gleditsia, DBL, DNY.
        line 37 pop. N; poplar DBL, DNY.

Page 163, line 6 [Hiton.] N; [Aiton.] DBL, DNY.
        line 14 Rossa, N; Rosa, DBL, DNY.
        line 34 *following creeper.* N; varieties very beau[tiful] DBL, varieties DNY.

Page 164, line 4 Hyrophylum, N; Hydrophylum, DBL, DNY.
        line 16 Preanthes N; Prenanthes DBL, DNY.
        line 44 Ranumculus N; Ranunculus DBL, DNY.

Page 165, line 17 Punetuata, N; Punctuata, DBL, DNY.
        line 19 Glycyrrhira N; Glycyrrhiza DBL, DNY.

Page 166, line 1 Ipicata, N; Spicata, DBL, DNY.
        line 4 *Rules drawn by hand to separate grasses from mush room,* DBL.

# ❧ Provenance and Census of Known Copies

Seven copies of this publication are currently known: one at the British Library, London (BL), three copies at Yale University's Beinecke Library (CtY Beinecke), and copies at the Newberry Library, Chicago (ICN); Western Reserve Historical Society Library and Archives, Cleveland (OCIWHi); and New York Public Library (NN). The Yale, Newberry, and New York copies were studied in person; those copies not viewed in person have been seen in microfilm or photocopy.

Four copies are complete: British Library, Yale Copy 1, Newberry Library, and New York Public Library.

The volume is octavo, in quarto signatures. Collation is as described for the British Library copy. There are no observed variants in the text. The title page has a variant, the addition of a comma after *SIBLEY* in line 6, seen in all copies apart from Yale Copy 1. The facsimile title page of Yale Copy 3 and its reproduction in Yale 2 both show a comma after *SIBLEY* and lack the period after DUNBAR and the colon after NATCHEZ. Two of these apparent variants are probably illusory. In the New York copy (source of the Yale facsimiles) the colon after NATCHEZ was badly inked and printed blind—where no ink is transferred to the paper—while the missing period after DUNBAR may be the victim of clean-up on the photographic plate. The third example, however, is a true variant, since the addition of a comma after *SIBLEY* exceeded the measure, and had to be accommodated by closing up space between *DOCTOR* and *SIBLEY*. The state lacking the comma is therefore presumably the first, uncorrected state.

Since no surviving copy shows end sheets from the original paper stock, it may be assumed that Marschalk originally delivered the edition as stabbed and sewn unbound sheets of the dimensions found in the untrimmed Copy 3 at Yale, 23 centimeters tall and 30 centimeters wide before folding to a page of 23 by 15 centimeters.

It is notable that at least three of the seven surviving copies of this publication (the British Library copy belonging to Sir Joseph Banks, Yale Copy 3 sent to Colonel Kingsbury, and the New York Public Library copy sent to John Swift) appear to have been direct gifts from the sponsor of the Natchez reprint. It is clear that William Dunbar designated a portion (perhaps a significant percentage) of this presumably limited edition to be sent to friends and associates.

### *British Library, Call Number 979.k.24*

PROVENANCE—Ownership stamp (on title page verso) of Sir Joseph Banks (1743–1820), botanist and natural historian, companion on Captain James Cook's first Pacific voyage of 1768, Fellow of the Royal Society from 1766, and its president from 1778.[1] The copy, with manuscript corrections by Dunbar in the botanical appendix, was presumably a gift from the author to Banks. The extensive Banks library was willed in 1820 to his librarian Robert Brown for use in his lifetime, but Brown soon transferred the volumes to the British Museum collection.

DESCRIPTION—A trimmed copy, 21.3 cm. tall x 13.0 cm wide, all pages present. Corrected state of title page, with comma after *SIBLEY*.

COLLATION—Title page, verso blank; [3]–4 MESSAGE. [of the President]; [5]–8 *Extract of a letter* [from Lewis at Fort Mandan]; [9]–64 [Lewis and Clark's] A STATISTICAL VIEW | OF THE | *INDIAN NATIONS* | INHABITING | THE TERRITORY OF LOUISIANA; [65]–83 [Sibley's] HISTORICAL SKETCHES | OF THE | SEVERAL INDIAN TRIBES

*References:* Coues, cx; Paltsits, lxiv; Wagner-Camp-Becker, 5: 4; *Literature*, 2b.5.
[1]For the influence of Banks on Jefferson as expedition planner, see Gilman, 15–16.

IN LOUISIANA,; 84–109 [Sibley's letter] TO GENERAL
HENRY DEARBORN, | *SECRETARY OF WAR.;* 110–112 [Sib-
ley's] *Distances up Red river by the course of the river.*; 113–127,
127–164 [Dunbar's] OBSERVATIONS | Made in a voyage
[on the Red, Black, and Washita rivers]; [165]–166,
[159]–169 EXTRACTS | FROM THE APPENDIX | TO MR.
DUNBAR'S JOURNAL.; 170–177 METEOROLOGICAL
*observations made by Mr. Dunbar and doctor Hunter,*; verso of
177 blank. No original endpapers before the title page or following [178].

Binding (probably twentieth-century) is marbled boards
and quarter cloth including the spine. End sheets of this
binding lack datable watermarks. Overall condition good.
Hardly any foxing, staining, or insect damage; slight brown-
ing throughout. Some letters partially failed to print (possibly obscured by a paper scrap) in the last line of 149. There is
a small hole, the width of two letters, in line 12 of 157.

There are manuscript corrections, certainly by the
author, on pages 114 and (second sequence) 161–166. See full
listing at the end of the previous chapter. The small corrections on page 4 are probably also authorial.

Microfilm (1992) pressmark PB. Mic. C. 16366.


*Beinecke Library, Yale Copy 1,*
*Call Number Zc10 806une, Copy 1*

PROVENANCE—Bookplate of William Robertson Coe
(1869–1955). Born in Britain, Coe emigrated to New Jersey
in 1883 and took his first job as office boy in a marine insur-
ance company, rising rapidly to become a claims adjust-
ment manager, and by 1910 was president of the company.
One of the claims Coe settled was that of the *Titanic,* on
which he had tickets for the return journey. He was married
three times. The father of his second wife, Mai Huttleston
Rogers, founded Standard Oil Company. Coe had strong
interests in the American West and in horticulture. His

benefactions included American Studies departments or professorships at over forty colleges and universities and paving the streets of Cody, Wyoming, where he had purchased Buffalo Bill's ranch. Coe's Frederick Remington Collection is also on display in Cody, at the Whitney Gallery. He deeded to New York his rhododendron garden of Planting Fields, and in 1948 Yale University received the magnificent Coe Collection of Western books, manuscripts, and photographs.[2]

Inscriptions of previous owners on back endpapers: Nicholas Cabler of Nashville and St. Louis; John Seales or Sealez. Nicholas Cabler may be the individual descended from Hans Frederick Kabler, immigrant from Germany in 1718/1719. Nicholas is visible in genealogical web sites[3] as born August 14, 1758, in Culpepper County, Virginia, and deceased September 21, 1840, in Davidson County, Tennessee. This Nicholas Cabler is also listed as purchaser of one of the first lots sold in Columbia (county seat of Maury County, Tennessee) soon after April 1, 1808. If this person is an early owner of the book, the St. Louis address may (as in the case of Colonel Kingsbury, likely first owner of Yale copy 3) indicate a connection with expeditions setting out from that point on the Missouri.

DESCRIPTION—A trimmed copy. Its title page is in the uncorrected state, lacking comma after *SIBLEY*. No other extant copy shows this reading, the only printing variant observed in the volume.

COLLATION—As for the British Library copy, all pages present. Two folded sheets front and back, not part of the original paper stock, form two free endpapers, their other half-sheets pasted down to the boards.

The early binding is in original gray boards, with raised bands on spine. No titling. The volume is in good condition.

[2]Information from www.plantingfields.org.
[3]RootsWeb.com, and Maury County, Tennessee, Early Settlers.

### Beinecke Library, Yale Copy 2, Call Number Zc10 806une, Copy 2

PROVENANCE—Bookplate of Frederick William Beinecke. A 1909 Yale graduate in civil engineering, Beinecke was an army captain in World War I. He worked in steel and railroads before becoming president of a New Jersey auto distributorship, and founder or chairman of a number of firms, including Sperry and Hutchinson. As a skilled engineer, he enjoyed constructing model trains and ships and repairing antique clocks. His collection of original source materials on the American West, now housed at the Yale Library named after him, was one of the greatest ever assembled.[4]

Item description (apparently from an Eberstadt sale) on two loose sheets laid in. Other names inscribed: Ben L. C. Wailey; John Close (with the note "John Close wishes this book might contain more real information and a more correct account of the travels than it appears to possess."); Covington. Nothing further is currently known about these three individuals.

DESCRIPTION—A trimmed copy, leading to the loss of some page numbers; height 21 cm.

COLLATION—As for the British Library copy. The title page is a facsimile, a reproduction of Yale copy 3's facsimile title. This was bound in before the volume was rebacked, and before its purchase by Beinecke, since it is noted in the sale description. There is one free endpaper front and back, not from the original paper stock.

The volume is bound in full contemporary leather, with a modern replacement spine. It includes an original handcolored manuscript map, bound in following page 113. This map appears to be a close copy of the southern portion of Nicholas King's chart, published with the 1806 Washington edition of the *Message* to Congress. On June 20, 1806, Dunbar wrote to his friend John Swift,[5] promising to send a copy of the Natchez edition with a map included, but no

[4] Information from www.beineckescholarship.org.
[5] See provenance notes for the New York Public Library copy.

surviving copy of the Natchez contains a printed map. It is possible, therefore, that the map of which this copy preserves a part was created by Dunbar to be interleaved in sections in one of his own copies, but it could have been made and inserted at any time before the early binding of the volume, and it is curious that only this part of King's map (showing the confluence of the Mississippi and the Red River, leading to the Ouachita) should have been inserted in the volume.

The volume's condition is good.

*Beinecke Library, Yale Copy 3,
Call Number Zc10 806une, Copy 3*

PROVENANCE—From the collection of Frederick Beinecke, bought in the Holliday sale of 1954. William Jaquelin Holliday (1895–1977) was the grandson of the founder of an Indianapolis hardware store in 1856 that sold carriage-making and blacksmith supplies. The company later manufactured auto parts, and then milling and mining equipment, becoming one of the nation's leading suppliers. The company was sold in 1954 to Jones & Laughlin Steel Corporation of Pittsburgh.[6]

Earlier inscription: "Colonel Jacob Kingsbury's property." Kingsbury was born in 1755 in Norwich, Connecticut and served with General "Mad Anthony" Wayne in the Ohio Indian wars, where he would most likely have encountered Meriwether Lewis, William Clark, and Andrew Marschalk, all officers under Wayne in the campaign leading to the Battle of Fallen Timbers in 1794. Kingsbury was appointed commandant at Detroit and later at New Orleans. His War of 1812 papers are housed at Lilly Library, Indiana University. He died in Franklin, Missouri, in 1837. Dunbar wrote from Natchez on June 6, 1807, to "Lt Col. Kingsbury."[7] At this time Kingsbury was probably still at Fort Belle Fontaine, on the Missouri near the confluence with the Mississippi. This was a Sauk and Fox trading post

[6]Information from www.indianahistory.org.
[7]Rowland, 354–55.

established by General Wilkinson and built by Kingsbury's First Infantry battalion. It was the start point for Zebulon Pike's 1805 and 1806 Mississippi and Missouri journeys, and the end point of Lewis and Clark's expedition on September 22, 1806. Dunbar requested Kingsbury to lay up expedition stores not needed in the remainder of 1807, together with a flat boat, that "may be of great use to the next Exploring party if preserved from damage." As the officer commanding the post of such importance to the Missouri explorations, it is easy to understand Kingsbury's interest in this reprint of the 1806 *Message*.

DESCRIPTION—Untrimmed and unbound sheets, loosely sewn through three stab-holes. Full page dimensions: 23 centimeters tall, 30 centimeters wide, before folding. The title page is a facsimile, perhaps printed from a photographically produced plate. Pages 7–8 and 175–[178] are also facsimiles. The source of these facsimiles was the copy now at New York Public Library. They were presumably created before sale to Beinecke, since the copy 3 title page was a source for that of copy 2. Since Kingsbury's ownership signature is at the top of page [3], the first genuine page, it seems possible that the original title page, the last two pages, and perhaps also the missing page 7 had already become separated from the volume while in his possession.

COLLATION—As for the British Library copy, all pages present, including facsimiles. No free endpapers. The volume's condition is good.

### *Newberry Library, Chicago,*
### *Call Number Ayer 128.3 L6 U5 1806a*

PROVENANCE—From the Ayer Collection, and apparently the personal copy of Edward E. Ayer, containing three pencil annotations in his hand. The first is a reference on page [3] to "Missouri River" in line 22, following "west from Greenwich." The other two, on pages 164 and [165] both note the difference in the remaining text of the volume from the 1806 edition of A. & G. Way. Edward E. Ayer (1841–1927) was the first major donor to the Newberry Library. Born in Wisconsin and raised in Illinois, as a young man he worked in a Nevada quartz mill, a San Francisco wood yard, and a Tucson silver mine, before serving as a cavalry-man in Indian Territory in the Civil War. The lumber business he began in 1871 in Chicago made him a fortune in railroad ties and telegraph poles. His entertaining note, "How I bought my first book," appeared in *The Newberry Library Bulletin* for December 1950.

DESCRIPTION—Pages trimmed, dimensions 20.1 centimeters tall, 12.0 centimeters wide. The title page is in the corrected state, with a comma after *SIBLEY*.

COLLATION—As for the British Library copy, all pages present. The end-sheets are not part of the original paper stock.

Newberry Library binding in red half morocco. Condition good, with some foxing.

Readex microfiche: Shaw-Shoemaker Early American Imprints. Second series, no. 10326.

### Western Reserve Historical Society Library and Archives, Call Number F42.5 J45 1806a Vault

PROVENANCE—Acquired for the Western Reserve Historical Society by William Pendleton Palmer, president of the Society from 1913 to 1927. Palmer (1861–1927) was president of American Steel & Wire Company in Cleveland. The title page also bears the faint inscription "J [?] Pickering Jr." and another indecipherable name in different ink. The stamped number 72584 appears on the title page verso and at the foot of page 48.

DESCRIPTION—Pages trimmed, dimensions 20.4 centimeters tall, 12.5 centimeters wide. All edges gilt, corresponding with the gold in the marbled flyleaves and pastedowns. Title page in the corrected state, with comma after *SIBLEY*.

COLLATION—As for the British Library copy, but lacking pages 175–[178]. End sheets are of similar laid stock to the text sheets, but of heavier weight.

Binding is leather with gold stamping. Authors' names in gold against red on spine. Some signs of wear, particularly along the crease line. Overall condition is good, with cracking along the left edge of front flyleaf and of page [3] and tears in a few upper corners of pages. No foxing, but some darkening of pages.

### New York Public Library Rare Book Room, Call Number *KF 1806

PROVENANCE—William Dunbar's presentation copy to John Swift, with corrections by Dunbar in the third part of the volume. The presentation leaf, now tipped in at the back of the volume, appears from its wear and staining to have been originally an extra leaf (not from the original paper stock) preceding the title page. The presentation reads "To Mr. John Swift from his friend William Dunbar of Natchez." The volume was presented by Swift to his grandson R. Maliphant in 1809, with the inscription "R. Maliphant the gift of his grandfather Mr. John Swift 1809." Swift, a London manufacturer and supplier of scientific instruments, was a frequent correspondent of William Dunbar's, addressed or mentioned in letters between 1802 and 1806.[8] Richard Maliphant, born in 1756 in Kidwelly, Wales (the ominous French form of the name is Malenfant), married Jane Swift, John Swift's daughter, in the early 1780s. Richard, the fifth of their seven children, born in 1794, was given this volume by his grandfather at the age of fifteen.

Dunbar wrote from Natchez to John Swift in London on June 20, 1806,

[8]Rowland, 117, 321–23, 326–27, 335–36, 345–47.

I shall very speedily send you a pamphlet now printing here, containing discoveries upon the River Missouri, Red River and upon the Washita with a map of my voyage up the latter, there will also be an appendix which I have lately added, these accounts were presented by the President to Congress, so that altho' you will not have all my Journal in the original words, you will have more than I think was worth preserving. . . .[9]

This brief passage is the only evidence for the presence of a map in the Natchez publication. It would have been presumably Nicholas King's chart, as presented in the Washington edition, but might possibly have been Dunbar's almost identical map, if he had decided to have it engraved at his own expense. No surviving copy of the Natchez contains a printed map.

Apparently in the late nineteenth century this copy was bound in full leather before being sold from the Museum Book Store, 45 Museum Street, London. This was probably when it became part of the Indian collection of Wilberforce Eames (1855–1937), secretary to James Lenox and in 1885 on the staff of the Lenox Library. This library formed the basis of the New York Public Library's Rare Book Collection in 1895, with Eames as its first director. Eames sold this copy to the New York Public Library on January 8, 1914, for twenty-six dollars.

DESCRIPTION—The copy is in fine condition. Pages trimmed; height 21 cm. Title page in corrected state, with comma after *SIBLEY*.

COLLATION—As for the British Library copy, all pages present.

The binding (see above) is full leather with gold stamping on the spine and boards, and with all edges gilt. Dunbar's authorial corrections relate this New York copy closely to the Banks copy now at the British Library, which contains most of the same corrections. These authorial corrections are listed at the end of the Textual Introduction.

[9]Rowland, 345.

# ❧ Discoveries Made in Exploring the Missouri, Red River and Washita.
## Natchez: Printed by Andrew Marschalk, 1806.

*Sources for the Shoulder Notes in the Facsimile*

C    William Clark's manuscript "A List of the Names of the different Nations," now at the American Philosophical Society.

D    William Dunbar's field notes, now at APS (1904 transcript).

DBL    William Dunbar's manuscript corrections on the British Library copy of N.

DNY    William Dunbar's manuscript corrections on the New York copy of N.

H    George Hunter's field notes, now at APS (edited by McDermott).

H(o)    George Hunter's Official Report to the Secretary of War (quoted by McDermott).

L    Meriwether Lewis's Fort Mandan letter to Jefferson (Jackson, *Letters*, item 149).

N    The Natchez edition of Andrew Marschalk, 1806.

S1    "Sibley's acct of the Indians" (Appendix B3).

S2    "Sibley's account of Red river" (Appendix B5).

S3    John Sibley letter to Governor Claiborne (Appendix B1).

S4    John Sibley letter to Calvin Jones (see Bibliography).

W    The Washington edition of A. & G. Way, 1806, Marschalk's copy text.

The shoulder notes accompanying the three sections of the facsimile represent different relationships between texts. An edited copy of Meriwether Lewis's April 7, 1805, Fort Mandan letter (L) was the direct source of its printing in A. & G. Way. William Clark's manuscript (C) is the closest surviving relative to the lost manuscript behind "A Statistical View." Citations from C are given only where they offer a guide to pronunciation, or diverge significantly from the printed text. No attempt was made to provide a full collation of this manuscript with the printed text. For a transcription of Clark's document, see Moulton, 3: 386–445.

Two of the John Sibley documents (S1 and S2) are notes for the lost manuscripts behind the two reports sent to General Dearborn. The two Sibley letters (S3 and S4) deal with related Louisiana material. Citations from all four documents are given only where they throw light on readings in the printed texts. The three unpublished documents are transcribed in Appendix B.

William Dunbar's manuscript (D) and George Hunter's official journal and field notes (H(o) and H) were almost certainly used by Nicholas King in preparing the Ouachita expedition narrative. In providing citations from D, we have generally ignored accidentals of capitalization and spelling, to clarify the relationship between D and either W or N, though original spellings from D are preserved. The manuscript changes made by Dunbar of two copies sent to friends (DBL and DNY) are provided as (incomplete) corrections of Marschalk's printing, and as an indication that Dunbar is unlikely to have proofed the Marschalk text while it was in press, though as noted in "Copy for the Natchez Edition," he certainly provided Marschalk and his compositor(s) with corrections to W.

# DISCOVERIES

MADE IN EXPLORING

## THE MISSOURI, RED RIVER AND WASHITA,

BY

*CAPTAINS LEWIS AND CLARK, DOCTOR SIBLEY,*

AND

WILLIAM DUNBAR, Esq.

WITH

A STATISTICAL ACCOUNT

OF THE

COUNTRIES ADJACENT.

〰〰〰〰〰〰〰〰〰

WITH AN APPENDIX BY Mr. DUNBAR.

〰〰〰〰〰〰〰〰〰

NATCHEZ:

PRINTED BY ANDREW MARSCHALK,

1806.

N *deletes the President's Message*
*information, and adds reference to*
*Dunbar's Appendix.*

## MESSAGE.

### TO THE SENATE AND HOUSE OF REPRESENTATIVES OF THE UNITED STATES.

IN purſuance of a meaſure propoſed to congreſs by a meſſage of January 18th, one thouſand eight hundred and three, and ſanctioned by their appropriation for carrying it into execution, captain Meriwether Lewis, of the firſt regiment of infantry, was appointed, with a party of men, to explore the river Miſſouri, from its mouth to its ſource, and croſſing the highlands by the ſhorteſt portage, to ſeek the beſt water communication thence to the Pacific ocean ; and lieutenant Clarke was appointed ſecond in command. They were to enter into conference with the Indian nations on their route, with a view to the eſtabliſhment of commerce with them. They entered the Miſſouri May fourteenth, one thouſand eight hundred and four, and on the firſt of November took up their winter quarters near the Mandan towns, 1609 miles above the mouth of the river, in latitude 47. 21. 47. north, and longitude 99. 24. 45. weſt from Greenwich. On the eighth of April, one thouſand eight hundred and five, they proceeded up the red river in purſuance of the objects preſcribed to them. A letter of the preceding day, April ſeventh, from captain Lewis, is herewith communicated. During his ſtay among the Mandans, he had been able to lay down the Miſſouri, according to courſes and diſtances taken on his paſſage up it, corrected by frequent, obſervations of longitude and latitude ; and to add to the actual ſurvey of this portion of the river, a general map of the country between the Miſſiſſippi and Pacific, from the thirty fourth to the fifty-fourth degres of latitude. Theſe additions are from information collected from Indians with whom he had opportunities of communicating, during his journey and reſidence with them Copies of this map are now preſented to both houſes of

47° 21′ 47″ W.
99° 24′ 45″ W.

up the river W.

frequent W.

from the thirty-fourth W.

them. W.

4

congrefs. With thefe I communicate alfo a ftatiftical view, procured and forwarded by him, of the Indian nations inhabiting the territory of Louifiana, and the countries adjacent to its northern and weftern borders; of their commerce, and of other interefting circumftances refpecting them.

be, of W.

In order to render the ftatement as complete as may be, o the Indians inhabiting the country weft of the Miffiffippi. I add doctor Sibley's account of thofe refiding in and adjacent to the territory of Orleans.

I communicate alfo, f om the fame perfon, an account of the Red river, according to the beft information he had been able to collect.

Having been difappointed, after confiderable prepara-ration, in the purpofe of fending an exploring party up that river, in the fummer of one thoufand eight hun-dred and four, it was thought beft to employ the au-tumn of that year in procuring a knowledge of an inte-refting branch of the river called the Wafhita. This was undertaken under the direction of Mr. Dunbar, of Natchez, a citizen of diftinguifhed fcience, who had aided, and continues to aid us, with his difinter-refted and valuable fervices in the profecution of thefe enterprizes. He afcended the river to the remarka-

34° 31' 4" 16, W; *added by hand,* DBL.
92° 50' 45" W; *added by hand,* DBL.

ble hot fprings near it, in latitude 34. 31. 4, 16, lon-gitude 92. 50. 45. weft from Greenwich, taking its courfes and diftances, and correcting them by frequent celeftial obfervations. Extracts from his obfervations, and copies of his map of the river, from its mouth to

springs, W.

the hot fpings, make part of the prefent communica-tions. The examination of the Red river itfelf, is but now commencing.

TH : JEFFERSON.

*February* 19, 1806.

*Extract of a letter from Captain Meriwether Lewis, to the President of the United States, dated*

## FORT MANDAN, April 17th, 1805.

DEAR SIR,

HEREWITH inclosed you will receive an invoice of certain articles, which I have forwarded to you from this place. Among other articles you will observe, by reference to the invoice, 67 specimens of earths, salts and minerals, and 60 specimens of plants ; these are accompanied by their respective labels, expressing the days on which obtained, places where found, and virtues and qualities when known. By means of these labels, references may be made to the chart of the Missouri, forwarded to the secretary of war, on which the encampment of each day has been carefully marked : thus the places at which these specimens have been obtained, may be easily pointed out, or again found, should any of them prove valuable to the community on further investigation.

You will also receive herewith enclosed, a part of capt. Clark's private journal ; the other part you will find inclosed in a seperate tin box. This journal will serve to give you the daily details of our progress and transactions.

I shall dispatch a canoe with three, perhaps four persons from the extreme navigable point of the Missouri, or the portage between this river and the Columbia river, as either may first happen. By the return of this canoe, I shall send you my journal, and some one or two of the best of those kept by my men. I have sent a journal kept by one of the sergeants, to captain Stoddard, my agent at St. Louis, in order as much as possible to multiply the chances of saving something. We have encouraged our men to keep journals, and seven of them do, to whom in this respect we give every assistance in our power.

I have transmitted to the secretary at war, every information relative to the geography of the country which we possess, together with a view of the Indian

April 7, 1805. Jackson, *Letters*, item 149; *National Intelligencer* for July 17, 1805.

and also their virtues and properties, when W.

reference W.

Secretary at War, L.

separate W.

do so, L.

6

nations, containing information relative to them, on those points with which I conceived it important that the government should be informed.

By reference to the muster rolls forwarded to the war department, you will see the state of the party; in addition to which we have two interpreters, one negro man, servant to capt. Clarke; one Indian woman, wife to one of the interpreters, and a Mandan man, whom we take with a view to restore peace between the Snake Indians, and those in the neighborhood, amounting in total with ourselves to 33 persons. By means of the interpreters and Indians, we shall be enabled to converse with all the Indians that we shall meet with on the Missouri.

I have forwarded to the secretary at war my public accounts, rendered up to the present day. They have been much longer delayed than I had any idea they would have been, when we departed from the Illenois; but this delay, under the circumstances which I was compelled to act, has been unavoidable. The provision peroque and her crew, could not have been dismissed in time to have been returned to St. Louis last fall, without evidently, in my opinion, hazarding the fate of the enterprize in which I am engaged; and I therefore did not hesitate to prefer the censure that I may have incurred by the detention of these papers, to that of risking in any degree the success of the expedition. To me the detention of these papers has formed a serious source of disquiet and anxiety; and the recollection of your particular charge to me on this subject, has made it still more poignant. I am fully aware of the inconvenience which must have arisen to the war department, from the want of these vouchers, previous to the last session of congress, but how to avert it was out of my power to devise.

From this place we shall send the barge and crew early to-morrow morning, with orders to proceed as expeditiously as possible to St. Louis; by her we send our dispatches, which I trust will get safe to hand. Her crew consists of ten able bodied men, well armed and provided with a sufficient stock of provision to last them to St. Louis. I have but little doubt but they will be

*Margin notes (left):*

this neighborhood L, W.

shall probably meet W.

Illinois; W.

have returned W.

divert it L.

**7**

fired on by the Siouxs : but they have pledged themselves to us that they will not yield while there is a man
of them living. Our baggage is all embarked in
six small canoes, and two peroques ; we shall set out
at the same moment that we dispatch the barge. One,
or perhaps both of these peroques, we shall leave at the
falls of the Missouri, from whence we intend continuing
our voyage in the canoes, and a peroque of skins, the
frame of which was prepared at Harper's ferry. This
peroque is now in a situation which will enable us to
prepare it in the course of a few hours. As our vessels
are now small, and the current of the river much more
moderate, we calculate upon travelling at the rate of 20
or 25 miles per day, as far as the falls of the Missouri.
Beyond this point, or the first range of rocky mountains, situated about 100 miles further, any calculation
with respect to our daily progress, can be little more
than bare conjecture. The circumstances of the Snake
Ind ans possessing large quantities of horses, is much in
our favor, as by means of horses the transportation of
our baggage will be rend red easy and expeditious over
land, from the Missouri to the Columbia river. Should
this river not prove navigable where we first meet with
it, our present intention is, to continue our march by
land down the river, until it becomes so, or to the Pacific ocean. The map, which has been forwarded to the
secretary of war, will give you the idea we entertain of
the connection of these rivers, which has been formed
from the corresponding testimony of a number of Indians, who have visited that country, and who have been
separately and carefully examined on that subject, and
we therefore think it entitled to some degree of confidence. Since our arrival at this place, we have subsist-
ted principally on meat, with which our guns have supplied us amply, and have thus been enabled to reserve
the parched meal, portable soup, and a considerable
proportion of pork and flour, which we had intended
for the more difficult parts of our voyage. If Indian
information can be credited, the vast quantity of game
with which the country abounds through which we are

embarked on board six L.

prepared W.

circumstance W.

Secretary at War, L.

8

to pafs, leaves us but little to apprehend from the want of food.

We do not calculate on completing our voyage within the prefent year, but expect to reach the Pacific ocean, and return as far as the head of the Miffouri, or perhaps to this place, before winter. You may therefore expect me to meet you at Montachello September, 1806. On our return we fhall probably pafs down the Yellow Stone river, which, from Indian information, waters one of the faireft portions of this continent.

I can fee no material or probable obftruction to our progrefs, and entertain, therefore, the moft fanguine hopes of complete fuceefs. As to myfelf, individually, I never enjoyed a more perfect ftate of good health than I have fince we commenced our voyage. My ineftimable friend and companion, captain Clarke, has alfo enjoyed good health generally. At this moment every individal of the party is in good health and excellent fpirits, zealoufly attached to the enterprize, and anxious to proceed ; not a whifper of difcontent or murmur is to be heard among them ; but all in unifon act with the moft perfect harmony. With fuch men I have every thing to hope and but little to fear.

Be fo good as to prefent my moft affectionate regard to all my friends, and be affured of the fincere and unalterable attachment of

Your moft obedient fervant,

MERIWETHER LEWIS,
*Captain 1ft of U. S. regiment of infantry.*

Th: Jefferson,
*Prefident of the United States.*

Montachello in September, W.

party are L.

hope, and W.

*Captain of 1st* W.

# A STATISTICAL VIEW

OF THE

## *INDIAN NATIONS*

INHABITING

## THE TERRITORY OF LOUISIANA

AND THE

COUNTRIES ADJACENT TO ITS NORTHERN AND WESTERN BOUNDARIES.

~~~~~~~~~~~~~

### EXPLANATORY REFERENCES.

A. The names of the Indian nations as ufually fpelt and pronounced in the Englifh language.

B. Primitive Indian names of nations and tribes, Englifh orthography, the fyllables producing the founds by which the Indians themfelves exprefs the name of their refpective nations.

C. Nick-names, or thofe which have generally obtained among the Canadian traders.

D. The language they fpeak, if primitive marked with a * otherwife derived from, and approximating to the     primitive, W.

E. Number of villages.

F. Number of tents or lodges of the roving bands.

G. Number of warriors.

H. The probable number of fouls.

B

# 10

I.   The rivers on which they rove, or on which their villages are situated.

J.   The names of the nations or companies with whom they maintain their principal commerce or traffic.

K.   The place at which their traffic is usually carried on.

**Merchandise W.**

L.   The amount of Merchandize necessary for their annual consumption, estimated in dollars at the St. Louis prices.

**M. The estimated amount in dollars, of their annual returns at the St. Louis prices. W;** *this category omitted* **N.**

N.   The species of peltries, furs and other articles which they annually supply or furnish.

O.   The species of peltries, furs and other articles which the natural productions of their country would enable them to furnish, provided proper encouragement was given them.

P.   The places at which it would be mutually advantageous to form the principal establishments, in order to supply the several Indian nations with merchandize.

**merchandise W.**

Q.   The names of the Indian nations with whom they are at war.

R.   The names of the Indian nations with whom they maintain a friendly alliance, or with whom they are united by intercourse or marriage.

S.   Miscellaneous remarks.

## NOTATIONS.

‒over *a*, denotes that *a* sounds as in caught, taught, &c.

ᴧ over *a*, denotes that it sounds as in dart, part. &c.

*a* without notation has its primitive sound as in ray, hay, &c. except only when it is followed by *r* or *w*, in which case it sounds as a.

*line 26*:
**sounds as â. W; sounds as a. N.** (*In transcriptions of Indian names in the remainder of signature B, the symbol* â *in W is rendered as* á *in N.*)

26

## 11

, set underneath denotes a small pause, the word being divided by it into two parts.

⤜⤜⤜ ⤜⤜⤜

THE INDIAN TRADE. The sums stated under and opposite "L" are the amounts of merchandize annually furnished the several nations of Indians, including all incidental expences of transportation, &c. incurred by the merchants which generally averages about one third of the whole amount. The merchandize is estimated at an advance of 125 per cent. on the sterling cost. It appears to me that the amount of merchandize which the Indians have been in the habit of receiving annually, is the best standard by which to regulate the quantities necessary for them in the first instance; they will always consume as much merchandize as they can pay for, and those with whom a regular trade has been carried on have generally received that quantity.

merchandise W.

expenses W.

merchandise W.

merchandise W.

merchandise W.

The amount of their returns stated under and opposite "M" are estimated by the peltry standard of St. Louis which is 40 cents per pound for deer skins; (i. e.) all furs and peltries are first reduced by their comparative value to lbs. of merchantable deer skins, which are then estimated at 40 cents per lb.

These establishments are not mentioned as being thought important at present in a govermental point of view.

A. Grand Oságe.

Osarge C; Osâge. W.

B. Bár-hár-cha.

Bâr-hâr-cha. W.

C. Grand Zo.

D. *

E. Two.

F.

G. 1.200.

H. 5.000.

I. At the three forks of the Arkansas river, and eighty leagues up the Osage river on the south side.

J. W.

J Merchants of St Louis.

## 12

K. At their villages.

L. 15.000.

M. 20.000.

N. Principally ſkins of the ſmall deer, black bear, ſome beaver, and a few otters and racoons.

rackoons. W.

O. Small deer ſkins, black bear, and a much larger proportion of beaver, otter, racoon, and muſkrats.

rackoon, W.

P. About the three forks of the Arkanſas river, 600 miles from its junction with the Miſſiſſippi.

Q. With all their Indian neighbours except the Little Oſage, until the United States took poſſeſſion of Louiſiana.

neighbors, W.

R. With the Little Oſage only.

S. Claim the country within the following limits, viz. commencing at the mouth of a ſouth branch of the Oſage river, called *Neangua*, and with the ſame to its ſource, thence ſouthwardly to interſect the Arkanſas about one hundred miles below the three forks of that river ; thence up the principal branch of the ſame, to the confluence of a large ſouthwardly branch of the ſame, lying a conſiderable diſtance weſt of the Great Saline, and with that ſtream nearly to its ſource ; thence northwardly, towards the Kanſas river, embracing the waters of the upper portion of the Oſage river, and thence obliquely approaching the ſame to the beginning.—— The climate is delightful, and the ſoil fertile in the extreme. The face of the country is generally level, and well watered ; the eaſtern part of the country is covered with a variety of excellent timber ; the weſtern and middle country high prairies. It embraces within its limits four ſalines, which are, in point of magnitude and excellence, unequalled by any known in North America : there are alſo many others of leſs note. The principal part of the Great Oſage have always reſided at their villages, on the Oſage river, ſince they have been known to the inhabitants of Louiſiana. About three years ſince, nearly one half of this nation, headed

Southerly C; northwardly W.

## 13

by their chief the *Big-track*, emigrated to the three forks of the Arkanſas, near which, and on its north ſide, they eſtabliſhed a village, where they now reſide. The little Oſage formerly reſided on the S. W. ſide of the Miſſouri, near the mouth of Grand river ; but being reduced by continual warfare with their neighbours, were compelled to ſeek the protection of the Great Oſage, near whom they now reſide. There is no doubt but their trade will increaſe : they could furniſh a much larger quantity of beaver than they do. I think two villages, on the Oſage river, might be prevailed on to remove to the Arkanſas, and the Kanſas, higher up the Miſſouri, and thus leave a ſufficient ſcope of country for the Shawnees, Dillewars, Miames, and Kickapoos. The Oſages cultivate corn, beans, &c.

A Oſáge.

B. Ood-zá-táu.

C. Petit Zo,

D. Oſáge.

E. One.

F.

G. 300.

A. 1.300.

I. Near the Great Osages.

J. Merchants of St. Louis.

K. At their village,

L. 5.000.

M. 8.000:

N. The ſame as the Great Oſages.

O. The ſame as the Great Oſages.

P. The ſame as the Great Oſages.

Q. With all their Indian neighbours, except the Great Oſage.

R. With the Great Oſage only.

S. See page 11, S. ⌇⌇⌇⌇

A. Kanzas.

*Margin notes:*

Little W.

neighbors, W.

Little Osarge C; Little Osâge. W.
Ood'-zâ-tau. W.

Osarge C; Osâge. W.

H. W.

8.000. W.

See page W.

## 14

| | |
|---|---|
| Kar sea C; Kar´-sa. W. | B. Kar-ſa. |
| Kâh. W. | C. Káh. |
| Osarge C; Osàge. W. | D. Oságe. |
| | E. One. |
| | F. |
| | G. 500. |
| | H. 1.300. |
| I. W. | I Eighty leagues up the Kanzas river, on the north ſide. |
| | J. Merchants of St. Louis. |
| | K. On the Miſſouri above the mouth of the Kanzas river, not ſtationary, and at their village. |
| 5.000 W. | L. 5.000. |
| | M. 8.000. |
| | N. The ſame as the Oſage, with buffaloe greaſe and robes. |
| | O. The ſame as the Oſage. |
| | P. On the north ſide of the Kanzas river, at a bluff one and a half miles from its confluence with the Miſſouri. |
| | Q. With all nations within their reach. |
| | R. They are ſometimes at peace with the Ottoes and Miſouris, with whom they are partially inter-married. |
| rivers: W. | S· The limits of the country they claim is not known. The country in which they reſide, and from thence to the Miſſouri, is a delightful one, and generally well watered and covered with excellent timber; they hunt on the upper part of the Kanzas and Arkanzas rivers; their trade may be expected to increaſe with proper management. At preſent they are a diſſolute, lawleſs banditti; frequently plunder their traders, and commit depredations on perſons aſcending and deſcending the Miſſouri river; population rather increaſing. Theſe people, as well as the Great and Little Oſages, are ſtationary, at their villages, from about the 15th of March to the 15th of May, and again from the 15th of |
| October: W. | Auguſt to the 15th of October the balance of the year is appropriated to hunting. They cultivate corn, &c. |

## 15

A. Ottoes.

{ *line 2*: War-doke-tar-tar C;
{ Wâd-doké-tâh-tâh. W.

B. Wád-doke-tàh-táh.

C. La Zóto

Zóto. W.

D. Miſſouri.

E. Ottoes and Miſſouris, one.

F.

G. 120.

H. 500.

I. South ſide of the river Platte, fifteen leagues from its mouth.

18 Lg up the platt C.

J. Merchants of St. Louis.

K. On the Miſſouri, below the river Platte ; not ſtationary, and at their villages.

L. 4.000, including the Miſſouris.

M 8.000, including the Miſſouris.

M. W.

N. Principally deer ſkins, black bear, a greater proportion of beaver than the Oſage, ſome otter and racoons.

rackoons. W.

O. Skins of the deer, black bear, beaver, otter, racoon, muskrats and woolves, buffaloe robes, tallow and greaſe, bear's oil, deer and elk tallow, elk skins dreſſed and in parchment, all in much larger quantities than they do at preſent.

rackoon, W.
wolves, W.
bears' W.

P. The Council Bluff, on the S. W. ſide of the Miſſouri, fifty miles above the mouth of the river Platte.

Q. With the Mahas, Poncars, Sioux, the Great and Little Oſage, Kanzas and Loups.

Pon'cârs, W.

R. With the Panis proper, Saukees and Renars.

S. They have no idea of an excluſive poſſeſſion of any country, nor do they aſſign themſelves any limits. I do not believe they would object to the introduction of any well diſpoſed indians : they treat the traders with reſpect and hoſpitality, generally. In their occupations of hunting and cultivation, they are the ſame with the Kanzas and Oſage. They hunt on the Saline, Nimmehaw rivers, and weſt of them in the plains. The country in which they hunt lies well ; it is extremely fertile and well watered ; that part of it which borders on the Nimmehaw and Miſſouri poſſeſſes a good portion of timber : popu-

believe that they W.

16

lation rather increafing. They have always refided near the place their village is fituated, and are the defcendants of the Miffouris.

❧❧ ❧❧❧❧

New'-dar-cha. W.

A. Miffouris.
B. New-dar-cha.
C. Miffouri.
D. *
E. See page 14, E.
F.

80. W.

G. 80
H. 300.
I. With the Ottoes.
J. Merchants of St. Louis.
K Same as Ottoes, fee page 15, K.
L. See page 15, L.
M. See page 15, M.
N. Same as the Ottoes, page 15, N.
O. Same as the Ottoes, do. O.
P.   The Council Bluff, on the S. W. fide of the Miffou-

the mouth of the river W.

ri, fifty miles above the river Platte.
Q. With the Mahas, Poncars, Sioux, the Great and Little Ofage, Kanzas and Loups.
R. With the Panis proper, Saukees and Renars.
S. Thefe are the remnant of the moft numerous nation inhabiting the Miffouri, when firft known to the French.   Their ancient and principal village was fituated in an extenfive and fertile plain on the

on the north bank of the Missouri, W.

Miffouri, juft below the entrance of the Grand ri-ver.   Repeated attacks of the fmall pox, together with their war with the Saukees and Renars, has reduced them to their prefent ftate of dependence on the Ottoes, with whom they refide, as well in their village as on their hunting excurfions.   The Ottoes view them as their inferiors, and fometime treat them amifs. Thefe people are the real propri-etors of an extenfive and fertile country lying on the

Missouri, W.

Miffouri above their ancient village for a confiderble diftance, and as low as the mouth of the Ofage river, and thence to the Miffiffippi.

## 17

A. Pānias proper.

B. Pâ-nee.

C. Grand Par.　　　　　　　　　　　　　　Parnee C.

D. *

E. One.

F.

G. 400.

H. 1600.

I. South side of the river Platte, thirty leagues from its mouth.

J. Merchants of St. Louis.

K. On the Missouri, below the river Platte, not stationary, and at their village.

L. 6.400 including the Panias Republican.

M. 10.000, including the Panias Republican.

N. Fine beaver principally, a considerable proportion of beaver, some robes and a few rackoons.

O. Skins of the beaver, otter, rackoon, muskrats and wolves, buffaloe robes, tallow and grease, elk skins and grease, also a number of horses.

P. The Council Bluff, on the S. W. side of the Missouri, fifty miles above the mouth of the river Platte.

Q. With the Pania-pique, great and little Osage, Kanzas, La Play, Sioux, Ricaras and Paducas.　　Pania Pickey C.

R. With the Loups, Mahas, Poncars, Ottoes, Missouris and Ayauwais.

S. With respect to their idea of the possession of soil, it is similar to that of the Ottoes: they hunt on the south side of the river Platte, higher up &　up and W.
on the head of Kanzas. A great proportion of　of the Kanzas. W.
this country is open plains, interspersed, however, with groves of timber, which are most generally found in the vicinity of the water courses. It is generally fertile and well watered; lies level, and free of stone. They have resided in the country which they now inhabit, since they were known to the whites. Their trade is a valuable one, from the large proportion of beaver & otter which they furnish, & it　　beaver and W. furnish, and W.

C

**18**

may be expected yet to increase, as those animals are still abundant in their country. The periods of their residence at their village and hunting, are similar to the Kanzas and Osages. Their population is increasing. They are friendly and hospitable to all white persons; pay great respect and deference to their traders, with whom they are punctual in the payment of their debts. They are, in all respects, a friendly, well disposed people. They cultivate corns, beans, melons, &c.

corn, C, W.

———

A. Pānias Republican.
B. Ar-râh´-pâ-hoó.
C. Republic.
D. Pania.
E. Pānias proper and Pānias Republican live in the same village.
F.
G. 300.
H. 1.400.
I. With the Panias proper.
J. Merchants of St. Louis.
K. See page 17 K.
L. See page 17 L.
M. See page 17 M.
N. See page 17 N.
O. See page 17 O.
P. See page 17 P.
Q. See page 17 Q.
R. See page 17 R.
S. Are a branch of the Pānias proper, or as they are frequently termed, the *Big Paunch*. About ten years since, they withdrew themselves from the mother nation, and established a village on a large northwardly branch of the Kanzas, to which they have given name; they afterwards subdivided and lived in different parts of the

Ar-râh´-pâ-hoo´. W.

Pānia W. or, W.

since W.

name: W.

**19**

country on the waters of the Kanzas river ; but being harassed by their turbulent neighbors, the Kanzas, they rejoined the Panias proper last spring. What has been said with respect to the Panias Proper is applicable to these people, except that they hunt principally on the Republican river, which is better stocked with timber than that hunted by the Panias.

of Kanzas W.

proper W.

———

A. Panias Loups (or Wolves).
B. Skec'-e-ree.
C. La Loup.
D. Pania.
E. One.
F.
G. 280.
H. 1.000.
I. On the N. E. side of the Wolf river, branch of the river Platte, 36 leagues from its mouth.
J. Merchants of St. Louis.
K. At the village of the Panias.
L. 2.400.
M. 3.500.
N. See page 17 N.
O. See page 17 Q.
P. See page 17 P.
Q. With Pania-picque, Great and Little Osage, Kanzas, Le Plays, Sioux, Ricaras, Mahas, Poncars, Ottoes and Missouris.
R. Panias proper, and Panias Republican.
S. These are also a branch of the Panias proper, who separated themselves from that nation many years since, and established themselves on a north branch of the river Platte, to which their name was also given ; these people have likewise no idea of any exclusive right to any portion of country. They hunt on the Wolf river above their village, and on the river Platte above

of an W.

**20**

the mouth of that river. This country is very similar to that of the Panias proper; though there is an extensive body of fertile well timbered land between the Wolf river below their village and the river Corn de Cerf, or Elkhorn river. They cultivate corn, beans, &c. The particulars related of the other Panias are also applicable to them. They are seldom visited by any trader, and therefore usually bring their furs and peltry to the village of the Panias proper, where they traffic with the whites.

———

*is also W.*

A. Māhâs.
B. O´-mâ´-hâ.
C. La Mar.
D. Osage, with different accent ; some words peculiar to themselves.
E.
F. 60.
G. 150.
H. 600.
I. The river Quicurre and the head of the Wolf river.
J. Merchants of St. Louis.
K. At their old village, though no trade latterly.

*including the W.*

L. 4.000, including Pon´cârs.
M. 7.000 including the Pon´cârs.
N. See page 17, N.
O. The same as the Ottoes' and Missouris', with the addition of the skins of the Missouri antelope, (called cabri´, by the inhabitants of Illinois.)
P. See page 17, P.

*Yanktons of the burnt woods C.*

Q. Great and Little Osages, Kanzas, Loups, Ottoes, Missouris, and all the Sioux, except the Yankton Ahnâ.
R. With the Panias proper, Panias Republicans, Yanktons Ahna, Saukees, Renars, and Ayouwais.

### 21

S. They have no idea of exclusive possession of soil. About ten years since, they boasted 700 warriors. They have lived in a village, on the west bank of the Missouri, 236 miles above the mouth of the river Platte, where they cultivated corn, beans and melons : they were warlike, and the terror of their neighbors. In the summer and autumn of 1802, they were visited by the small-pox, which reduced their numbers to something less than 300; they burnt their village, and have become a wandering nation, deserted by the traders, and the consequent deficiency of arms and ammunition has invited frequent aggressions from their neighbors, which have tended to reduce them still further. They rove principally on the waters of the river Quicurre, or Rapid river. The country is generally level, high, and open; it is fertile, and tolerably well watered. They might easily be induced to become stationary : they are well disposed towards the whites, and are good hunters : their country abounds in beaver and otter, and their trade will increase and become valuable, provided they become stationary, and are at peace. The Tetons Bois brûlé killed and took about 60 of them last summer.

—

A. Pon´cârs.
B. Poong-câr.
C. la Pong.
D. Mâhâ.
E.
F. 20.
G. 50.
H. 200.
I. With the Mahas.
J. Merchants of St. Louis.
K. No place of trade latterly.

**22**

L. See page 20, **L.**
M. See page 20, **M.**
N. See page 17, **N.**
O. See page 20, **O.**
P. See page 17, **P.**
Q. See page 20, **Q.**
R. See page 21, **R.**
S. The remnant of a nation once respectable in point of numbers. They formerly resided on a branch of the Red river of lake Winnipie : being oppressed by the Sioux, they removed to the west side of the Missouri, on Poncar river, where they built and fortified a village, and remained some years ; but being pursued by their ancient enemies the Sioux, and reduced by continual wars, they have joined, and now reside with the Mahas, whose language they speak.

—

A. Ric'ârâs.
B. Stâr-râh-hé.
C. la Ree.

Pania Corrupted C.

D. Pania, with a different accent, and a number of words peculiar to themselves.
E. Three.
F.
G. 500
H. 2.000.
I. On the S. W. side of the Missouri, 1,440 miles from its mouth.
J. Merchants of St. Louis.
K. At their villages.
L. 2.500.
M. 6.000.
N. Buffaloe robes principally, a small quantity of beaver, small foxes and grease.
O. Buffaloe robes, tallow and grease, skins of beaver, small and large foxes, wolves, antelopes and elk in great abundance ; also, some otter, deer and grizzly bears.

abundance: W.

## 23

**P.** About the mouth of the river Chyenne, on the Missouri, or at the mouth of the Yellow Stone River.

**Q.** With the Crow Indians, Snake Indians, Panias Loups, Assinnibains, Nemosen, Alitan, la Plays, and Paunch Indians.

**R.** Chyennes, Wetepahatoes, Kiawas, Kanenavich, Staetan, Cattako, Dotame, Castahanas, Mandans, Ah-wah-haway's, Minetares, and partially with the Sioux.

**S.** Are the remains of ten large tribes of Panias, who have been reduced, by the small pox and the Sioux, to their present number. They live in fortified villages, and hunt immediately in their neighborhood. The country around them, in every direction, for several hundred miles, is entirely bare of timber, except on the water courses and steep declivities of hills, where it is sheltered from the ravages of fire. The land is tolerably well watered, and lies well for cultivation. The remains of the villages of these people are to be seen on many parts of the Missouri, from the mouth of Tetone river to the Mandans. They claim no land except that on which their villages stand, and the fields which they cultivate. The Tetons claim the country around them. Though they are the oldest inhabitants, they may properly be considered the farmers or *tenants at will* of that lawless, savage and rapacious race the Sioux *Teton*, who rob them of their horses, plunder their gardens and fields, and sometimes murder them, without opposition. If these people were freed from the oppression of the Tetons, their trade would increase rapidly, and might be extended to a considerable amount. They maintain a partial trade with their oppressors the Tetons, to whom they barter horses, mules, corn, beans, and a species of tobacco which they cultivate : and inhabiting the Missouri. They are brave, hu-

remains of Eight different tribes C.

*last line of page superfluous (see Textual Introduction).*

**24**

receive in return guns, ammunition, kettles, axes, and other articles which the Tetons obtain from the Yanktons of the N. and Sissatones, who trade with Mr. Cammeron, on the river St. Peters. These horses and mules the Ricaras obtain from their western neighbors, who visit them frequently for the purpose of trafficking.

———

A. Mandans.
B. Măn-dân { Ma-too-ton´-ka, 1st village.  
{ Roop-tar´-ha, 2d village.
C. Mandans.
D. *, some words resembling the Osage.
E. Two.
F.
G. 350.
H. 1,250.
I. On both sides of the Missouri, 1612 miles from its mouth.
J. The Hudson Bay and N. W. companies, from their establishment on the Assinniboin.
K. At their villages.
L. 2.000.
M. 6.000.
N. Principally the skins of the large and small wolves, and the small fox, with buffaloe robes, some skins of the large fox and beaver, also corn and beans.
O. The same as the Ricars (see page 23 O.) except the grizzly bear. They could furnish, in addition, the skins of a large species of white hare, a very delicate fur.
P. At or near the mouth of the Yellow Stone river.
Q. With no nation except a defensive war with the Sioux.
R. With all nations who do not wage war against them.
S. These are the most friendly, well disposed Indians

25

inhabiting the Miſſouri.   They are brave, hu-
mane and hospitable.   About 25 years since
they lived in six villages, about forty miles below
their present villages, on both sides of the Missouri.   Repeated viſitations of the small pox,
aided by frequent attacks of the Sioux, has reduced them to their present number.   They
claim no particular traƈt of country.   They live
in fortified villages, hunt immediately in their
neighbourhood, and cultivate corn, beans,
squashes and tobacco, which forms articles of
traffic with their neighbors the Assinniboin ; they
also barter horses with the Assinniboins for arms,
ammunition, axes, kettles and other articles of
European manufaƈtures, which these laſt obtain
from the British establishments on the Assinniboin river.   The articles which they thus obtain
from the Assinniboins and the Britiſh traders
who visit them, they again exchange for horses
and leather tents with the Crow Indians, Chyennes, Wetepahatoes, Kiawas, Kanenavich, Staƈtan
and Cataka, who visit them occasionally for the
purpose of traffic.   Their trade may be much
increased.   Their country is similar to that of
the Ricaras,   Population increasing.

form W.
Assiniboin: W.

kettles, W.

Ricaras. W.

———

A. Ahwáhháway.
B. Ah-wáh-há-way.
C. Gens des Soulier.
D. Menetarres.
E. One.
F.
G. 50.
H. 200
I. On the S. W. side of the Missouri, three miles
   above the Mandans.
J. See page 24, J.

Shoes Men C; Ahwâhhâway. W.
Mah-har-ha C; Ah-wâh-hâ-way. W.

200. W.

D

26

K. At the Mandan and Menetare villages.

L. 300.

M. 1.000.

N. See page 24, **N.**

O. See page 24, **O.**

P. See page 25, **P.**

Q. Defensive war with the Sioux, and offensive with the Snake Indians and Flatheads.

R. With all who do not wage war againſt them, except the Snake Indians and Flatheads.

S. They differ but very little, in any particular, from the Mandans, their neighbors, except in the unjuſt war which they, as well as the Menetares, prosecute against the defenceless Snake Indians, from which, I believe, it will be difficult to induce them to desist. They claim to have once been a part of the Crow Indians, whom they still acknowledge as relations. They have resided on the Missouri as long as their tradition will enable them to inform.

———

A. **Menetares.**

B. **E-hát-sár,** } Me-ne-tar-re, 1st village.
Me-ne-tar-re-me-te-har-tar, 2d village.

C. Gross Ventres.

D. *

E. Two.

F.

G. 600.

H. 2.500.

I. On both sides of Knife river, near the Missouri, 5 miles above the Mandans.

J. See page 24, **J.**

K. At their village and hunting camps.

L. 1.000.

M. 3.000.

N. See page 24, **N;**

page 25, P. (i.e., page 24, P.) W, N.

Big bellies C; Minetares, W.

Minetares. W.

E-hât′-sâr, W.

### 27

O. The same as the Mandans (see p. 24, O.) with the addition of the white bear.

P. See p. 25, P.

p. 25, P. (i.e., p. 24, P.) W, N.

Q. Defensive war with the Sioux, and offensive with the Snake Indians and Flatheads.

R. With all except the Snake Indians and Flatheads, who do not wage war against them.

S. They claim no particular country, nor do they assign themselves any limits: their tradition relates that they have always resided at their present villages. In their customs, manners and dispositions, they are similar to the Mandans and Ahwahhaways. The scarcity of fuel induces them to reside, during the cold season, in large bands, in camps, on different parts of the missouri, as high up that river as the mouth of the river Yellow Stone, and west of their villages, about the Turtle mountain. I believe that these people, as well as the Mandans and Ahwahhaways, might be prevailed on to remove to the mouth of Yellow Stone river, provided an establishment is made at that place. They have as yet furnished scarcely any beaver, although the country they hunt abounds with them; the lodges of these animals are to be seen within a mile of their villages. These people have also suffered considerably with the small pox; but have successfully resisted the attacks of the Sioux. The N W. company intend to form an establishment in the course of the next summer and antumn, on the Missouri, near these people, which, if effected, will most probably prevent their removal to any point which our government may hereafter wish them to reside.

Missouri, W.

small-pox; W.

summer, W.

reside at. W.

———

A. Ayauwais.

B. Ah-e-a-war.

Ah'-e-o-war'. W.

C. Ne Perce.

ne persa C; Ne Perce'. W.

D. Missouri.

28

E. One.

F

G. 200.

H. 800.

I. 40 leagues up the river Demoin on the S. E. side.

36 Lgs up Demoin C.

J. Mr. Crawford, and other merchants from Michilimackinac.

K. At their village and hunting camps.

L 3.800.

M. 6.000.

N. Deer skins principally, and the skins of the black
bear, beaver, otter, grey fox, rackoon, muskrat,
and mink.

O. Deer skins, beaver, black bear, otter, grey fox,
rackoon, muskrat and mink; also, elk and deers'
tallow, and bears' oil.

P. At the mouth of the Kanzas.

Q. Particularly with the Osage, Kanzas, and Chippeways, la Fallorine, and those of the Leach and
Sand Lakes: sometimes with the Mahas and
Sioux Wahpatone, Mindawarcarton and Wahpacoota.

of Leach W.

R. With the Ottoes, Missouris, Siouxs, Yankton
ahnah, and all the nations east of the Mississippi
and south of the Chippeways.

Mississippi, W.

S. They are the descendants of the ancient Missouris,
and claim the country west of them to the Missouri; but as to its precise limits or boundaries,
between themselves and the Saukees and Foxes,
I could never learn. They are a turbulent savage race, frequently abuse their traders, and commit depredations on those ascending and descending the Missouri. Their trade cannot be expected to increase much.

limits, W.

—— ——

A Saukees.

B. Osaw-kee.

C. la Sauk.

D. ✿

O'saw-kee. W.

29

E. Two.

F.

G. 500.

H. 2.000.

I. On the west side of the Mississippi, 140 leagues above St. Louis.

J. Merchants from Michilimakinac and St. Louis.      Michilimackinac W.

K. At their villages, on the Mississippi in sundry places, and at Eel river on the Waubash.

L. 4.000.

M 6.000.

N. See p. 28, N.

O. See p. 28, O.

P. At Prairie de chien, (or dog plain.)      Chien, W.

Q. With the Ofage, Chippeways generally, and Sioux, except the Yangton ahnah.      Yankton W.

R. Kanzas, Ottoes, Missouris, Panias, Mahas, Pon cars, and Ayauways, and all the nations eaft of the Mississippi, and south of the Chippeways, also with the Yankton ahnahs.      Pon— W.

S. Saukees and Renars or Foxes. These nations are so perfectly consolidated that they may, in fact, be confidered as one nation only. They speak the same language : they formerly resided on the east side of the Mississippi, and ftill claim the land on that side of the river, from the mouth of the Oisconsin to the illinois river, and eastward towards lake Michigan ; but to what particular boundary, I am not informed : They also claim, by conquest, the whole of the country belonging to the ancient Missouris, which forms one of the most valuble portions of Louisiana, but what proportion of this territory they are willing to assign to the Ayouways, who also claim, a part of it, I do not know, as they are at war with the Sioux, who live N. and N. W. of them, except the Yankton ahnah. Their boundaries in that quarter are also undefined : their trade would become much more valuable if peace was established between them and the nations west of the Missouri, with whom they are at

(margin notes for S paragraph: Renars, W. — Illinois W. — they W.)

30

war : their population has remained nearly the same for many years : they raise an abundance of corn, beans, and melons · they sometimes hunt in the country west of them, towards the Missouri, but their principal hunting is on both sides of the Mississippi, from the mouth of the Oisconsin to the mouth of the Illinois river. These people are extremely friendly to the whites, and seldom injure their traders ; but they are the most implacable enemies to the Indian nations with · hom they are at war.   To them is justly attributable the almost entire destruction of the Missouris, the Illinois, Cahokias, Kaskaskias and Piorias.

*whom W.*

——————

A. Foxes.
B. Ot-tár-gár-me,
C. la Renar.
D. Saukee.
E. One.
F.
G. 300.
H. 1.200.
I· Near the Saukees.
J. Merchants of Michilimackinac and St. Louis.
K. See p. 29, K.
L. 2.500.
M. 4. 000.
N. See page 29, N.
O. See page 28, O.
P. At Prairie de chein (or dog plain.)
Q See page 29, Q.
R. See page 29, R.
S. See page 29, S.
    S. WAHPATONE.  Claim the country in which they rove on the N. W. side of the river St. Peters, from their village to the mouth of the Chippeway river, and thence north eastwardly towards the head of the Mississippi, including the Crow-wing

*Ot-târ-gâr-me. W.*

*4.000. W.*
*28, W.*

*Chien W.*

*See Appendix A1 for text missing in N, a chart describing the Sioux.*

**31**

river. Their lands are fertile, and generally well timbered. They are only stationary while the traders are with them, which is from the beginning of October to the last of March. Their trade is supposed to be at its greatest extent. They treat their traders with respect, and seldom attempt to rob them. This, as well as the other Sioux bands, act, in all respects, as independently of each other as if they were a distinct nation.

S. MINDAWARCARTON. 'Tis the only band of Siouxs that cultivates corn, beans, &c. and these even cannot properly be termed a stationary people. They live in tents of dressed leather, which they trasport by means of horses and dogs, and ramble from place to place during the greater part of the year. They are friendly to their own traders; but the inveterate enemies to such a supply their enemies, the Chippeways, with merchandise. They also claim the country in which they hunt, commencing at the entrance of the river St. Peters, and extending upwards on both sides of the Mississippi river, to the mouth of the Crow-wing river. The land is fertile, and well watered; lies level and sufficiently timbered. Their trade cannot be expected to increase much.

S. WAHPACOOTA. They rove in the country south west of the river St. Peters, from a place called the *Hardwood* to the mouth of the Yellow Medicine river; never stationary but when their traders are with them, and this does not happen at any regular or fixed point. At present they treat their traders tolerably well. Their trade cannot be expected to increase much. A great proportion of their country is open plains, lies level, and is tolerably fertile. They maintain a partial traffic with the Yanktons and Tetons to the west of them; to these they barter the articles which they obtain from the traders on the river St. Peters, and receive in return horses, some robes and leather lodges.

transport W.

such as W.

river: W.

32

**S. SISSATONE.** They claim the country in which they rove, embracing the upper portions of the Red river, of lake Winnipie, and St. Peters : it is a level country, intersected with many small lakes ; the land is fertile and free of stone ; the Majority of it open plains. This country abounds more in the valuable fur animals, the beaver, otter and marten, than any portion of Louisiana yet known. This circumstance furnishes the Sissatones with the means of purchasing more merchandise, in proportion to their number than any nation in this quarter. A great proportion of this merchandise is reserved by them for their trade with the Tetons, whom they annually meet at some point previously agreed on upon the waters of James river, in the month of May. This Indian fair is frequently attended by the Yanktons of the North and ahnah. The Sissatones and Yanktons of the North here supply the others with considerable quantities of arms, ammunition, axes, knives, kettles, cloth and a variety of other articles ; and receive in return principally horses, which the others have stolen or purchased from the nations on the Missouri and west of it. They are devoted to the interests of their traders.

**S. YANKTONS of the NORTH.** This band, although they purchase a much smaller quantity of merchandise than the Sissatones, still appropriate a considerable proportion of what they do obtain in a similar manner with that mentioned of the Sissatones. This trade, as small as it may appear, has been sufficient to render the Tetones independent of the trade of the Missouri, in a great measure, and has furnished them with the means, not only of distressing and plundering the traders of the Missouri, but also, of plundering and massacreeing the defenceless savages of the Missouri, from the mouth of the river Platte to the Minetares, and west to the Rocky mountains. The country these people inhabit is almost one entire

majority W.

number, W.

agreed on, W.

Ahnah. W.

cloth, W.

proportion W.

massacreing W.

**33**

plain, uncovered with timber: it is extremely level; the soil fertile, and generally well watered.

S. YANKTONS AHNAH. These are the best disposed Sioux who rove on the banks of the Missouri, and these even will not suffer any trader to ascend the river, if they can possibly avoid it: they have, heretofore, invariably arrested the progress of all those they have met with, and generally compelled them to trade at the prices, nearly, which they themselves think proper to fix on their merchandize; they seldom commit any further acts of violence on the whites.    They sometimes visit the river Demoin, where a partial trade has been carried on with them, for a few years past, by Mr. Crawford.    Their trade, if well regulated, might be rendered extremely valuable.    Their country is a very fertile one; it consists of a mixture of wood lands and priaries.    The land bordering on the Missouri is principally plains with but little timber.

S.  TETONS BOIS BRULE'.    } These are
    TETONS ORKANDANDAS.    } the vilest
    TETONS MINNAKINEAZZO. } miscreants
    TETONS SAHONE.    } of the savage race, and must ever remain the pirates of the Missouri, until such measures are pursued, by our government, as will make them feel a dependence on its will for their supply of merchandize. Unless these people are reduced to order, by coercive measures, I am ready to pronounce that the citizens of the United States can never enjoy but partially the advantages which the Missouri presents. Relying on a regular supply of Merchandize, through the channel of the river St. Peters, they view with contempt the merchants of the Missouri, whom they never fail to plunder, when in their power. Persuasion or advice, with them, is viewed as supplication, and only tends to inspire them with contempt for those who offer either. The tameness with which the traders of the Missouri have heretofore submitted to their rapacity, has tended not a little to inspire them with contempt for

E

merchandise: W.

a Mr. W.

wood-lands and prairies. W.

OKANDANDAS. W.

merchandise. W.

merchandise, W.

them, through that channel. W.

merchandise W.

water-courses, W.

alum, . . . sulphur, W.

of Red W.

**34**

the white persons who visit them through the channel  A prevalent idea among them, and one which they make the rule of their conduct, is, that the more illy they treat the traders the greater quantites of merchandize they will bring them, and that they will thus obtain the articles they wish on better terms ; they have endeavored to inspire the Ricaras with similar sentiments, but, happily, without any considerable effect. The country in which these four bands rove is one continued plain, with scarcely a tree to be seen, except on the water courses, or the steep declivities of hills, which last are but rare : the land is fertile, and lies extremely well for cultivation ; many parts of it are but badly watered.  It is from this country that the Missouri derives most of its coloring matter : the earth is strongly impregnated with glauber salts, allum, copperas and sulpher, and when saturated with water, immense bodies of the hills precipitate themselves into the Missouri, and mingle with its waters.  The waters of this river have a purgative effect on those unaccust med to use it.— I doubt whether these people can ever be induced to become stationary ; their trade might be made valuable if they were reduced to order.  They claim jointly with the other bands of the Sioux, all the country lying within the following limits, viz. beginning at the confluence of the river Demoin and Mississippi, thence up the west side of the Mississippi to the mouth of the St. Peters river, thence on both sides of the Mississippi to the mouth of Crow-wing river, and upwards with that stream, including the waters of the upper part of the same : thence to include the waters of the upper portion of the Red river, of lake Winnipie, and down the same nearly to Pembenar river, thence a south westerly course to intersect the Missouri at or near the Mandans, and with that stream downwards to the entrance of the Warrecunne creek, thence passing the Missouri it goes to include the lower portion of the river Chyenne, all the waters of White river and river

### 35

Teton, including the lower portion of the river Quicurre, and returns to the Missouri, and with that
stream downwards to the mouth of Waddipon river,
and thence eastwardly to intersect the Mississippi at
the beginning.

———

A. Chyenne.
B. Shâr´-ha.
C. la Chien.
D. *
E.
F. 110.
G. 300.
H. 1200.
I. About the source of the river Chyenne, in the
    black hills.
J. Mr. Loiselle, & Co. of St. Louis.
K. On the river Chyenne, not stationary and at the
    Ricaras village.
L. 1.500.
M. 2.000.
N. Buffaloe robes of best quality.
O. Buffaloe robes, tallow, grease, and dried meat,
    skins of the beaver, small and large foxes, small
    and large wolf, antelo e, elk and deer in great
    abundance ; also, elk and deers' tallow, a few
    grizzly bear, skins of the white bear, and big
    horned antelopes.
P. At or near the mouth of Chyenne river.
Q. A defensive war with the Sioux, and at war with
    no other within my knowledge.
R. With all their neighbours except the Sioux.
S. They are the remnant of a nation once respectable
    in point of number: formerly resided on a branch
    of the Red river of Lake Winnipie, which still
    bears their name. Being oppressed by the Sioux,
    they removed to the west side of the Missouri,
    about 15 miles below the mouth of Warricunne

*See Appendix A2 for text missing in N, the second folding chart describing the Sioux.*

Chyennes. W.

No trader C; Mr. Loiselle, W, N. stationary, W.

At, W.
Siouxs, W.

**36**

creek, where they built and fortified a village, but being pursued by their ancient enemies the Sioux, they fled to the Black hills, about the head of the Chyenne river, where they wander in quest of the buffaloe, having no fixed residence. They do not cultivate. They are well dispose towards the whites, and might easily be induced to settle on the Missouri, if they could be assured of being protected from the Sioux. Their number annually diminishes. Their trade may be made valuable.

disposed W.

———

A. Wetepâhâ´toes.
B. We-te-pâ-hâ´-to.
C. Wete-pahatoes.
D. ✳
E.
F. 70, including the Kiâwâs.
G. 200, including the Kiawas.
H. 700, including the Kiawas.
I. On the Paduca fork of the river Platte.
J. No trader.
K.        L.        M.        N.
O. The same as the Tetons, (see first table) also horses.
P. At or near the mouth of the Chyenne river.
Q. A defensive war with the Sioux, and at war with no other to my knowledge.
R. With all their wandering neighbors to the west, and particularly with Ricaras, Mandans, Minatares, and Awahhaways whom they occasionally visit for the purpose of trafficking their horses, mules, &c. for European manufactures.
S. They are a wandering nation, inhabit an open country, and raise a great number of horses, which they barter to the Ricaras, Mandans, &c. for articles of European manufactory. They are a well disposed people, and might be readily

Tetons. W.

of Chyenne W.

trafficking W.

### 37

induced to visit the trading establishments on the Missouri. From the animals their country produces, their trade would, no doubt, become valuable. These people again barter a considerable proportion of the articles they obtain from the Menetares, Ahwahhaways, Mandans, and Ricaras, to the Dotames and Castapanas.

———

A. Kiâwâs.
B. Kí-â-wâ.
C. Kí´âwâs.
D. *
E.
F. See page 36, F.
G. See page 36, G.
H. See page 36, H.
I. On the Paduca, and frequently with the Wetepahatoes.
J. No trader.
K.         L.         M.         N.
O. See page 35, O.
P. At, or near the mouth of Chyenne river.
Q. See page 36, Q.
R. See page 36, R.
S. What has been said of the Wetepehatoes is in all respects applicable to these people also. Neither these people, the Wetepahotoes, nor the Chyennes have any idea of exclusive right to the soil.

———

A. Kanenavish.
B. Kan-e-nâ´-vish.
C. Gens-des-vache.
D. *
E.
F. 150.
G. 400.

150 W.

38

H. 1.500.

I. On the heads of the Paducas fork of the river
    Platte, and south fork of Chyenne river.

S. fork W.

J. No trade.

K.    L.    M.    N.

O. See page 35, O.

Chyenne W.

P. At, or near the mouth of Chayenne river.

Q. See page 36, Q.

R. See page 36. R.

S. See page 37, S.

—

A. Staetan.

B. Sta´-e-tan.

C. Kites.

D. *

E.

F. 40.

G. 100.

H. 400.

I. On the head of the Chyenne, and frequently with
    the Kanenavish.

J.    K.    L.    M.    N.

O. See page 36, O.

P. At, or near the mouth of Chyenne river.

Q. See page 36, Q.

R. See page 36, R.

S. See page 37, S.

—

A. Cataka.

B. Cat´-a-kâ.

C. Cat´akâ.

D. *

E.

F. 25.

G. 75.

H. 300.

### 39

I. Between the heads of the north and south forks of the river Chyenne.

J.     K.     L.     M.     N.

O. See page 35, O.

P. At, or near the mouth of the Chyenne river.

Q. See page 36, Q.

R. See page 36, R.

S. See page 37, S.

— — —

A. Nemousin.

B. Ne´-mo-sin.

C. Allebome.

D. *

E.

F. 15.

G. 50.

H. 200.

I. On the head of the north fork of the river Chyenne.

J. No trader.

K.     L.     M.     N.

O. See page 35, O.

P. At, or near the mouth of the Chyenne river.     At W.

Q. A defensive war with the Ricaras and Sioux.

R. The same as the Wetepahatoes (See page 36, R.) except the Ricaras.     see W.

S. These differ from the others (viz. Wetepahatoes, Kiawas, Kenenavich, Staetan and Cataka) in as much as they never visit the Ricaras; in all other respects they are the same, see page 37, S.     Kanenavich, W.

— — —

A. Dotame.

B. Do-ta´-me.

C. Dotame.

D. *

E.

40

F. 10.

G. 30.

H. 120.

heads W.    I. On the head of the river Chyenne.

J. No trader.

K.    L.    M.    N.

O. See page 35, O.

P. At, or near the mouth of the Chyenne river.

Q. See page 36, Q.

R. See page 36, R.

information: W.    S. The information I possess, with respect to this nation, is derived from Indian information; they are said to be a wandering nation, inhabiting an open country, and who raise a great number of

friendly, W.    horses and mules. They are a friendly well disposed people, and might, from the position of their country, be easily induced to visit an establishment on the Missouri, about the mouth of Chyenne river. They have not, as yet, visited the Missouri.

———

A. Castahana.

B. Cas-ta-ha´-na.

Gens des Vache C; Castahana. W.    C. Castahana.

D. *

E.

F. 500.

G. 1.300.

H. 5.000.

I. Between the sources of the Padoucas fork, of the rivers Platte and Yellow Stone.

J. No trader.

K.    L.    M.    N.

Chyennes W.    O. The same as the Chyenne (see page 35, O) and

louverin, W.    the skins of the lynx, or louvering, and martens in addition.

At W.    P. At, or near the mouth of the river Yellow Stone, on the Missouri.

### 41

Q. A defensive war with the Sioux and Assinniboin.
R. See page 36, R.
S. What has been said of the Dotames is applicable to these people, except that they trade principally with the Crow Indians, and that they would most probably prefer visiting an establishment on the Yellow Stone river, or at its mouth on the Missouri.

———

A. Crow Indians.
B. Kee´-kât´-sâ.
C. Gens des Corbeau.
D. Minetarre.
E.
F. 350.
G. 900.
H. 3.500.
I. On each side of the river Yellow Stone, about the mouth of the Big-horn river.
J. No trader.
K.
L.      M.      N.
O. See page 40, O.
P. At, or near the mouth of the river Yellow Stone, on the Missouri.
Q. Denfensive with the Sioux and Ricaras.
R. The same as the Wetepahatoes, (see page 36, R.) except the Ricaras.
S. These people are divided into four bands, called by themselves Ahâh-âr-ro´-pir-no-pah, Noo´-ta-, Pa-rees-car, and E-hârt´-sâr. They annually visit the Mandans, Minetares, and Awahhaways, to whom they barter horses, mules. leather lodges, and many articles of Indian apparel, for which rhey receive in return guns, ammunition, axes, kettles, awls, and other European manufactures. When they return to their country, they are in turn visited by the Paunch and Snake

F

Siouxs and Assinniboins. W.

Defensive W.
See W.

Ahâ´-âr-ro´-pir-no-pah, W.

they . . . return, W.

obtain of the Snake Indians,
bridle-bits W.

bridle-bits W.

Kee-hât-sâ C; Al-la-kâ'-we-âh. W.

42

Indians, to whom they barter most of the articles they have obtained from the nations on the
Missouri, for horses and mules, of which those
nations have a greater abundance than themselves.
They also obtain from the Snake Indians bridle-
bitts and blankets, and some other articles which
those Indians purchase from the Spaniards. The
bridle-bitts and blankets I have seen in the possession of the Mandans and Minetares. Their
country is fertile, and well watered, and in most
parts well timbered.

———

A. Paunch Indians.
B. Al-la-kâ-we-âh.
C. Gens de Panse.
D. *
E.
F. 300.
G. 800.
H. 2.300.
I. On each side of the Yellow Stone river, near the
rocky mountains, and heads of the Big-horn ri-
ver.
I. No trader.
K.    L.    M.    N.
O. See page 40, O.
P. At, or near the mouth of the river Yellow Stone,
on the Missouri.
Q. Defensive with the Sioux and Ricaras.
R. The same as the Wetepehatoes, (see page 36, R.)
except the Ricaras.
S. These are said to be a peaceable, well disposed
nation. Their country is a variegated one, con-
sisting of mountains, vallies, plains, and wood-
lands, irregularly interspersed. They might be
induced to visit the Missouri, at the mouth of the
Yellow Stone river; and from the great abundance of valuable fured animals which their

**43**

country, as well as that of the Crow Indians. produces, their trade must become extremely valuable. They are a roving people, and have no idea of exclusive right to the soil.

of of W.

*column B, line 3*  O-ee-gah C; O-seé-gâh. W.
*column C, line 4*  Gens des fees or Girls C; Gens des Tee. W.
*column C, line 8*  Big Devils C; Gens des grand Diable. W.
*column I, line 6*  of Little W.

44

| A. | B. | C. | D. | E. | F. | G. | H. | I. |
|---|---|---|---|---|---|---|---|---|
| ASSINNIBOIN. / NACOTA. | Ma-ne-to´-pâ. | Gens des Canoe. | Sioux, with some few words peculiar to themselves. | | 100 | 200 | 750 | On the Mouse river, between the Assinniboin and the Missouri. |
| | O-see-gâh. | Gens des Tee. | | | 100 | 250 | 850 | From the Missouri, about the mouth of the Little Missouri, to the Assinniboin, at the mouth of Capelle river. |
| | Mâh´-to,-pâ-nâ-to. | Gens des grand Diable. | | | 200 | 450 | 1.600 | On the Missouri, about the mouth of the White Earth river, and on the head of Assiniboin and Capelle rivers. |

45

CONTINUED.

| A. ASSINNIBOIN. NACOTA. | | J. | K. | L. | M. | N. |
|---|---|---|---|---|---|---|
| B. | Me-ne-to'-pâ. | British Hudson's Bay, and the N.W. and X.Y. Canadian companies. | Establishments on the Assinniboin river. | 4.500 | 7.000 | Buffaloe meat dried or pounded, and grease in bladders, principally; also, wolves, a few beaver and buffaloe robes. |
| | O-seé-gâh. | | Establishments on the Assinniboin and Capelle rivers. | 6.000 | 6.500 | |
| | Mâh'-to,-pâ-nâ-to. | | Ditto, and occasionally at the establishments on the river Saskashawan. | 8.000 | 8.000 | |

*column B, line 2* Ma-ne-to-par C; Ma-ne-to'-pâ. W.

*column B, line 4* Mah-ta-pa-nar-to C; Mâh'-to,-pâ-nâ-to. W, N.

*column O line 10* also, W.
*column P* Yellow Stone, W.
*column R line 9* Prairie, W.

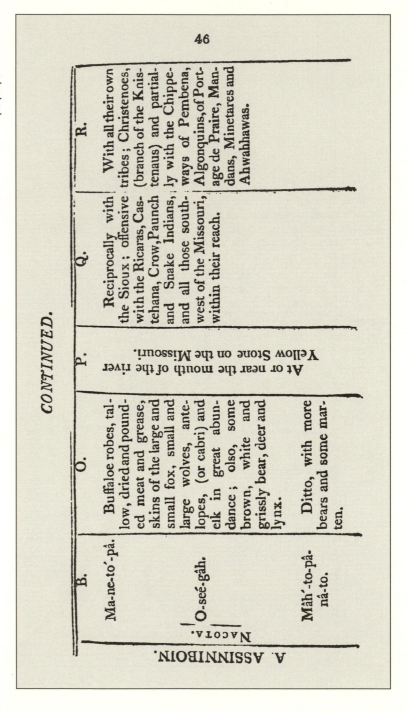

*CONTINUED.*

46

A. ASSINNIBOIN.

| B. | O. | P. | Q. | R. |
|---|---|---|---|---|
| Ma-ne-tó-pá.<br>O-seé-gáh.<br>NACOTA. | Buffaloe robes, tallow, dried and pounded meat and grease, skins of the large and small fox, small and large wolves, antelopes, (or cabri) and elk in great abundance; olso, some brown, white and grissly bear, deer and lynx. | At or near the mouth of the river Yellow Stone on the Missouri. | Reciprocally with the Sioux; offensive with the Ricaras, Castehana, Crow, Paunch and Snake Indians, and all those south-west of the Missouri, within their reach. | With all their own tribes; Christenoes, (branch of the Knistenaus) and partially with the Chippeways of Pembena, Algonquins, of Portage de Praire, Mandans, Minetares and Ahwahhawas. |
| Máh'-to-pá-ná-to. | Ditto, with more bears and some marten. | | | |

### 47

S. MANETOPA.
OSEEGAH.
MAHTOPANATO. } Are the descendants of the Sioux, and partake of their turbulent and faithless disposition : they frequeutly plunder, and sometimes murder, their own traders The name by which this nation is generally known was borrowed from the Chippeways, who call them *Assinniboan*, which, literally translated, is *Stone Sioux*, hence the name of Stone Indians, by which they are sometimes called. The country in which they rove is almost entirely uncovered with timber ; lies extremely level, and is but badly watered in many parts ; the land, however, is tolerably fertile and unincumbered with stone. They might be induced to trade at the river Yellow Stone ; but I do not think that their trade promises much. Their numbers continue about the same. These bands, like the Sioux, act entirely independant of each other, altho' they claim a national affinity and never make war on each other. The country inhabited by the Mahtopanato possesses rather more timber than the other parts of the country. They do not cultivate.

traders. W.

although W.

*column A* CHIPPEWAYS. W.
*column I line 11* Pembanar W.

48

**A. CHIPPEWAY.**

| B. | C. | D. | E. | F. | G. | H. | I. | J. |
|---|---|---|---|---|---|---|---|---|
| O-jib'-â-way. | La Sauteur. | * | 1 | | 400 | 1.600 | On an island in a small lake, called Leach Lake, formed by the Mississippi river. | N. W. Company. |
| Ditto. | | Chippeway. | | | 20c | 700 | About the head of the Mississippi and around Red Lake. | Ditto. |
| Ditto. | | Ditto. | | | 10c | 350 | On the Red river of Lake Winnipie, and about the mouth of Pembenar river. | N. W. and X. Y. Conpanies. |

**CONTINUED.**

49

| O. | K. | L. | M. | N. | O. |
|---|---|---|---|---|---|
| **G A. CHIPPEWAYS.** | | | | | |
| Ojibaway. | At their villages and hunting camps on the Mississippi. | 12.000 | 16.000 | Beaver, otter, black bear, rac-koon, fox, marten, mink, fisher, and deer skins. | Beaver, otter, black bear, rac-koon, grey fox. martin, mink. fisher, and deer skins. |
| Ditto. | At an establishment on Red lake, and at their hunting camps. | 8.000 | 10.000 | Ditto, and bark canoes. | Ditto, and bark canoes. |
| Ditto. | Establishments near the mouth of Pembenar river, and at their hunting camps. | 7.000 | 10.000 | Ditto, principally beaver and otter, but no canoes, with some wolverine and lynx. | Ditto, except canoes, with wolverine and lynx in addition. |

*first column heading* B. W, O. N.
*column K line 11* Pembanar W.

*column B line 2* Ojibaway. W.

50

CONTINUED.

| A. CHIPPEWAYS. | B. | P. | Q. | R. |
|---|---|---|---|---|
| | O-jib-â-way. | On the north side of the Mississippi, at Sandy Lake. | With all the tribes of Sioux, Saukees, Renars, and Ayouwais. | All the tribes of Chippeways, and the nations inhabiting lakes Superior, Michigan, and the country east of the Mississippi. |
| | Ditto. | On the Red Lake, near the head of the Mississippi. | ! The Sioux only. | |
| | Ditto. | On the Red river of Lake Winnipie, about the mouth of the Assinniboin river. | † The Sioux, and partially with the Assinniboins. | Ditto, and with the Christenoes and Algonquins. |

**51**

**S. CHIPPEWAYS,** *of Leach Lake.* Claim the country on both sides of the Mississippi, from the mouth of the Crow-wing river to its source, and extending west of the Mississippi to the lands claimed by the Sioux, with whom they still contend for dominion. They claim, also, east of the Mississippi, the country extending as far as lake Superior, including the waters of the river St. Louis. This country is thickly covered with timber generally; lies level, and generally fertile, though a considerable proportion of it is intersected and broken up by small lakes, morasses and swamps, particularly about the heads of the Mississippi and river St. Louis. They do not cultivate, but live principally on the wild rice, which they procure in great abundance on the borders of Leach Lake and the banks of the Mississippi. Their number has been considerably reduced by wars and the small pox. Their trade is at its greatest extent.

*Of Red lake.* Claim the country about Red lake and Red lake river, as far as the Red river of lake Winnipie, beyond which last river they contend with the Siox for territory. This is a low level country, and generally thickly covered with timber, interrupted with many swamps and morasses. This, as well as the other bands of Chippeways, are esteemed the best hunters in the north west country; but from the long residence of this band in the country they now inhabit, game is becoming scarce; therefore, their trade is supposed to be at its greatest extent. The Chippeways are a well disposed people, but excessively fond of spiritous liquor.

*Of river Pembena.* These people formerly resided on the east side of the Mississippi, at Sand lake, but were induced, by the north west company, to remove, about two years since, to the river Pembena. They do not claim the lands on which they hunt. The country is level and the soil good. The west side of the river is principally prairies or open plains; on the east side there is a greater proportion of tim-

Sioux W.

spirituous W.

## 52

ber.   Their trade at present is a very valuable one, and will probably increase for some years.   They do not cultivate, but live by hunting.   They are well disposed towards the whites.

53

| A. ALGONQUINS. | B. | C. | D. | E. F. G. | H. | I. | J. |
|---|---|---|---|---|---|---|---|
| | O-jib'-â-way. | Algonquins. | Chippeways. | 100 | 300 | On the south side of Rainy Lake, Rainy Lake river, and the Lake of the Wood. | N. W. and X. Y. Companies. |
| | Ditto. | Algonquins. | Chippeways. | 200 | 600 | About the mouth of the Assinniboin, on Red river. | Ditto. |

*column B line 2*  O-jib'-â-way. W.

*column N line 2*  Beaver Otter, racoon, fox Min[k], Deer & B[lack] Bear Skins & marten C; Principally birch bark canoes. W, N.

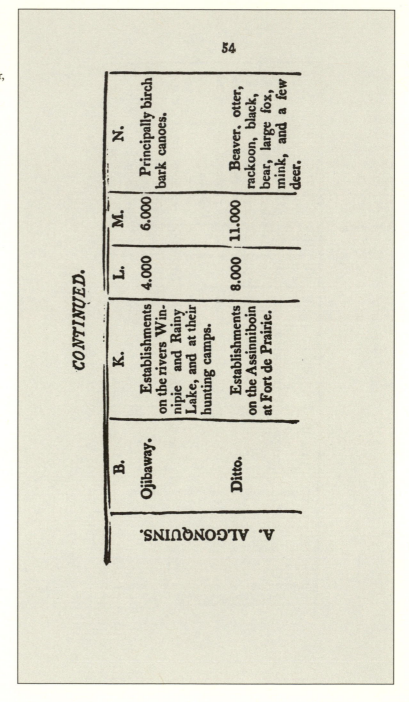

54

CONTINUED.

| A. ALGONQUINS. | B. | K. | L. | M. | N. |
|---|---|---|---|---|---|
| | Ojibaway. | Establishments on the rivers Winnipie and Rainy Lake, and at their hunting camps. | 4.000 | 6.000 | Principally birch bark canoes. |
| | Ditto. | Establishments on the Assinniboin at Fort de Prairie. | 8.000 | 11.000 | Beaver. otter, rackoon, black, bear, large fox, mink, and a few deer. |

55

**CONTINUED.**

| A. ALGONQUINS. | B. | .O. | P. | Q. | R. |
|---|---|---|---|---|---|
| | Ojibaway. | The same as the Chippeways, but in small quantities. and canoes, (see page 48, O.) | At the Red Lake establishment. | The Sioux, and partially with the Assiniboins. | All the tribes of the Chippeways, Algonquins, and Christenoes. |
| | Ditto. | Beaver, otter, raccoon, black bear, large fox, mink, deer, wolves and muskrats. | At the Red river establishment, | | |

*heading* CONTINUED. (*roman*) W.

*column O line 4* quantities, W.

*column Q line 1* Siouxs, W.

**56**

**S. ALGONQUINS,** *of Rainy Lake,* &c. With the precise limits of the country they claim, I am not informed. They live very much detached, in small parties. The country they inhabit is but an indifferent one ; it has been much hunted, and the game, of course, nearly exhausted. They are well disposed towards the whites. Their number is said to decrease. They are extremely addicted to spiritous liquor, of which large quantities are annually furnished them by the N. W. traders, in return for their bark canoes. They live wretchedly poor.

*Of Portage de Priarie.* These people inhabit a low, flat, marshy country, mostly covered with timber, and well stocked with game. They are emigrants from the lake of the Woods and the country east of it, who were introduced, some years since, by the N. W. traders, in order to hunt the country on the lower parts of Red river, which then abounded in a variety of animals of the fur kind. They are an orderly, well disposed people, but like their relations on Rainy lake, extremely addicted to spiritous liquors. Their trade is at its greatest extent.

—

A. Christenoes or Knistenaus.
B. Chris- 'te-no.
C. Cree.
D. Chippeways, with a different accent, and many words peculiar to themselves.
E.
F. 150.
G. 300.
H. 1.000
I. On the heads of the Assinniboin, and thence towards the Saskashawan.
J. Hudson's Bay, N. W. and X. Y. companies.
K. Establishments on the Assinniboin, Swan Lake river and the Saskashawan.

*Marginal notes:*

spirituous W.

*Prairie.* W.

spirituous W.

Corrupted Chipaway C; Chippeways, with a different accent, W, N.

### 57

L. 15.000.

M. 15.000.

N. Beaver, otter, lynx, wolverine, marten, mink, wolf, small fox(or kitts) dressed elk and moose deer skins.

O. The skins of the beaver, otter, lynx, wolf, wolverine, marten, mink, and fox, brown and grizzly bear, dressed elk and moose-deer skins, muskrat skins, and some buffaloe robes, dried meat, tallow and grease. — mink, small fox, W.

P. On the Missouri, at, or near the mouth of the Yellow Stone river.

Q. With the Sioux, Fall, Blood and Crow Indians. — Siouxs, W.

R. With the Assinniboin, Algonquins, Chippeways, Mandans, Minatares, and Awahhaways. — Assinniboins, W. Ahwahhaways. W.

S. They are a wandering nation; do not cultivate, nor claim any particular tract of country. They are well disposed towards the whites, and treat their traders with respect. The country in which they rove is generally open plains, but in some parts, particularly about the head of the Assinniboin river, it is marshy and tolerably well furnished with timber, as are also the Fort Dauphin mountains, to which they sometimes resort.— From the quantity of beaver in their country, they ought to furnish more of that article than they do at present. They are not esteemed good beaver hunters. They might, probably be induced to visit an establishment on the Missouri, at the Yellow Stone river. Their number has been reduced by the small pox, since they were first known to the Canadians. — reduced, W.

———

A. Fall Indians.

B. A-lân-sâr.

C. Fall Indians. — Fall Indians or Gen de rapid C;

D. Minetare. — Fall Indians. W, N.

H

58

E.
F. 260.
G. 660.
H. 2.500.
I. On the head of the south fork of the Saskashawan river, and some streams supposed to be branches of the Missouri.
J. N. W. company.
K. Upper establishment on the Saskashawan; but little trade.
L. 1.000.
M. 4.000.
N. Beaver and marten.
O. Skins of the beaver, brown, white and grizzly bear, large and small foxes, muskrat, marten, mink, lynx, wolverine, wolves, white hares, deer, elk, moose-deer, antelopes of the Missouri, and some buffaloe.

At W.

P. At, or near the falls of the Missouri.
Q. Defensive war with the Christenoes.
R.
S. The country these people rove in is not much

known: W.

known, it is said to be a high, broken, woody,

Missouri: W.

country. They might be induced to visit an establishment at the falls of the Missouri; their trade may, no doubt, be made profitable.

———

A. Cattanahaws.
B. Cat-tan-a-hâws.
C. Cattanahâws.
D. *
E.      F.      G.      H.
I. Between the Saskashawan and the Missouri, on waters supposed to be of the Missouri.
J. No trader.
K.      L.      M.      N.
O. See page 57, O.

59

P.  At, or near the falls of the Missouri.
Q.    R.
S.  What has been said of the Fall Indians is, in all
    respects, applicable to this nation.   They are
    both wandering nations.

———

A.  Black-foot Indians.
B.
C.  Blackfoot Indians.
D.  *
E.    F.    G.    H.
I.  Between the Saskashawan and the Missouri, on
    waters supposed to be of the Missouri.
J.  No trader.
K.    L.    M.    N.
O.  See page, 57, O.
P.  At, or near the falls of the Missouri.
Q.    R.
S.  See page 58, S.

———

A.  Blue Mud and Long Hair Indians.
B.
C.  Blue Mud and Long Hair Indians.
D.  *
E.    F.    G.    H.
I.  West of the Rocky mountains, and near the same
    on water courses supposed to be branches of the
    Columbia river.
J.  No trader.
K.    L.    M.    N.
O.  Not known, but from the position of their coun-
    try supposed to abound in animals similar to
    those mentioned in page 57, O.
P.    Q.    R.
S.  Still less is known of these people, or their coun-
    try.   The water courses on which they reside,

60

are supposed to be branches of the Columbia river.  They are wandering nations.

———:

A.  Flatheads.
B.  Tut-see'-wâs.
C.  Flat-head Indians.
D.  *
E.      F.      G.      H.
I.  On the west side of a large river, lying west of the Rocky mountains, and running north, supposed to be the south fork of the Columbia river.
J.  No trader.
K.      L.      M.      N.
O.  See page 58, O.
P.

Defensive war with W.  Q  Defensive with the Minetares.
R.

posses W.  S.  The information I possess with respect to these people has been received from the Minetares, who have extended their war excursions as far westerly as that nation, of whom they have made several prisoners, and brought them with them

Missouri: W.  to their villages on the Missouri; these prisoners have been seen by the Frenchmen residing in this neighborhood.  The Minetares state, that this nation resides in one village on the west side of a large and rapid river, which runs from south

Rocky W.  to north, along the foot of the rocky mountains
their west W.  on the west side; and that this river passes at a small distance from the three forks of the Missouri.  That the country between the mountains and the river is broken, but on the opposite side

river it is W.  of the river is an extensive open plain, with a number of barren sandy hills, irregularly distributed over its surface as far as the eye can reach.  They are a timid, inoffensive, and defenceless people.  They are said to possess an abundance of horses.

61

| A. ALIATANS. | B. | C. | D. | E. | F. | G. | H. | I. |
|---|---|---|---|---|---|---|---|---|
| Snake Indians. | So-so-na´, So-so-bâ, and I´-â-kâr. | Gens des Serpent. | Aliatan. | | | Very numerous. | | Among the rocky mountains, on the heads of the Missouri, Yellow Stone and Platte river. |
| Of the West. | A-li-a-tân. | Aliata. | * Aliatan. | | | | | Among the rocky mountains, and in the plains at the heads of the Platte and Arkansas rivers. |
| La Plays. | La Plays. | La Plays. | Aliatan. | | | | | The mountains on the borders of New Mexico, and the extensive plains at the heads of the Arkansas and Red rivers. |

*column C line 4* Aliatâ. W.
*column I line 4* Mis— W.

62

*CONTINUED.*

| A. ALIATANS. | J. | K. | L. | M. | N. | O. |
|---|---|---|---|---|---|---|
| Snake Indians. | With the Spaniards of New Mexico. | The place at which this trade is carried on is not known. | | | | The same with the Fall, Cattanahaws and Black Foot Indians, except buffaloes; but they have in addition immense quantities of horses, mules and asses. |
| Of the West. | | | | | | |
| La Plays. | | | | | | Immense quantities of horses, mules, asses, buffaloe, deer, elk, black bear, and large hares; and in the northern regions of their country, big horn and Missouri antelopes, with many animals of the fur kind. |

63

CONTINUED.

| A. ALIATANS. | P. | Q. | R. |
|---|---|---|---|
| Snake Indians. | At or near the Falls of the Missouri. | Defensive war with the Ricaras, Sioux, Assinniboin, Christenoes, Minetares, Ahwahhaways, and all the nations inhabiting the Saskashawan river. | Mandans and Crow Indians, and all those who do not attack them. |
| Of the West.<br>La Plays. | On the Arkansas, as high up as possible. It would be best that it should be west of the source of the Kansas, if it should be necessary even to supply it some distance by land. | Defensive war with the Great and Little Osages, Paniapique, Kansas, Pania Proper, Pania Republican, Pania Loups, Ricaras, and Sioux. | At Peace with all who do not wage war against them. |

*column Q line 3* Assiniboins, W.

**64**

**S. ALIATANS,** *Snake Indians.* These are a very numerous and well disposed people, inhabiting a woody and mountainous country; they are divided into three large tribes, who wander at a considerable distance from each other; and are called by themselves So-so-na, So-so'bu-bar, and I-a-kar; these are again subdivided into smaller tho' independent bands, the names of which I have not yet learnt; they raise a number of horses and mules which they trade with the Crow Indians, or are stolen by the nations on the east of them. They maintain a partial trade with the Spaniards, from whom they obtain many articles of cloathing and ironmongery, but no warlike implements.

*Of the West.* The people also inhabit a mountainous country, and sometimes venture in the plains east of the Rocky mountains, about the heads of the Arkansas river. They have more intercourse with the Spaniards of New Mexico, than the Snake Indians. They are said to be very numerous and warlike, but are badly armed. The Spaniards fear these people, and therefore take the precaution not to furnish them with any warlike implements. In their present unarmed state, they frequently commit hostilities on the Spaniards. They raise a great many horses.

*La Playes.* They principally inhabit the rich plains from the head of the Arkansas, embracing the heads of Red river, and extending with the mountains and high lands eastwardly as far as it is known towards the gulph of Mexico. They possess no fire arms, but are warlike and brave. They are as well as the other Aliatans, a wandering people. Their country abounds in wild horses, besides great numbers which they raise themselves. These people and the West Aliatans, might be induced to trade with us on the upper part of the Arkansas river. I do not believe that any of the Aliatans claim a country within any particular limits.

These people W.

They are, as W.

people, W.

*See Appendix A3 for text missing in* N, *relating to the Pania Pique and the Paducas.*

# HISTORICAL SKETCHES

### OF THE

## SEVERAL INDIAN TRIBES IN LOUISIANA,

#### SOUTH OF

## THE ARKANSA RIVER,

#### AND BETWEEN

## *THE MISSISSIPPI AND RIVER GRAND.*

———————

CADDOQUES, live about 35 miles west of the main branch of Red river, on a bayau or creek, called by them Sodo, which is navigable for perogues only within about six miles of their village, and that only in the rainy season. They are distant from Natchitoches about 120 miles, the nearest route by land, and in nearly a north west direction. They have lived where they now do only five years. The first year they moved there the small pox got amongst them and destroyed nearly one half of them ; it was in the winter season, and they practised plunging into the creek on the first appearance of the eruption, and died in a few hours. Two years ago they had the measles, of which several more of them died. They formerly lived on the south bank of the river, by the course of the river 375 miles higher up, at a beautiful priarie, which has a clear lake of good water in the middle of it, surrounded by a pleasant and fertile country, which had been the residence of their ancestors from time immemorial.

I

peroques W.

prairie, W.

65

They have a traditionary tale which not only the Caddos, but half a dozen other smaller nations believe in, who claim the honor of being descendants of the same family; they say, when all the world was drowned by a flood that inundated the whole country, the great spirit placed on an eminence, near this lake, one family of Caddoques, who alone were saved; from that family all the Indians originated.

The French, for many years before Louisiana was transferred to Spain, had, at this place, a fort and some soldiers; several French families were likewise settled in the vicinity, where they had erected a good flour mill with burr stones brought from France. These French families continued there till about 25 years ago, when they moved down and settled at Campti, on the Red river, about 20 miles above Natchitoches, where they now live; and the Indians left it about 14 years ago, on account of a dreadful sickness that visited them. They settled on the river nearly opposite where they now live, on a low place, but were driven thence on account of its overflowing, occasioned by a jam of timber choking the river at a point below them.

The whole number of what they call warriors of the ancient Caddo nation, is now reduced to about 100, who are looked upon somewhat like knights of Malta, or some distinguished military order. They are brave, despise danger or death, and boast that they have never shed white man's blood. Besides these, there are of old men and strangers who live amongst them, nearly the same number, but there are 40 or 50 more women than men. This nation has great influence over the Yattasses, Nandakoes, Nabadaches, Inies or Yaches, Nagogdoches, Keychies, Adaize and Natchitoches, who all speak the Caddo language, look up to them as their fathers, visit and intermarry among them, and join them in all their wars.

The Caddoques complain of the Choctaws incroaching upon their country; call them lazy, thievish, &c. There has been a misunderstanding be-

family: W.

Tachies, SI; Yachies, W.

**66**

tween them for several years, and small hunting parties will kill one another when they meet.

The Caddos raise corn, beans, pumpkins, &c. but the land on which they now live is priarie, of a white clay soil, very flat : their crops are subject to injury either by too wet or too dry a season. They have horses, but few of any other domestic animal, except dogs : most of them have guns and some have rifles ; they and all other Indians that we have any knowledge of, are at war with the Osages.

The country, generally, round the Caddos is hilly, not very rich; growth a mixture of oak, hickory and pine, interspersed with priaries, which are very rich generally, and fit for cultivation. There are creeks and springs of good water frequent.

YATTASSEES, live on Bayau Pierre, (or Stony creek) which falls into Red river, western division, about 50 miles above Natchitoches. Their village is a large priarie about half way between the Caddoques and Nachitoches, surrounded by a settlement of French families. The Spanish government at present, exercise jurisdiction over this settlement, where they keep a guard of a noncommissioned officer and eight soldiers.

A few months ago, the Caddo chief with a few of his young men were coming to this place to trade, and came that way which is the usual road. The Spanish officer of the guard threatened to stop them from trading with the Americans, and told the chief if he returned that way with the goods he should take them from him : The chief and his party were very angry, and threatened to kill the whole guard, and told them that road had been always theirs, and that if the Spaniards attempted to prevent their using it as their ancestors had always done, he would soon make it a bloody road. He came here, purchased the goods he wanted, and might have returned another way and avoided the Spanish guard, and was advised to do so ; but he said he would pass by them,

parties kill W.

prairie, W.

Candos W.

prairies, W.

is in a large prairie W.
Natchitoches, W.

that that road W.

**67**

and let them attempt to stop him if they dared. The guard said nothing to him as he returned.

This settlement, till some few years ago, used to belong to the district of Natchitoches, and the rights to their lands given by the government of Louisiana, before it was ceded to Spain. Its now being under the government of Texas, was only an agreement between the commandant of Natchitoches and the commandant of Nagadoches. The French formerly had a station and factory there, and another on the *Sabine* river, nearly one hundred miles north west from the Bayau Pierre settlement. The Yattassees now say the French used to be their people and now the Americans.

But of the ancient Yattassees there are but eight men remaining, and twenty-five women, besides children ; but a number of men of other nations have intermarried with them and live together. I paid a visit at their village last summer ; there were about forty men of them altogether : their original language differs from any other : but now, all speak Caddo. They live on rich land, raise plenty of corn, beans, pumpkins, tobacco, &c. have horses, cattle, hogs and poultry.

NANDAKOES, live on the Sabine river, 60 or 70 miles to the westward of the Yattassees, near where the French formerly had a station and factory. Their language is Caddo : about 40 men only of them remaining. A few years ago they suffered very much by the small pox. They consider themselves the same as Caddos, with whom they intermarry, and are, occasionally, visiting one another in the greatest harmony : have the same manners, customs and attachments.

ADAIZE, live about 40 miles from Natchitoches below the Yattassees, on a lake called Lac Macdon, which communicates with the division of Red river, that passes by Bayau Pierre. They live at or near

Taxus, W.

Nagogdoches. W.

Yattasses W.

other; W.

river that W.

68

where their ancestors have lived from time immemorial. They being the nearest nation to the old Spanish fort, or Mission of Adaize, that place was named after them, being about 20 miles from them, to the south. There are now but 20 men of them remaining, but more women. Their language differs from all other, and is so difficult to speak or understand, that no nation can speak ten words of it ; but they all speak Caddo, and most of them French, to whom they were always attached, and joined them against the Natchez Indians, After the massacre of Natchez, in 1798, while the Spaniards occupied the post of Adaize, their priests took much pains to proselyte these Indians to the Roman Catholic religion, but, I am informed, were totally unsuccessful.

ALICHE, (commonly pronounced Eyeish) live near Nagadoches, but are almost extinct, as a nation, not being more than 25 souls of them remaining : four years ago the small pox destroyed the greater part of them. They were, some years ago, a considerable nation, and lived on a bayau which bears their name, which the road from Nachitoches to Nagadoches crosses, about 12 miles west of Sabine river, on which a few French and American families are settled. Their native language is spoken by no other nation, but they speak and understand Caddo, with whom they are in amity, often visiting one another.

ALICHE W.
Nacogdoches, W.

Natchitoch to Nacogdoches W.

KEYES, or KEYCHIES, live on the east bank of Trinity river, a small distance above where the road from Natchitoches to St. Antoine crosses it. There are of them 60 men : have their peculiar native language, but mostly now speak Caddo ; intermarry with them, and live together in much harmony, formerly having lived near them, on the head waters of the Sabine. They plant corn and some other vegetables.

INIES, or TACHIES (called indifferently by

69

or Taxus W.

both names.) From the latter name the name of the province of Tachus or Texas is derived. The Inies live about 25 miles west of Natchitoches, on a small

of Sabine, called the Naches. W.
like all their W.

river a branch of the Sabine, called Natches. They are, like their neighbours, diminishing: but have now 80 men. Their ancestors, for a long time, lived where they now do. Their language the same as

amity. W.

that of the Caddos, with whom they are in great amity, These Indians have a good character, live on excellent land, and raise corn to sell.

of the same river, W.
them; have W.

NABEDACHES, live on the west side of said river, about fifteen miles above them: have about the same number of men; speak the same language; live on the best of land; raise corn in plenty; have the same manners, customs and attachments.

Nacogdoches; W.

BEDIES, are on the Trinity river, about 60 miles to the southward of Nagadoches: have 100 men; are good hunters for deer, which are very large and plenty about them; plant, and make good crops

other, W.
peaceable, W.

of corn; language differs from all others, but speak Caddo; are a peacable, quiet people, and have an excellent character for their honesty and punctuality.

Colerado W.
miles W. Nacogdoches, W.

ACCOKESAWS. Their ancient town and principal place of residence is on the west side of Calerado or Rio Rouge, about 200 mlies south west of Nagadoches, but often change their place of residence for a season; being near the bay make great use of fish, oysters, &c. kill a great many deer, which are

province; W.

the largest and fattest in the province: and their country is universally said to be inferior to no part of the province in soil, growth of timber, goodness of water, and beauty of surface; have a language peculiar to themselves, but have a mode of communica-

dum W. understand; W.

tion by dumb signs, which they all understand: number about 80 men. 30 or 40 years ago the Spaniards had a mission here, but broke it up, or moved

Nacogdoches. W.

it to Nagadoches. They talked of resettling it, and speak in the highest terms of the country.

**70**

MAYES, live on a large creek called St. Gabriel, on the bay of St. Bernard, near the mouth of Guadaloupe river : are estimated at 200 men; never at peace with the Spaniards, towards whom they are said to possess a fixed hatred, but profess great friendship for the French, to whom they have been strongly attached since Mons. de Salle landed in their neighborhood. The place where there is talked of the Spaniards opening a new port, and making a settlement, is near them ; where the party, with the governor of St. Antoine, who were there last fall to examine it, say they found the remains of a French block house ; some of the cannon now at Labahie are said to have been brought from that place, and known by the engravings now to be seen on them.

The French speak highly of these Indians for their extreme kindness and hospitality to all Frenchmen who have been amongst them ; have a language of their own, but speak Attakapa, which is the language of their neighbours the Carankouas ; they have likewise a way of conversing by signs.

CARANKOUAS, live on an island, or peninsula, in the bay of St. Bernard, in length about ten miles, and five in breadth ; the soil is extremely rich and pleasant ; on one side of which there is a high bluff, or mountain of coal, which has been on fire for many years, affording always a light at night, and a strong, thick smoke by day, by which vessels are sometimes deceived and lost on the shoaly coast, which shoals are said to extend nearly out of sight of land. From this burning coal there is emitted a gummy substance the Spaniards call *cheta*, which is thrown on the shore by the surf, and collected by them in considerable quantities, which they are fond of chewing ; it has the appearance and consistence of pitch, of a strong, aromatic, and not disagreeable smell. These Indians are irreconcileable enemies to the Spaniards, always at war with them, and kill them whenever they can. The Spaniards call them can-

is a talk of W.

Labahie S1; Laverdee S3; Laberdee S4.

them: W.

neighbors W.

**71**

nibals, but the French give them a different character, who have always been treated kindly by them since Mons. de Salle and his party were in their neighbourhood.   They are said to be 500 men strong, but I have not been able to estimate their numbers from any very accurate information ; in a short time expect to be well informed.   They speak the Attakapa language; are friendly and kind to all other Indians, and, I presume, are much like all others notwithstanding what the Spaniards say of them, for nature is every where the same.

Last summer an old Spaniard came to me from Labahie, a journey of about 500 miles, to have a barbed arrow taken out of his shoulder, that one of these Indians had shot into it. I found it under his shoulder-blade, near nine inches, and had to cut a new place to get at the point of it, in order to get it out the contrary way from that in which it had entered; it was made of a piece of an iron hoop, with wings like a fluke and an inche.

CANCES, are a very numerous nation, consisting of a great many different tribes, occupying different parts of the country, from the bay of St. Bernard, cross river Grand, towards La Vera Cruz.   They are not friendly to the Spaniards, and generally kill them when they have an opportunity.   They are attached to the French; are good hunters, principally using the bow.   They are very particular in their dress, which is made of neatly dressed leather ; the women wear a long loose robe, resembling that of a Franciscan friar ;  nothing but their heads and feet are to be seen.   The dress of the men is straight leather leggings, resembling pantaloons, and leather hunting shirt, or frock.   No estimate can be made of their number.

Thirty or forty years ago the Spaniards used to make slaves of them when they could catch them; a considerable number of them were brought to Natchitoches and sold to the French inhabitants at 40 or

neighborhood. W.

others, notwithstanding W.

entered: W.

and a leather W.

could take them; W.

**72**

50 dollars a head, and a number of them are still liv-ing here, but are now free.   About twenty years ago an order came from the king of Spain that no more Indians should be made slaves,  and those that were enslaved should  be emancipated ; after which some of the women who had been  servants  in good fami-lies, and  taught  spinning,  sewing,  &c. as  well as managing household affairs, married maitiffs of the country,  and became respectable well  behaved wo-men,  and  have  now growing up  decent families of children : have a language  peculiar  to  themselves, and are  understood,  by signs,  by all others.   They are at amity with all other Indians except the Hietans.

respectable, W.

TANKAWAYS (or TANKS, as the French call them) have no land, nor claim the exclusive right to any, nor have any particular place of abode, but are always moving, alternately occupying the country watered by the Trinity, Braces and Calerado, towards St. a Fe.   Resemble, in their dress, the Cances and Hietans, but all in one horde or tribe.   The number of men is estimated at about 200 ; are good hunters; kill buffaloe and  deer with the bow: have the best breed of horses ; are alternately the friends and ene-mies of the Spaniards.  An old trader lately informed me that  he had received 5000 deer skins from them in one  year, exclusive of tallow, rugs and tongues. They  plant nothing,  but live upon  wild fruits and flesh ; are strong, athletic people, and excellent horse-men.

Colerado, Si, W.
Fé. W.
Their number W.

alternately friends W.

flesh: W.

TAWAKENOES, or THREE CANES.  They are called by  both names  indifferently ; live on the west side of the Braces, but are often for some months at a time, lower down than their usual place of resi-dence, in the great priarie at the Tortuga, or Turtle, called so from its being a hill in the priarie, which at a distance, appears in the form of a turtle, upon which there are some remarkable springs of water.   Their usual residence  is about 200 miles  to the westward

often, W.

prairie W.
prairie, which, W.

**K**

**73**

Nacogdoches, W. Fé. W.
men: W.
bow: W.
Nacogdoches, W.

of Nagadoches, towards St. a Fe. They are estimated at 200 men; are good hunters; have guns, but hunt principally with the bow; are supplied with goods from Nagadoches, and pay for them in rugs, tongues, tallow and skins. They speak the same language as the Panis, or Towiaches, and pretend to have descended from the same ancestors.

PANIS, or TOWIACHES. The French call them Panis, and the Spaniards Towiaches: the latter is the proper Indian name. They live on the south bank of Red River; by the course of the river upwards of 800 miles above Natchitoches, and by land

land, W.

by the nearest path, is estimated at about 340. They have two towns near together; the lower town, where the chief lives, is called Niteheta, and the other is

Witcheta Sɪ; Niteheta, W.
Towaahach. W.

called Towaahah. They call their present chief the Great Bear. They are at war with the Spaniards, but friendly to those French and American hunters who have lately been among them. They are likewise at war with the Osages, as are every other nation. For many hundreds of miles round them, the

prairie, W.

country is rich priarie, covered with luxuriant grass, which is green summer and winter, with skirts of wood on the river bank, by the springs and creeks.

They have many horses and mules. They raise more corn, pumpkins, beans and tobacco, than they want for their own consumption: the surplusage they

Hietans for W.

exchange with the Hietans, for buffaloe rugs, horses and mules; the pumpkins they cut round in their shreads, and when it is in a state of dryness that it is so tough it will not break, but bend, they plait and work it into large mats, in which state they sell it to the Hietans, who, as they travel, cut off and eat it as they want it. Their tobacco they manufacture and cut as fine as tea, which is put into leather bags of a certain size, and is likewise an article of trade. They have but few guns, and very little ammunition; what they have they keep for war, and hunt with the bow;

bow. Their meat W.

their meet is principally buffaloe; seldom kill a deer,

**74**

though they are so plenty they come into their villages, and about their houses, like a domestic animal; elk, bear, wolves, antelope and wild hogs are likewise plenty in their country, and white rabbits, or hares, as well as the common rabbit: white bears sometimes come down amongst them, and wolves of all colours. The men generally go entirely naked, and the women nearly so, only wearing a small flap of a piece of skin. They have a number of Spaniards amongst them, of fair complection, taken from the settlement of St. a Fe, when they were children, who live as they do, and have no knowledge of where they came from. Their language differs from that of any other nation, the Tawakenoes excepted.— Their present number of men is estimated at about 400. A great number of them, four years ago, were swept off by the small pox.

HIETANS, or Comanches, who are likewise called by both names, have no fixed place of residence; have neither towns nor villages; divided into so many different hordes or tribes, that they have scarcely any knowledge of one another. No estimate of their numbers can well be made. They never remain in the same place more than a few days, but follow the buffaloe, the flesh of which is their principal food.— Some of them occasionally purchase of the Panis, corn, beans and pumpkins; but they are so numerous, any quantity of these articles the Panis are able to supply them with, must make but a small proportion of their food. They have tents made of neatly dressed skins, fashioned in the form of a cone, sufficiently roomy for a family of ten or twelve persons; those of the chiefs will contain occasionally 50 or 60 persons. When they stop, their tents are pitched in very exact order, so as to form regular streets and squares, which in a few minutes has the appearance of a town, raised, as it were, by inchantment: and they are equally dexterous in striking their tents and preparing for a march when the signal is given; to

animal: W.

complexion, W.
Fé, W.

**75**

tent, and W.

Antoine; W.

men as fat W.

significations: W.
is, close W.

every tent two horses or mules are allotted, one to
carry the tent, & another the poles or sticks, which are
neatly made of red cedar ; they all travel on horseback,
Their horses they never turn loose to graze, but always keep them tied with a long cabras or halter ;
and every two or three days they are obliged to move
on account of all the grass near them being eaten up,
they have such numbers of horses,   They are good
horsemen and have good horses,  most of which are
bred by themselves,  and being accustomed from
when very young to be handled, they are remarkably
docile and gentle,   They sometimes catch wild horses, which are every where amongst them in immense
droves.   They hunt down the buffaloe on horseback,
and kill them either with the bow or a sharp stick like
a spear, which they carry in their hands.   They are
generally at war with the Spaniards, often committing
depredations upon the inhabitants of St. a Fe and St.
Antoine : but have always been friendly and civil to
any French or Americans who have been amongst
them.   They are strong and athletic, and the elderly
men are as fat as though they had lived upon English beef and porter.

It is said the man who kills a buffaloe, catches the
blood and drinks it while warm ; they likewise eat
the liver raw, befor it is cold, and use the gaul by
way of sauce.   They are, for savages, uncommonly
cleanly in their persons: the dress of the women is a
long, loose robe, that reaches from their chin to the
ground, tied round with a fancy sash, or girdle, all
made of neatly dressed leather, on which they paint
figures of different colours and significations ; the
dress of the men is close leather pantaloons, and a
hunting shirt, or frock of the same,   They never remain long enough in the same place to plant any
thing: the small Cayenne pepper grows spontane-
ously in the country, with which, and some wild
herbs and fruits, particularly a bean that grows in
great plenty on a small tree resembling a willow, called masketo, the women cook their buffaloe beef in a

**76**

manner that would be grateful to an English squire.
They alternately occupy the immense space of country from the Trinity and Braces, crossing the Red
River, to the heads ef Arkansa and Missouri, to river Grand, and beyond it, about St. a Fe, and over
the dividing ridge on the waters of the Western O-
cean, where they say they have seen large perogues,
with masts to them : in describing which, they make
a drawing of a ship, with all its sails and rigging: and
they describe a place where they have seen vessels
ascending a river, over which was a draw bridge that
opened to give them a passage. Their native language of sounds differs from the language of any other
nation, and none can either speak or understand it ;
but they have a language by signs that all Indians understand, and by which they converse much among
themselves. They have a number of Spanish men
and women among them, who are slaves, and who
they made prisoners when young.

An elderly gentleman now living at Natchitoches
who, some years ago, carried on a trade with the Hietans, a few days ago related to me the following
story :

About 20 years ago a party of these Indians passed
over the river Grand to Chewawa, the residence of
the governor-general of what is called the five internal
provinces ; lay in ambush for an opportunity, and
made prisoner the governor's daughter, a young lady,
going in her coach to mass, and brought her off.
The governor sent a message to him (my informant)
with a thousand dollars, for the purpose of recovering
his daughter : he immediately dispatched a confidential trader, then in his employ, with the amount of
the 1000 dollars in merchandise, who repaired to the
nation, found her, and purchased her ransom ; but,
to his great surprise, she refused to return with him
to her father, and sent by him the following message:
that the Indians had disfigured her face by tattooing
it according to their fancy and ideas of beauty, and a
young man of them had taken her for his wife, by

Red river, S1, W.
heads of W.
Fé, W.
ocean, W.
peroques, W.
them; in W.

Natchitoches, W.

## 77

whom she believed herself pregnant; that she had become reconciled to their mode of life, and was well treated by her husband; and that she should be more unhappy by returning to her father, under these circumstances, than by remaining where she was. Which message was conveyed to her father, who rewarded the trader by a present of 300 dollars more for his trouble and fidelity; and his daughter is now living with her Indian husband in the nation, by whom she has three children.

Natchitoch; W.

NATCHITOCHES, formerly lived where the town of Natchitoches is now situated, which took its name from them. An elderly French gentleman, lately informed me, he remembered when they were 600 men strong. I believe it is now 98 years since the French first established themselves at Natchitoches; ever since, these Indians have been their steady and faithful friends. After the massacre of the French inhabitants of Natchez, by the Natchez Indians, in 1728, those Indians fled from the French, after being reinforced, and came up Red river, and camped about 6 miles below the town of Natchitoches, near the river, by the side of a small lake of clear water, and erected a mound of considerable size, where it now remains. Monsieur St. Dennie, a French Canadian, was then commandant at Natchitoches; the Indians called him the Big Foot, were fond of him, for he was a brave man. St. Dennie, with a few French soldiers, and what militia he could muster, joined by the Natchitoches Indians, attacked the Natchez in their camp, early in the morning; they defended themselves desperately for 6 hours, but were at length totally defeated by St. Dennie, and what of them that were not killed in battle, were drove into the lake, where the last of them perished, and the Natchez, as a nation, became extinct. The lake is now called by no other name than the Natchez lake. There are now remaining of the Natchitoches, but 12 men and 19 women, who live in a village about

78

25 miles by land above the town which bears their name, near a lake, called by the French *Lac de Muire.* Their original language is the same as the Yattassee, but speak Caddo, and most of them French.

The French inhabitants have great respect for this nation, and a number of very decent families have a mixture of their blood in them. They claim but a small tract of land, on which they live, and I am informed, have the same rights to it from government, that other inhabitants in their neighbourhood have. They are gradually wasting away; the small pox has been their great destroyer. They still preserve their Indian dress and habits; raise corn and those vegetables common in their neighborhood.

neighborhood W.

BOLUXAS, are emigrants from near Pensacola. They came to Red River about 42 years ago, with some French families, who left that country about the time Pensacola was taken possession of by the English. They were then a considerable numerous tribe, and have generally embraced the Roman Catholic religion, and were ever highly esteemed by the French. They settled first at Avoyall, then moved higher up to Rapide Bayau, and from thence to the mouth of Rigula de Bondieu, a division of Red river, about 40 miles below Natchitoches, where they now live, and are reduced to about 30 in number. Their native language is peculiar to themselves, but speak Mobilian, which is spoken by all the Indians from the east side of Mississippi. They are honest, harmless and friendly people.

Natchitoch, W.

APPALACHES, are likewise emigrants from West Florida, from off the river whose name they bear; came over to Red river about the same time the Boluxas did, and have, ever since, lived on the river, above Bayau Rapide. No nation have been more highly esteemed by the French inhabitants; no complaints against them are ever heard; there are only 14 men remaining; have their own language, but speak French and Mobilian.

**79**

ALLIBAMIS, are likewise from West Florida, off the Allibami river, and came to Red river about the same time of the Boluxas and Appalaches. Part of them have lived on Red river, about 16 miles above the Bayau Rapide, till last year, when most of this party, of about 30 men, went up Red river, and have settled themselves near the Caddoques, where, I am informed, they last year made a good crop of corn. The Caddos are friendly to them, and have no objection to their settling there. They speak the Creek and Chactaw languages, and Mobilian ; most of them French, and some of them English.

Appalousa S1; Appelousa W.
Appalousa. S1; Appelousa. W.

There is another party of them, whose village is on a small creek, in Appalousa district, about 30 miles north west from the church of Appalousa. They consist of about 40 men. They have lived at the same place ever since they came from Florida ; are said to be increasing a little in numbers, for a few years past. They raise corn, have horses, hogs and cattle, and are harmless, quiet people.

CONCHATTAS, are almost the same people as the Allibamis, but came over only ten years ago ; first lived on bayau Chico, in Appalousa district, but, four years ago, moved to the river Sabine, settled themselves on the east bank, where they now live, in nearly a south direction from Natchitoches, and distant about 80 miles. They call their number of men 160, but say, if they were all together, they would amount to 200. Several families of them live in detached settlements. They are good hunters, and game is plenty about where they are. A few days ago, a small party of them were here, consisting of 15 persons, men, women and children, who were on their return from a bear hunt up Sabine. They told me they had killed 118 ; but this year an uncommon number of bears have come down. One man alone, on Sabine, during the summer and fall, hunting, killed 400 deer, sold his skins at 40 dollars a hundred. The bears this year are not so fat as com-

Bayau W. Appelousa W.

Natchitoch, W.

80

mon; they usually yield from eight to twelve gallons of oil, each of which never sells for less than a dollar a gallon, and the skins a dollar more; no great quantity of the meet is saved; what the hunters don't use when out, they generally give to their dogs. The Conchattas are friendly with all other Indians, and speak well of their neighbors the Carankouas, who, they say, live about 80 miles south of them, on the bay, which, I believe, is the nearest point to the sea from Natchitoches. A few families of Chactaws have lately settled near them from Bayau Beauf. The Conchattas speak Creek, which is their native language, and Chactaw, and several of them English, and one or two of them can read it a little.

*skin* Sı, W.
*meat* W.

PACANAS, are a small tribe of about 30 men, who live on the Quelqueshoe river, which falls into the bay between the Attakapa and Sabine, which heads in a priarie called Cooko priarie, about 50 miles south-west of Natchitoches. These people are likewise emigrants from West Florida, about 40 years ago. Their village is about 30 miles south east of the Conchattas; are said to be encreasing a little in number; quiet, peaceable and friendly people.— Their own language differs from any other, but speak Mobilian.

*prairie . . . prairie,* W.
*south west* W.

50 *miles* W.
*increasing* W.

ATTAKAPAS. This word I am informed when translated into English, means man-eater, but is no more applicable to them than any other Indians.— The district they now live in is called after them. Their village is about 20 miles to the westward of the Attakapa church, towards Quelqueshoe. Their number of men is about 50, but some Tunicas and Humas, who have married in their nation and live with them, makes them altogether about 80. They are peaceable and friendly to every body: labor occasionally, for the white inhabitants: raise their own corn: have cattle and hogs. Their language and the Carancouas is the same. They were, or near, where

*word, . . . informed,* W.

*they live in* W.

*body; labor,* W.
*inhabitants;* W.
*corn;* W.
*Carankouas* W.

L

**81**

they now live, when that part of the country was first discovered by the French.

APPALOUSAS. It is said the word Appalousa, in the Indian language, means black head or black skull. They are aborigines of the district called by their name. Their village is about 15 miles west from the Appalousa church: have about 40 men. Their native language differs from all other; understand Attakapa and French: plant corn; have cattle and hogs.

Appalousa church. Si;
Appelousa church; W.
and speak French; W.

TUNICAS. These people lived formerly on the Bayau Tunica, above Point Coupee, on the Mississippi, east side; live at Avoyall; do not at present exceed twenty-five men. Their native language is peculiar to themselves, but speak Mobilian; are employed, occasionally, by the inhabitants as boatmen; &c. in amity with all other people, and gradually diminishing in numbers.

*line 13*: now at Avoyall. Si;
live now at Avoyall; W.
25 W.

boatmen, W.

13

PASCAGOLAS, live in a small village on Red river, about 60 miles below Natchitoches: are emigrants from Pascagola river, in West Florida; 25 men only of them remaining; speak Mobilian, but have a language peculiar to themselves; most of them speak and understand French. They raise good crops of corn, and garden vegetables; have cattle, horses, and poultry plenty. Their houses are much like the poorer kind of French inhabitants on the river, and appear to live about as well.

Their horses W.

TENISAWS, are likewise emigrants from the Tenesau river, that falls into the bay of Mobile: have been on Red river about 40 years; are reduced to about 25 men. Their village is within one mile of the Pascagolas, on the opposite side, but have lately sold their land, and have, or are about moving, to Bayau Beauf, about 25 miles south from where they lately lived: all speak French and Mobilian, and live much like their neighbours the Pascagolas.

Bay of Mobile; W.

82

CHACTOOS, live on Bayau Beauf, about 10 miles to the southward of Bayau Rapide, on Red river, towards Appalousa; a small, honest people; are aborigines of the country where they live; of men about 30; diminishing; have their own peculiar tongue: speak Mobilian. The lands they claim on Bayau Beauf are inferior to no part of Louisiana in depth and richness of soil, growth of timber, pleasantness of surface and goodness of water. The Bayau Beauf falls into the Chaffeli, and discharges through Appalousa and Attakapa, into Vermilion Bay.

diminishing: W.

Appalousa S1; Appelousa W.

WASHAS. When the French first came into the Mississippi, this nation lived on an island to the south west of New-Orleans, called Barritaria, and were the first tribe of Indians they became acquainted with, and were always friends. They afterwards lived on Bayau La Fosh; and, from their being a considerable nation, are now reduced to five persons only, two men and three women, who are scattered in French families; have been many years extinct as a nation, and their native language is lost.

from being W.

extinct, W.

CHACTAWS. There are a considerable number of this nation on the west side of the Mississippi, who have not been home for several years. About 12 miles above the post on Oacheta, on that river, there is a small village of them of about 30 men, who have lived there for several years, and made corn; and likewise on Bayau Chico, in the northern part of the district of Appalousa, there is another village of them of about 50 men, who have been there about 9 years, and say they have the governor of Louisiana's permission to settle there. Besides these, there are rambling hunting parties to be met with all over Lower Louisiana. They are at war with the Caddoques, and liked by neither red nor white people.

there about S1; there for about W.

parties of them to W.

ARKANSAS, live on the Arkansa river, south side, in three villages, about 12 miles above the post

Arkensaws S1; ARKENSAS, W.
post, W.

83

*Ousotu.* S1. *Oufotu,* W.

or station. The name of the first village is *Tawani-ma*, second *Oufotu*, and the third *Ocapa* ; in all, it is believed, they do not at present exceed 100 men, and diminishing. They are at war with the Osages, but friendly with all other people, white and red ; are the original proprietors of the country on the river, to all which they claim, to about 300 miles above them, to the junction of the river Cadwa with the Arkansa ; above this fork the Osages claim. Their language is Osage. They generally raise corn to sell ; are called honest and friendly people.

*claim, for about* W.
*with Arkensa;* S1, W.

————

*of, or* W.
*Arkensa,* S1, W.

The forementioned are all the Indian tribes that I have any knowledge of or can obtain an account of, in Louisiana, south of the river Arkansa, between the Mississippi and river Grand. At Avoyall there did live a considerable tribe of that name, but, as far as I can learn, have been extinct for many years, two or three women excepted, who did lately live among the French inhabitants at Washita.

*on Washita.* W.

There are a few of the Humas still living on the east side of the Mississippi, in Ixsusees parish, below Manchack, bnt scearcely exist as a nation.

*scarcely exist,* W.
*sketches is not to be* W.

That there are errors in these sketches cannot be doubted, but in all cases out of my own personal knowledge I have endeavored to procure the best information, which I have faithfully related ; and I am confident any errors that do exist are too unim-portant to affect the object for which they are intended.

I am, sir, &c.

*(Signed)* JOHN SIBLEY.

General H. Dearborn.

*Natchitoches, April 5, 1805.*

84

## TO GENERAL HENRY DEARBORN,

*SECRETARY OF WAR.*

SIR,

YOU request me to give you some account of Red river, and the country adjacent : I will endeavor to comply with your request, to the best of my knowledge and capacity.  My personal knowledge of it is only from its mouth to about 70 or 80 miles above Natchitoches, being, by the course of the river, near 400 miles.  After that, what I can say of it is derived from information from others, on whose veracity I have great reliance : principally from Mr. Francis Grappe, who is my assistant and Interpreter of Indian languages ; whose father was a French officer, and superintendant of Indian affairs, at a post or station, occupied by France, where they kept some soldiers, and had a factory, previous to the cession of Louisiana to Spain, situate nearly 500 miles, by the course of the river, above Natchitoches, where he, my informant was born, and lived upwards of 30 years ; his time, during which, being occupied alternately as an assistant to his father, an Indian trader and hunter, with the advantage of some learning, and a very retentive memory, acquired an accurate knowledge of the river, as well as the languages of all the different Indian tribes in Louisiana, which, with his having been Indian interpreter for the Spanish government for many years past, and (I believe) deservedly esteemed by the Indians, and all others, a man of strict integrity, has, for many years, and does now possess their entire confidence, and a very extensive influence over them ; and I have invariably found, that whatever information I have received from him, has been confirmed by every other intelligent person, having a knowledge of the same, with whom I have conversed.

post, W.

**85**

NOTE. Contrary to geographical rules, as I ascended the river, I called the right bank the northern one, and the left the southern.

———

THE confluence of Red river with the Mississippi is, by the course of the latter, estimated about 220 miles from New-Orleans. Descending the Mississippi, after passing the Spanish line at the 31st degree of north latitude, it makes a remarkable turn to the westward, or nearly north west, for some distance before you arrive at the mouth of Red river, as though, notwithstanding the immense quantity of its waters already, from its almost numberless tributary streams, it was still desirous of a farther augmentation, by hastening its union with Red river (which, perhaps, is second only in dignity to it) that they might, from thence, flow on and join the ocean together, which, for many leagues, is forced to give place to its mighty current. But there are reasons for believing the Red river did not always unite with the Mississippi, as it does at present ; and that no very great length of time has elapsed since the Mississippi left its ancient bed, some miles to the eastward, and took its course westwardly for the purpose of intermarrying with Red river. The mouth of the Chaffeli, which is now, properly speaking, one of the outlets of the river Mississippi to the ocean, is just below, in sight of the junction of Red river with the Mississippi ; and from its resemblance to Red river in size, growth on its banks, appearance and texture of soil, and differing from that of the Mississippi, induces strongly the belief that the Chaffeli was once but the continuation of Red river to the ocean, and that it had, in its bed, no connection with the Mississippi. There is no doubt but the Mississippi has alternately occupied different places in the low grounds through which it meanders, almost from the high lands of one side to those of the other, for the average space of near 30

## 86

miles. These two great rivers happening to flow, for a distance, through the same mass of swamp, that annually is almost all inundated, it is not extraordinary that their channels should find their way together; the remarkable bend of the Mississippi, at this place, to the westward, seems to have been for the express purpose of forming this union; after which it returns to its former course.

In the month of March, 1803, I ascended Red river, from its mouth to Natchitoches, in an open boat, unless when I chose to land and walk across a point, or by the beauty of the river bank, the pleasantness of its groves, or the variety of its shrubs and flowers, I was invited ashore to gratify or please my curiosity. On entering the mouth of the river I found its waters turgid, of a red colour, and of a brackish taste; and as the Mississippi was then falling, and Red river rising, found a current, from its mouth upwards, varying considerably in places, but averaging about two miles an hour, for the first hundred miles, which, at that time, I found to be about the same in the Mississippi: but, when that river is high, and Red river low, there is very little current in the latter, for sixty or seventy miles: the river, for that distance, is very crooked, increasing the distance, by it, from a straight line, more than two-thirds; the general course of it nearly west: that I was able to ascertain, from hearing the morning gun at Fort Adams, for three or four mornings after entering the river, which was not at the greatest height by about fourteen feet; and all the low grounds, for near seventy miles, entirely overflowed like those of the Mississippi, which, in fact, is but a continuation of the same. Some places appeared, by the high water mark on the trees, to overflow not more than two or three feet, particularly the right bank, below the mouth of Black river, and the left bank above it; the growth, on the lowest places, willow and cotton wood, but on the highest, handsome oaks, swamp hickory, ash, grape vines, &c.

miles: W.

two thirds; W.

**87**

I made my calculation of our rate of ascent and distances up the river, by my watch, noting carefully with my pencil the minute of our stops and settings off, the inlets and outlets, remarkable bends in the river, and whatever I observed any way remarkable. About six miles from the mouth of the river, left side, there is a bayan, as it is called, comes in, that communicates with a lake called lake Long, which, by another bayau, communicates again with the river, through which, when there is a swell in the river, boats can pass, and cut off about 30 miles, being only 14 or 15 through it, and about 45 by the course of the river; and through the lake there is very little or no current; but the passage is intricate and difficult to find; a stranger should not attempt it without a pilot; people have been lost in it for several days; but not difficult for one acquainted; we, having no pilot on board to be depended on, kept the river.

From the mouth of Red river to the mouth of Black river, I made it 31 miles: the water of Black river is clear, and when contrasted with the water of Red river has a black appearance. From the mouth of Black river, Red river makes a regular twining to the left, for about 18 miles, called the Grand Bend, forming a segment of nearly three-fourths of a circle; when you arrive at the bayau that leads into lake Long, which, perhaps, is in a right line, not exceeding 15 miles from the mouth of the river. From Bayau Lake Long, to Avoyall landing, called Baker's landing, I made 33 miles, and the river is remarkably crooked. At this place the guns at Fort Adams are distinctly heard, and the sound appears to be but little south of east. We came through a bayau called Silver Bayau, that cut off, we understand, six miles; it was through the Bayau about four miles. Until we arrived at Baker's landing, saw no spot of ground that did not overflow; the high water mark generally from 3 to 15 feet above its banks. After passing Black river, the edge of the banks near the river are highest; the land falls, from the river back. At

three fourths W.

**88**

Baker's landing I went ashore; I understood, from Baker's landing, cross the point, to Le Glass' landing, was only 3 or 4 miles, and by water 15; but I found it 6 at least, and met with some difficulty in getting from where I landed to the high land at Baker's house, for water, though at low water it is a dry cart road, and less than a mile. I found Baker and his family very hospitable and kind; Mr. Baker told me he was a native of Virginia, and had lived there upwards of 30 years. He was living on a tolerable good high piece of land, not priarie, but joining it. After leaving Baker's house, was soon in sight of the priarie, which, I understand, is about 40 miles in circumference, longer than it is wide, very level, only a few clumps of trees to be seen, all covered with good grass. The inhabitants are settled all around the out edge of it, by the woods, their houses facing inwards, and cultivate the priarie land. Though the soil, when turned up by the plough, has a good appearance; what I could discover by the old corn and cotton stalks, they made but indifferent crops; the timber land that I saw cleared and planted, produced the best; the priarie is better for grass than for planting. The inhabitants have considerable stocks of cattle, which appears to be their principal dependence, and I was informed their beef is of a superior quality: they have likewise good pork; hogs live very well; the timbered country all round the priarie is principally oak that produces good mast for hogs. Corn is generally scarce: they raise no wheat, for they have no mills. I was informed that the lower end of the priarie that I did not see was much the richest land, and the inhabitants lived better, and were more wealthy; they are a mixture of French, Irish and Americans, generally poor and ignorant. Avoyall, at high water, is an island, elevated 30 or 40 feet above high water mark; the quantity of timbered land exceeds that of the priarie, which is likewise pretty level, but scarcely a second quality of soil. Le Glass' landing, as it is called, I found about a mile and a half from the upper

**M**

*Margin notes:*

prairie, W.
prairie, W.

prairie W.

prairie W.

prairie W.

prairie W.

mark W.
prairie, W.

La W.

**89**

prairie; W.

end of the priarie; the high lands bluff to the river. After leaving this place found the banks rise higher and higher on each side, and fit for settlements; on the right side pine woods sometimes in sight. I left the boat again about eight miles from Le Glass' land-ing, right side; walked two and a half miles cross a point, to a Mr. Holmes';

Hoome's; W.

round the point is called 16 miles. I found the lands through which I passed high, moderately hilly; the soil a good second qua-lity, clay; timber, large oak, hickory, some short leaved pine; and several small streams of clear run-ning water. This description of lands extended back 5 or 6 miles, and bounded by open pine woods, which continue, for 30 miles, to Ocatahola. I found Mr.

Hoomes's S2; Hoomes' W.

Holmes' house on a high bluff very near the river; his plantation the same description of land through which I had passed, producing good corn, cotton and tobacco, and he told me he had tried it in wheat, which succeeded well, but having no mills to manu-facture it, had only made the experiment. Mr.

Hoomes' W

Holmes' told me all the lands round his, for many miles, were vacant. On the south side there is a large body of rich, low grounds, extending to the borders of Appalousa, watered and drained by Bayau Robert and Bayau Beauf, two handsome streams of clear water that rise in the high lands between Red river and Sabine, and after meandering through this im-mense mass of low grounds of 30 or 40 miles square, fall into the Chaffeli, to the southward of Avoyall. I believe, in point of soil, growth of timber, goodness of water, and conveniency to navigation, there is not a more valuable body of land in this part of Louisiana.

Hoomes' W.

From Mr. Holmes' to the mouth of Rapide Bayau is, by the river, 35 miles. A few scattering settlements on the right side, but none on the left; the right is preferred to settle on, on account of their stocks being convenient to the high lands; but the settlers on the right side own the lands on the left side too; the lands on the Bayau Rapide are the same quality as those on

and, in W.

Bayaus Robert and Beauf, and in fact, are a continu-

## 90

ation of the same body of lands. Bayau Rapide is somewhat in the form of a half moon ; the two points, or horns, meeting the river about 20 miles from each other : the length of the bayau is about 30 miles: on the back of it there is a large bayau falls in, on which there is a saw mill, very advantageously situated, in respect to a never failing supply of water ; plenty of timber ; and the plank can be taken from the mill tail by water. This bayau is excellent water ; rises in the pine woods, and discharges itself each way into the river, by both ends of Bayau Rapide. Boats cannot pass through the bayau, from the river to the river again, on account of rafts of timber choaking the upper end of it, but can enter the lower end and ascend it more than half through it. On the lower end of the bayau, on each side, is the principal Rapide settlement, as it is called ; no country whatever can exhibit handsomer plantations, or better lands. The Rapide is a fall, or shoal, occasioned by a soft rock in the bed of the river, that extends from side to side, over which, for about five months in the year, (viz.) from July to December, there is not sufficient water for boats to pass without lightening, but at all other seasons it is the same as any other part of the river. This rock, or hard clay, for it resembles the latter almost as much as the former, is so soft it may be cut away with a pen-knife, or any sharp instrument, and scarcely turn the edge, and extends up and down the river but a few yards ; and I have heard several intelligent persons give it as their opinion, that the extraordinary expense and trouble the inhabitants were at, in one year, in getting loaded boats over this shoal, would be more than sufficient to cut a passage through it ; but it happens at a season of the year when the able planters are occupied at home, and would make no use of the river were there no obstructions in it ; but at any rate, the navigation of the river is clear a longer proportion of the year than the rivers in the northern countries are clear of ice. But this obstruction is certainly remov-

year W.

pen knife, W.

## 91

able, at a very trifling expense, in comparison to the importance of having it done ; and nothing but the nature of the government we have lately emerged from, can be assigned as a reason for its not having been effected long ago.

After passing the Rapides there are very few settlements to be seen, on the main river, for about 20 miles, though both sides appeared to me to be capable of making as valuable settlements as any on the river; we arrive then at the Indian villages, on both sides, situated exceedingly pleasant, and on the best lands ; after passing which you arrive at a large, beautiful plantation of Mr. Gillard ; the house is on a point of a high pine woods bluff, close to the river, 60 or 70 feet above the common surface of the country, overlooking, on the east, or opposite side, very extensive fields of low grounds, in high cultivation, and a long reach of the river, up and down ; and there is an excellent spring of water issues from the bluff, on which the house is situated, from an aperture in the rock that seems to have been cloven on purpose for it to flow, and a small distance, back of the house, there is a lake of clear water, abounding with fish in summer and fowl in winter. I have seen in all my life, very few more beautiful or advantageously situated places.

Six miles above Gillard's, you arrive at the small village of Boluxa Indians, where the river is divided into two channels, forming an island of about fifty miles in length, and three or four in breadth. The right hand division is called the Rigula de Bondieu, on which are no settlements : but, I am informed, will admit of being well settled ; the left hand division is the boat channel, at present, to Natchitoches : the other is likewise boatable. Ascending the left hand branch for about 24 miles, we pass a thick settlement and a number of wealthy inhabitants. This is called the *River Cane* settlement ; called so, I believe, from the banks some years ago, being a remarkable thick cane-brake.

After passing this settlemen of about 40 families,

apperture W.

Natchitiches: W.

settlement of about forty W.

92

the river divides again, forming another island of about thirty miles in length, and from two to four in breadth, called the *Isle Brevel*, after a reputable old man now living on it, who first settled it. This island is sub-divided by a bayau that communicates from one river to the other, called also Bayau Brevel. The middle division of the river, is called *Little* river, and it is thickly settled, and is the boat channel; the westward division of the river is called False river, is navigable but not settled, the banks are too low; it passes through a lake called *Lac Occassa*. When you arrive at Natchitoches, you find it a small, irregular, and meanly built village, half a dozen houses excepted, of the west side of that division of the river it is on, the high pine and oak woods approach within two or three hundred yards of the river. In the village are about forty families, twelve or fifteen are merchants or traders, nearly all French. The fort built by our troops since their arrival, called fort Claiborne, is situated on a small hill, one street from the river, and about thirty feet higher than the river banks. All the hill is occupied by the fort and barracks, and does not exceed two acres of ground. The southern and eastern prospects from it are very beautiful. One has an extensive view of the fields and habitations down the river, and of the whole village. This town thirty or forty years ago, was much larger than at present, and situated on a hill about half a mile from its present site. Then most of the families of the district lived in the town, but finding it inconvenient on account of the stocks and farms, they filed off, one after another, and settled up and down the river. The merchants and trading people found being on the bank of the river more convenient for loading and unloading their boats, left the hill on that account; and others, finding the river ground much superior for gardens, to which they are in the habit of paying great attention, followed the merchants; after them the priests and commandant; then the church and

living in it, W.

navigable, W.

excepted, on W.

river, and the other a similar view over the river, and W.

**93**

calleboose), W.

sandy, W.

rain water, W.
spring water. The planters along
the river generally use rain
water; though W.
price), W.

thirty: W.

mill-tale, W.

copernican W.

jail (or calleboose) and now nothing of the old town is left, but the form of their gardens and some ornamental trees. It is now a very extensive common of several hundred acres, entirely tufted with clover and covered with sheep and cattle. The hill is a stiff clay, and used to make miry streets; the river soil, though much richer, is of a loose, sandy texture: the streets are neither miry nor very dusty. Our wells do not afford us good water, and the river water, in summer, is too brackish to drink, and never clear. Our springs are about half a mile back from the river, but the inhabitants, many of them, have large cisterns, and use, principally, rain-water, which is preferred to the spring water; though when the river is high, and the water taken up and settled in large earthen jars, (which the Indian women make of good quality and at a moderate price) it can be drank tolerably well, but it makes bad tea.

Near Natchitoches there are two large lakes, one within a mile, the other six miles to the nearest parts. One of them is fifty or sixty miles in circumference, the other upwards of thirty; these lakes rise and fall with the river. When the river is rising the bayaus that connect with the lakes, run into the lakes like a mill-tail, till the lakes are filled; and when the river is falling, it is the same the contrary way, just like the tide, but only annual. On these creeks good mills might be erected, but the present inhabitants know nothing of mills by water, yet have excellent cotton gins worked by horses. I do not know a single mechanic in the district, who is a native of it, one tailor excepted. Every thing of the kind is done by strangers, and mostly Americans. Though Natchitoches has been settled almost one hundred years, it is not more than twelve or fifteen years since they ever had a plough, or a flat to cross the river with; both of which were introduced by an Irish Pennsylvanian, under a similar opposition to the Copernican system. 'Tis almost incredible the quantity of fish and fowl these lakes supply. It is not uncommon in

**94**

winter for a single man to kill from two to four hundred fowls in one evening; they fly between sundown and dark; the air is filled with them; they load and fire as fast as they can, without taking any particular aim, continuing at the same stand till they think they have killed enough, and then pick up what they have killed; they consist of several kinds of ducks, geese, brant, and swan.   In summer the quantities of fish are nearly in proportion.   One Indian will with a bow and arrow, sometimes kill them faster than another, with two horses, can bring them in; they weigh, some of them, upwards of thirty or forty pounds.—— The lakes likewise afford plenty of shells for lime: and at low water, the greater of them is a most luxuriant meadow, where the inhabitants fatten their horses.   All round these lakes above high water mark, there is a border of rich land generally wide enough for a field.   On the bank of one of them, there is plenty of stone coal, and several quarries of tolerable good building stone; at high water, boats can go out of the river into them.   Similar lakes are to be found all along Red river, for five or six hundred miles, which besides the uses already mentioned, nature seems to have provided as reservoirs for the immense quantity of water beyond what the banks of the river will contain; otherwise no part of them could be inhabited; the low grounds from hill to hill, would be inundated.   About twelve miles north of Natchitoches, on the north-east side of the river, there is a large lake called *Lac Noiz*; the bayau of it communicates to the Rigula de Bondieu, opposite to Natchitoches, which is boatable the greater part of the year.   Near this lake are the salt works, from which all the salt that is used in the district, is made; and which is made with so much ease, that two old men both of them cripples, with ten or twelve old pots and kettles, have for several years past made an abundant supply of salt for the whole district; they informed me they made six bushels per day.   I have not been at the place but have a bottle of the water

fowl W.

duck, W.
summer, W.
will, W.

them, thirty W.
lime; W.

water W.
are found W.

inhabited: W.
grounds, W.

opposite Natchitoch, W.

men, W.

have, W. past, W.
district: W.
inform W.
place, W.

**95**

brought to me, which I found nearly saturated. The salt is good. I never had better bacon than I make with it. I am informed, there are twelve saline springs now open; and by digging for them, for aught any one knows, twelve hundred might be opened.— A few month ago, captain Burnet, of the Mississippi territory, coming to this place by the Washita, came by the salt works, and purchased the right of one of the old men he found there, and has lately sent up a boat, with some large kettles and some negroes, under the direction of his son; and expects, when they get all in order, to be able to make thirty or forty bushels per day. Captain Burnet, is of opinion, that he shall be able to supply the Mississippi territory, and the settlements on the Mississippi, from Point Coupee, upwards, lower than they can get it in New-Orleans and bring it up. Cathartic salts, and magnesia, might likewise be made in large quantities, if they understood it. The country all round the Sabine and Black lake is vacant, and from thence to Washita, a distance of about one hundred and twenty miles, which I am informed affords considerable quantities of well timbered good uplands, and well watered. There is a small stream we cross on the Washita road, the English call it *Little river*, the French *Dogdimona*, affording a wide rich bottom; this stream falls into the Ocatahola river; its course is eastwardly, and falls into Washita, near the mouth of Tensaw, where the road from Natchitoches to Natchez, crosses it; from the confluence of these three rivers, downwards, it is called Black river, which falls into Red river, sixty miles below. There is a good salt spring near the Ocatahola lake.

Ascending Red river above Natchitoches, in about three miles arrive at the upper mouth of the Rigula de Bondieu; there are settlements all along; plantations adjoining. From the upper mouth of the Rigula de Bondieu, the river, is in one channel through the settlement called Grand Ecore, of about six miles; it is called Grand Ecore. (or in English the Great

*Marginal notes (left):*

by Washita, W.

Burnet is W.

on Mississippi, W.
New Orleans W.

bottom: W.
into the Acatahola lake; from thence to Washita, it is called Acatahola river; its course W.

Acatahola W.

Bondieu: W.

river is W.

**96**

Bluff) being such a one on the left hand side, near one hundred feet high. The face next the river, almost perpendicular, of a soft, white rock; the top, a gravel loam, of considerable extent, on which grow large oaks, hickory, black cherry, and grape vines. At the bottom of one of these bluffs, for there are two near each other, is a large quantity of stone-coal, and near them several springs of the best water in this part of the country; and a lake of clear water within two hundred yards, bounded by a gravelly margin. I pretend to have no knowledge of military tactics, but think, from the river in this place being all in one channel, the goodness of the water, a high, healthy country, and well timbered all round it, no height near it so high, its commanding the river, and a very public ferry just under it, and at a small expense, would be capable of great defence with a small force. The road from it to the westward, better than from Natchitoches, and by land only about five miles above it, and near it plenty of good building stone. These advantages it possesses beyond any other place within my knowledge on the river, for a strong fort, and safe place of deposit. Just about this bluff, the river makes a large bend to the right, and a long reach nearly due east and west by it: the bluff overlooks, on the opposite side, several handsome plantations. I have been induced, from the advantages this place appeared to me to possess, to purchase it, with four or five small settlements adjoining, including both bluffs, the ferry, springs and lake, the stone quarries, and coal; and a field of about five hundred acres of the best low grounds, on the opposite side. After leaving Grand Ecore, about a mile, on the left side comes in a large bayau, from the Spanish lake, as it is called, boatable the greater part of the year. This lake is said to be about fifty miles in circumference, and rises and falls with the river, into which, from the river, the largest boats may ascend, and from it, up the mouths of several large bayaus that fall into it, for some distance, one in particular called bayau

N

Natchitoch, W.

**97**

Dupong, up which boats may ascend within one and a half mile of old fort Adaize. Leaving this bayau about two miles, arrive at a fork or division of the river; the left hand branch bears westwardly for sixty or eighty miles; then eastwardly, meeting the branch it left, after forming an island of about one hundred miles long, and, in some places, nearly thirty miles wide. Six or seven years ago, boats used to pass this way into the main river again: its communication with which being above the great raft or obstruction; but it is now choaked, and requires a portage of three miles; but at any season, boats can go from Natchitoches, about eighty miles, to the place called the point, where the French had a factory, and a small station of soldiers to guard the Indian trade, and is now undoubtedly a very eligible situation for a similar establishment. The country bounded to the east and north, by this branch or divison of the river, is called the bayau Pierre settlement, which was begun, and some of the lands granted before Louisiana was ceded to Spain by France, and continued under the jurisdiction of the commandant of Natchitoches until about twenty years ago, when, by an agreement between a Mr. Vogone, then commandant of this place, and a Mr. Elibarbe, commandant at Nagadoches, the settlement called bayau Pierre, was placed under the jurisdiction of the latter, and has so continued ever since. The settlement, I believe, contains about forty families, and generally they have large stocks of cattle: they supply us with our cheese entirely, and of a tolerable quality, and we get from them some excellent bacon hams. The country is interspersed with priaries, resembling, as to richness, the river bottoms, and, in size, from five to five thousand acres. The hills are a good grey soil, and produce very well, and afford beautiful situations. The creek called Bayau Pierre, (stony creek) passes through the settlement, and affords a number of good mill seats, and its bed and banks lined with a good kind of building stone,

Natchitoches, W.

prairies, W.

98

but no mills are erected on it. Some of the inhabitants have tried the uplands in wheat, which succeeded well. They are high, gently rolling, and rich enough ; produce good corn, cotton and tobacco. I was through the settlement in July last, and found good water, either from a spring or well, at every house. The inhabitants are all French, one family excepted. A few miles to the westward, towards Sabine, there is a Saline where the inhabitants go and make their salt. On the whole, for health, good water, good living, plenty of food for every kind of animal, general conveniency, and handsome surface, I have seen few parts of the world more inviting to settlers.

cotton, W.

Returning back again to the fork of the main river we left, for the purpose of exploring the Bayau Pierre branch, we find irregular settlements, including Campti, where a few families are settled together on a hill near the river, north-east side. For about 20 miles the river land is much the same every where, but the Campti settlement is more broken with bayaus and lagoons than any place I am acquainted with on the river, and for want of about a dozen bridges is inconvenient to get to, or travel through. The upper end of this settlement is the last on the main branch of Red river, which, straight by land, does not exceed 25 miles above Natchitoches. At the upper house the great raft or jam of timber begins ; this raft choaks the main channel for upwards of 100 miles, by the course of the river ; not one entire jam from the beginning to the end of it, but only at the points, with places of several leagues that are clear. The river is very crooked, and the low grounds are wide and rich, and I am informed, no part of Red river will afford better plantations than along its banks by this raft, which is represented as being so important as to render the country above it of little value for settlements ; this opinion is founded entirely upon incorrect information. The first or lowest part of the raft is at a bend or point in the river, just below

north east W.

**99**

the upper plantation, at which, on the right side, a large bayau, or division of the river, called Bayau Channo, comes in, which is free of any obstructions, and the greater part of the year boats of any size may ascend it, into lake Bistino, through which, to its communication with the lake, is only about three miles; the lake is about 60 miles long, and lays nearly parrallel with the river, from the upper end of which it communicates again with the river, by a bayau called *Daichet*, about 40 miles above the upper end of the raft; from the lake to the river, through Bayau Daichet, is called nine miles : there is always in this bayau sufficient water for any boat to pass ; from thence upwards Red river is free of all obstructions to the mountains. By lake Bistino, and these two bayaus, an island is formed, about 70 miles long, and three or four wide, capable of affording settlements inferior to none on the river. From the above account you will perceive, that the only difficulty in opening a boat passage by this raft, through the lake, which is much shorter than by the course of the river, and avoid the current, and indeed were the river unobstructed, would always be preferred, is this small jam of timber at the point just below the bayau Channo, as it is called.

After the receipt of your letter I had an opportunity of seeing some of the inhabitants who live near this place, who informed me, that that small raft was easily broken, and that they had lately been talking of doing it. I persuaded them to make the attempt, and they accordingly appointed the Friday following, and all the neighbors were to be invited to attend and assist. They met accordingly, and effected a passage next to one bank of the river, so that boats could pass, but did not entirely break it : they intend to take another spell at it, when the water falls a little, and speak confidently of succeeding.

The country about the head of lake Bistino, is highly spoken of, as well the highlands as the river bottom. There are falling into the river and lake,

parallel W.

indeed, was W.

high lands, W.
lake in W.

## 100

in the vicinity, some handsome streams of clear wholsome water from towards Washita, one in particular called Badkah by the Indians, which is boatable at some seasons ; this bayau passes through a long, narrow, and rich priarie, on which my informant says 500 families might be desirably settled ; and from thence up to where the Caddos lately lived, the river banks are high, bottoms wide and rich as any other part of the river.   From thence it is much the same to the mouth of the Little river of the left; this river is generally from 50 to a hundred yards wide ; heads in the great priaries, south of Red river, and interlocks with the head branches of the Sabine and Trinity rivers ; and in time of high water is boatable 40 or 50 leagues, affording a large body of excellent, well timbered and rich land, the low grounds from 3 to 6 miles wide ; but the quality of the water, tho' clear, is very inferior to that of the streams that fall into Red river on the north side.   The general course of the Red river from this upwards is nearly from west to east, till we arrive at the Panis towns, when it turns northwestwardly.   After leaving the mouth of the Little river of the left, both banks are covered with strong, thick cane for about 20 miles : the low grounds very wide, rich and do not overflow ; the river widening in proportion as the banks are less liable to overflow ; you arrive at a handsome, rich priarie, 25 miles long on the right side, and 4 or 5 miles wide ; bounded by handsome oak and hickory woods, mixed with some short leaved pine, interspersed with pleasant streams and fountains of water. The opposite, or left side is a continuation of thick cane : the river or low lands 10 or 12 miles wide. After leaving the priarie, the cane continues for about 40 miles ; you then arrive at another priarie, called Little priarie, left side, about 5 miles in length, and from 2 to 3 in breadth ; opposite side continues cane as before ; low lands wide, well timbered, very rich and overflow but little ; the river still widening.— Back of the low grouuds, is a well timbered, rich up-

called bayau Badkah W.

prairie, W.  says, W.

to an 100 W.
prairies, W.

times W.

wide: W.  though W.

prarie, W.

cane; W.
prairie, W.
prairie, W.
prairie, W.

rich, W.

**101**

prairie, W.  miles, W.

land country ; gently rolling and well watered ; from the Little priarie both banks cane for 10 or 12 miles when the oak and pine woods come bluff to the river for about 5 miles : left hand side, cane as before : then the same on both sides, for from 10 to 20 miles wide, for about 15 miles, when the cedar begins on both sides, and is the principal growth on the wide, rich river bottom for 40 miles ; in all the world there is scarcely to be found a more beautiful growth of cedar timber ; they, like the cedars of Libanus, are large, lofty and straight.

prairies W.

inundation at W.

prairie, W.

You now arrive at the mouth of the Little river of the right ; this river is about 150 yards wide ; the water clear as chrystal ; the bottom of the river stony, and is boatable, at high water, up to the great priaries near 200 miles by the course of the river ; the low grounds generally from 10 to 15 miles wide, abounding with the most luxuriant growth of rich timber, but subject to a partial inundation, at particular rainy seasons.  After leaving this river, both banks of Red river are cane as before, for about 20 miles, when you come to the round priarie, right side, about 5 miles in circumference.  At this place Red river is fordable at low water ; a hard stony bottom, and is the first place from its mouth where it can be forded.  This round priarie is high and pleasant ; surrounded by high oak and hickory uplands :

prairie W.

prairie, W.

Long prairie S2; prairie, W.

Caddoquies W.
which, W.

left side cane as before, and then the same both sides for 20 miles, to the long priarie, left side, 40 miles long; opposite cane as before ; near the middle of this priarie, there is a lake of 5 miles in circumference, in an oval form, neither tree nor shrub near it, nor stream of water running in or out of it ; it is very deep and the water so limpid that a fish may be seen 15 feet from the surface.  By the side of this lake the Caddoques have lived from time immemorial.  About one mile from the lake is the hill on which they say, the great spirit placed one Caddo family, who were saved when, by a general deluge, all the world were drowned; from which family all the In-

## 102

dians have originated. For this little natural emi-
nence, all the Indian tribes as well as the Caddoques, **Caddoquies, W.**
for a great distance pay a devout and sacred homage. **distance, W.**
Here the French, for many years before Louisiana
was ceded to Spain, had erected a small fort; kept
some soldiers to guard a factory they had here established for the Indian trade, and several French families were settled in the vicinity, built a flour mill, and
cultivated wheat successfully for several years; and
it is only a few years ago that the mill irons and mill
stones were brought down; it is about 25 years since **down: W.**
those French families moved down, and 14 years
since the Caddoques left it. Here is another fording **Caddoquies W.**
place when the river is low. On the opposide side
a point of high oak, hickory, and pine land comes
bluff to the river for about a mile; after which,
thick cane to the upper end of the priarie; then the **prairie; W.**
same on both sides for about 12 miles; then priarie **prairie W.**
on the left side for 20 miles, opposite side cane;
then the same for 30 miles, then an oak high bluff
three miles, cane again for about the same distance,
on both sides; then for about one league, left side,
is a beautiful grove of pacans, intermixed with no
other growth; after which cane both sides for 40
miles; then priarie, left side, for 20 miles, and from **prairie, W.**
one to two miles only in depth; about the middle
of which comes in a bayau of clear running water,
about 50 feet wide; thence cane again both sides of **then cane W.**
the river for about 40 miles; then, on the right side **side, W.**
a point of high pine woods bluff to the river for about
half a mile, cane again for 15 or 16 miles; then a **again 15 W.**
bluff of large white rocks for about half a mile, near
100 feet high, cane again for about 45 miles, to a **again about 45 W.**
priarie on the right side, of about thirty miles long **prairie W. 30 W.**
and twelve or fifteen miles wide; and there is a thin **12 or 15 miles wide; there W.**
skirt of wood along the bank of the river, that when
the leaves are on the trees, the priarie is, from the ri- **prairie W.**
ver, scarcely to be seen. From the upper end of this
priarie it is thick cane again for about six miles, when **prairie W.**
we arrive to the mouth of Bayau Galle, which is on

**103**

the right side, about 30 yards wide, a beautiful, clear, running stream of wholesome well tasted water; after passing which it is thick cane again for 25 miles, when we arrive at a river that falls in on the right side, which is called by the Indians *Kiomitchie*, and by the French *La Riviere la Mine*, or Mine river, which is about 150 yards wide, the water clear and good, and is boatable about 60 miles to the silver mine, which is on the bank of the river, and the ore appears in large quantities, but the richness of it is not known. The Indians inform of their discovering another, about a year ago, on a creek that empties into the Kiomitchie, about three miles from its mouth, the ore of which they say resembles the other. The bottom land of this river is not wide, but rich; the adjoining high lands are rich, and well timbered, well watered and situated. About the mine the current of the river is too strong for boats to ascend it, the country being hilly. After passing the Kiomitchie, both banks of the river are covered with thick cane for 25 miles, then, left side, a high pine bluff appears again to the river for about half a mile, after which nothing but cane again on each side for about forty miles, which brings you to the mouth of a handsome bayau, left side, called by the Indians *Nahaucha*, which, in English, means the Kick; the French call it *Bois d' Arc*, or bow-wood creek, from the large quantity of that wood that grows upon it. On this bayau trappers have been more successful in catching beaver than on any other water of Red river; it communicates with a lake, three or four miles from its mouth, called Swan lake, from the great number of swan that frequent it; it is believed that this bayau is boatable at high water, for twenty or thirty leagues, from what I have been informed by some hunters with whom I have conversed, who have been upon it.— low grounds are from three to six miles wide, very rich, the principal growth on it is the bois d' arc. The great priaries approch pretty near the low grounds on each side of this creek; leaving which it

*Margin notes:*

rich, well W.

40 W.

Bow-wood W.

20 or 30 W.

The low W.
d'arc. W.
prairies approach W.

**104**

is cane both sides for about eight miles, when we arrive at the mouth of the Vazzures, or Boggy river, which is about 200 yards wide, soft miry bottom, the water whitish, but well tasted. Attempts have been made to ascend it in perogues, but it was found to be obstructed by a raft of logs, about 20 miles up it. The current was found to be gentle, and depth of water sufficient; were the channel not obstructed might be ascended far up it. The low grounds on this river are not as wide as on most of the rivers that fall into Red river, but very rich; the high lands are a strong clay soil; the principal growth oak. After leaving this river the banks of Red river are alternately cane and prairie; timber is very small and scattered along only in places; it is now only to be seen along the water courses. From the Boggy river to the Blue river is about 50 miles, which comes in on the right side. The water of this river is called *blue*, from its extreme transparency; it is said to be well tasted, and admired, for its quality, to drink. The bed of this river is lined generally with black and greyish flint stones; it is about 50 yards wide, and represented as a beautiful stream; perogues ascend it about 60 or 70 miles. The low grounds of Blue river are a good width for plantations, very rich; the growth pacan, and every species of the walnut. The whole country here, except on the margin of the water courses, is one immense prairie. After passing this river copses of wood only are to be seen here and there along the river bank for about 25 miles, to a small turgid river, called by the Indians *Bahachaha*, and by the French *Fouxoacheta*; some call it the Missouri branch of Red river; it emits a considerable quantity of water; runs from north to south and falls into Red river nearly at right angles, and heads near the head of the Arkansa, and is so brackish it cannot be drank. On this river, and on a branch of the Arkansa, not far from it, the Indians find the salt rock; pieces of it have often been brought to Natchitoches by hunters, who procured it from the In-

**O**

was the channel W.

is only now to be W.

Fauxoacheta, S2; *Fouxoacheta;* W.

Arkansa S2; Arkensa, W.

Arkansa S2; Arkensa, W.

## 105

dians. From the mouth of this river, through the priarie, to the main branch of the Arkansa, is three days journey; perhaps 60 or 70 miles in a straight line. From this to the Panis, or Towiache towns, by land, is about 30 miles, and by water, double that distance; the river is nearly a mile wide. The country on each side, for many hundreds of miles, is all priarie, except a skirt of wood along the river bank, and on the smaller streams; what trees there are, are small; the grass is green summer and winter. In between 33 and 34 degrees of north latitude, the soil is very rich, producing, luxuriously, every thing that is planted in it: the river, from this upwards, for 150 miles, continues at least a mile wide, and may be ascended in perogues.

Mr. Grappe, to whom I am indebted for the foregoing accurate description of Red river, informed me, that his personal knowledge of it did not extend but little above the Panis towns; but Mr. Brevel, of the Isle Brevel, who was born at the Caddo old towns, where he was, had been farther up it, and that whatever account he gave me might be relied on.

I therefore sought an opportunity, a few days after, to obtain from Mr. Brevel the following narrative, which I wrote down from his own mouth, as he related it:

" About 40 years ago, I sat off, on foot, from the Panis nation (who then lived about 50 leagues above where they now live) in company with a party of young Indian men, with whom I had been partly raised, on a hunting voyage, and to procure horses. We kept up on the south side of Red river, as near it as we could conveniently cross the small streams that fall in, sometimes at some distance, and at others very near it, and in sight of it. We found the country all priarie, except small copses of wood, cedar, cotton wood, or musketo, amongst which a stick six inches in diameter could not be found; the surface becoming more and more light, sandy and hilly, with ledges of clifts of a greyish sandy rock, but every

prairie, W.  Arkensa, W.

Towiaches S1; Towrache W.

prairie, W.

prairie, S1, W.

106

where covered with herbage. We found many small streams falling into the river, but none of any considerable size, or that discharged much water in dry seasons, but many deep gullies formed by the rain water. After travelling for several days over a country of this description, the country became more broken, the hills rising into mountains, amongst which we saw a great deal of rock salt, and an ore the Indians said was my (meaning the white people's) treasure, which I afterwards learned was silver. And that amongst these mountains of mines, we often heard a noise like the explosion of a cannon, or distant thunder, which the Indians said was the spirit of the white people working in their treasure, which, I afterwards was informed, was the blowing of the mines, as it is called, which is common in all parts of Spanish America where mines exist. The main branch of the river becoming smaller, till it divided into almost innumerable streams that issued out of the vallies amongst these mountains ; the soil very light and sandy, of a reddish grey color. We travelled on from the top of one mountain to the top of another, in hopes the one we were ascending was always the last, till the small streams we met with ran the contrary way, towards the setting sun, and the lands declining that way. We continued on till the streams enlarged into a river of considerable size, and the country became level, well timbered, the soil a rich black loam ; the waters were all clear and well tasted. Here we found a great many different tribes of the Hietan, Appaches and Concee Indians; we likewise fell in with them frequently from the time we had been a few days out from the Panis towns, and were always treated kindly by them. I believe the distance from the Panis old towns to where we saw the last of Red river water, is at least one hundred leagues ; and in crossing over the ridge, we saw no animals that were not common in all the country of Louisiana, except the spotted tyger, and a few white bears. After spending some days on the western

Cansas. S2; Concee W, N.

**107**

prairies, S2; prairie; W.

Fe′ W.

Fe′ W.

Fe′ W.

Fe′ W.
prairie. S2, W.

waters, we sat off for the settlements of St. a Fe; steering nearly a south-east course, and in a few days were out of the timbered country in to priarie; the country became broken and hilly; the waters all running westwardly; the country cloathed with a luxuriant herbage, and frequently passing mines of silver ore.  We arrived, at length, at a small, meanly built town in the St. a Fe settlement, containing about one hundred houses, round which were some small, cultivated fields, fenced round with small cedar and musketo brush, wattled in stakes.  This little town was on a small stream of water that ran westwardly, and in a dry season scarcely run at all; and that the inhabitants were obliged to water their cattle from wells. And I understood that the bayau upon which this town is situated, was no part of Rio Grandi, but fell into the western ocean; but of that I might have been mistaken.  I understood that similar small towns, or missions, were within certain distances of each other for a great extent southwardly, towards Mexico; and that the inhabitants were mostly christianised Indians and Matiffs.  That the mines in that settlement afforded very rich ore, which was taken away in large quantities, packed on mules, and had the same appearance of what we met with about the head branches of Red river.  After furnishing ourselves with horses at this place, we sat off again for the Panis towns, from whence we started, steering at first southwardly, in order to avoid a high, mountainous country that is difficult to cross, that lies between St. a Fe and Red river.  After travelling some distance south, we turned our course northeastwardly, and arrived at the Panis towns in eighteen days from the day we left St. a Fe settlements; and three months and twenty days from the time we started."

He is of the opinion that from the Panis towns to St. a Fe, in a right line, is nearly three hundred miles, and all the country priarie, a few scattering cedar knobs excepted.  After he had finished his narrative, I asked him how far Red river was boatable.  He said, not

**108**

much above the Panis old towns ; not that he knew of any particular falls or obstructions, but that the head branches of the river came from steep mountains, on which the rain often poured down in torrents, and runs into the river with such velocity, sweeping along with it large quantities of loose earth, of which these hills and mountains are composed; that it rolls like a swell in the sea, and would either sink or carry along with it any boat that it might meet in the river.   But, he observed at the same time, that his opinion was founded on no experiment that he had ever known made. I asked him if the Indians had no perogues high up in the river.   He told me, that the Indians there knew nothing of the use of them, for instead of their being for hundreds of miles a tree large enough for a canoe, one could scarcely be found large enough to make a fowl trough.   I asked him what animals were found in the Great priaries.   He told me that from Blue river, upwards, on both sides of Red river, there were innumerable quantities of wild horses, buffaloe, bears, wolves, elk, deer, foxes, sangliers or wild hogs, antelopes, white hares, rabbits, &c. and on the mountains, the spotted tiger, panther, and wild cat. He farther told me, that about 23 years ago, he was employed by the governor of St Antoine, to go from that place into some of the Indian nations that lived towards St. a Fe, who were at war with the Spaniards, to try to make a peace with them, and bring in some of the chiefs to St. Antoine.   He sat off from that place with a party of soldiers, and was to have gone to St. a Fe ; they passed on a northwestwardly course for about 200 miles, but after getting into the Great Priarie, being a dry season, they were forced to turn back for want of water for themselves and horses,  and that he does not know how near he went to St, a Fe, but believes he might have been half way.

The accounts given by Mr. Brevel, Mr. Grappe, and all other hunters with whom I have conversed, of the immense droves of animals that, at the beginning of winter descend from the mountains down south-

composed: W.

prairies. W.

antelope, S2, W.
tyger, S2, W.
twenty-three W.

Fe', W.

Fe'; W.
two hundred W.
Prairie, W.

St. a Fe', W.

winter, W.

that blacken W.

### 109

wardly, into the timbered country, is almost incredible. They say the buffaloe and bear particularly, are in droves of many thousands together, and blacken the whole surface of the earth, and continue passing, without intermission, for weeks together, so that the whole surface of the country is, for many miles in breadth, trodden like a large road.

I am, sir, &c. &c.

(Signed)

**JOHN SIBLEY.**

*Natchitoches,* 10th *April,* 1805.

## 110

*Distances up Red river by the course of the river.*

MILES.

| | |
|---|---|
| From the mouth of Red river to Black river, | 31 |
| to Baker's landing, lower end Avoyall, | 51 |
| La Glee's ditto, upper end Avoyall, . | 15 |
| Rice's, . . . . . . . . | 6 |
| Holmes' . . . . . . . . | 18 |
| Nicholas Grubb's, . . . . . | 21 |
| mouth of bayau Rapide, . . . . | 15 |
| | — 157 |
| Indian villages, . . . . . . . | 22 |
| Mount pleasant, Gillard's place, . . | 7 |
| mouth of Rigula de Bondieu, . . . | 6 |
| Mounete's plantation, . . . . . | 10 |
| mouth of Little river, . . . . . | 24 |
| bayau Brevel. . . . . . . . | 20 |
| Natchitoches, . . . . . . . | 20 |
| | — 109 |
| Grand Ecore, . . . . . . . | 10 |
| Campti, . . . . . . . . . | 20 |
| bayau Channo, . . . . . . ., | 15 |
| lake Bistino, through bayau Channo, | 3 |
| through lake Bistino, to the upper end of Channo, . . . . . . . | 60 |
| through bayau Daichet to the river again, . . . . . . . . . | 9 |
| late Caddo villages where they lived 5 years ago, . . . . . . . | 80 |
| | — 196 |
| Little river of the left, . . . . . | 80 |
| long priarie, right side, . . . . | 25 |
| upper end of ditto, . . . . . . | 25 |
| little priarie, left side, . . . . . | 40 |
| upper end ditto, . . . . . . | 5 |
| | — 175 |
| | 638 |

avoyal W.
avoyal W.

Hoome's, W.

Pleasant, W.

Brevell, W.

Compti, W.

197 W.

prairie, W.

prairie, W.

### 111

|  | *Continued,* . . *miles.* | 638 |
|---|---|---|
| Bluff, W. | pine bluff, right side, . . . . | 12 |
|  | upper end ditto, . . . . . | 5 |
|  | cedars, . . . . . . . . | 15 |
| river of W. | upper end ditto and mouth of Little river to the right, . . . . | 40 |
|  |  | — 72 |
| prairie, W. | round priarie, right side (first fording place) . . . . . . . . | 20 |
| prairie, W. | lower end of long priarie, left side, | 25 |
|  | upper end ditto, . . . . . | 40 |
| prairie W. | next priarie, same side, . . . | 12 |
|  | upper end of the same, . . . . | 20 |
| Bluff, W. | 3 mile oak and pine bluff, . . . | 30 |
|  | Pacan grove, . . . . , . . | 9 |
|  | upper end of the same, . . . . | 6 |
|  |  | — 162 |
| prairie W. | priarie next above the pacans, . . | 40 |
|  | upper end of the same, . . . . | 25 |
|  | pine Bluff right side, . . . . | 45 |
| oak bluff, W. | white oak Bluff, . . . . . . | 15 |
| prairie W. | next priarie right side, . . . . | 45 |
|  | upper end ditto, . . . . . | 30 |
|  | bayau Galle, right side, . . . | 6 |
|  | mouth of Kiomitchie, or mine river, | 25 |
|  |  | — 231 |
| Bluff left W. | pine Bluff, left side, . . . . | 25 |
|  | bayau Kick, or Bois d' arc creek, . | 40 |
|  | the Vazzures, or Boggy river, right side, . . . . . , , . | 8 |
| river right W. | Blue river, right side, . . . . | 50 |
| Oacheto or Missouri W. | Faux Ocheto or the Missouri branch, | 25 |
|  | Panis or Towiache towns, . . . | 70 |
|  | Panis or ditto old towns, . . | 150 |
|  | Head branch of Red river, or dividing ridge, . - . . . . | 300 |
|  |  | — 668 |
|  |  | 1,771 |

**112**

Continued, . . . *miles,* 1,771
To which may be added for so much the distance being shortened by going through lake
Bistino, and the course of the river, . . 60       than the course W.
                              —————
                              1,831

Computed length of Red river from where it
falls into the Mississippi, to which add the
distance from the mouth of Red river to the
ocean, by either the Mississippi, or the
Chaffeli, which was once probably the       Cheffeli, W.
mouth of Red river, . . . . . . . 320

Total length of Red river,     *miles.* 2,151       lenth W.

**P**

**113**

# OBSERVATIONS

Made in a voyage commencing at St. Catharine's landing, on the east bank of the Mississippi, proceeding downwards to the mouth of Red river, and from thence ascending that river, the Black river, and the Washita river, as high as the hot springs in the proximity of the last mentioned river, extracted from the journals of William Dunbar, esquire, and Doctor Hunter.

MR. DUNBAR, Doctor Hunter, and the party employed by the United States to make a survey of, and explore the country traversed by the Washita river left St. Catharine's landing, on the Mississippi, in latitude 31. 26m. 30s. N. and longitude 6h. 5m. 56s. W. from the meridian of Greenwich, on Tuesday the 16th of October, 1804. A little distance below St. Catharine's creek, and five leagues from Natchez, they passed the White Cliffs, composed chiefly of sand, surmounted by pine, and from one hundred to two hundred feet high. When the waters of the Mississippi are low, the base of the cliff is uncovered, which consists of different colored clays, and some beds of ochre, over which there lies, in places, a thin lamina of iron ore. Small springs possessing a petrifying quality flow over the clay and ochre, and numerous logs and pieces of timber, converted into stone, are strewed about the beach. Fine pure argil of various colors, chiefly white and red, is found here.

On the 17th they arrived at the mouth of Red river, the confluence of which with the Mississippi, agreeably to the observations of Mr. de Ferrer, lies in latitude 31d. 1m. 15s. N. and longitude 6h. 7m. 11s. west of Greenwich. Red river is here about five hundred yards wide, and without any sensible current. The banks of the river are clothed with willow ; the land low and subject to inundation, to the height of thirty feet or more above the level of the water at this time. The mouth of the Red river is

river, W.
31°. 26'. 30". W. 6h. 5'. 56". W.

Natchez D; Natches, W.

in some places, W.

31°. 1'. 15". W. 6h. 7'. 11". W.

## 114

accounted to be seventy five leagues from New-Or-leans, and three miles higher up than the Chaffeli, or Opelousa river, which was probably a continuation of the Red river, when its waters did not unite with the Mississippi but during the inundation.

On the 18th the survey of the Red river was commenced, and on the evening of the 19th the party arrived at the mouth of the Black river, in latitude 31d. 15m. 48s. N. and about 26 miles from the Mississippi. The Red river derives its name from the rich fat earth, or marle, of that colour, borne down by the floods; the last of which appeared to have deposited on the high bank a stratum of upwards of half an inch in thickness. The vegetation on its banks is surprisingly luxuriant; no doubt owing to the deposition of marle during its annual floods. The willows grow to a good size; but other forest trees are much smaller than those seen on the banks of the Mississippi. As you advance up the river, it gradually narrows; in latitude 31d. 08m. N. it is about two hundred yards wide, which width is continued to the mouth of Black river, where each of them appears one hundred and fifty yards across. The banks of the river are covered with pea vine and several sorts of grass, bearing seed, which geese and ducks eat very greedily; and there are generally seen willows growing on one side, and on the other a small growth of black oak, pacan, hickory, elm, &c. The current in Red river is so moderate as scarcely to afford an impediment to its ascent.

On sounding the Black river a little above its mouth, there was found twenty feet of water, with a bottom of black sand. The water of Black river is rather clearer than that of the Ohio, and of warm temperature, which it may receive from the water flowing into it from the valley of the Mississippi, particularly by the the Ocatahola. At noon on the 23d, by a good meridian observation, they ascertained their latitude to be 31d. 36m. 29s. N. and were then a little below the mouth of the Ocatahola, Washita

37

New-orleans D; New Orleans, W.
Chafalaya D; Chafalaya, W;
 Chaffalaïa DBL, DNY.
Red river when W.

31°. 15′. 48″. W.

31°. 08′. W.

packawn, D, W.
in the Red W.

{ *line 37*:
Catahoola. D, W; Ocatahola. N,
*corrected to* Catahoo[la.] DBL;
*corrected to* Catahoola. DNY.
30°. 36′. 29″. D, W.
Catahoola, D, W; Ocatahola, N,
 *corrected to* [Catahoola] DNY.

**115**

and Bayau Tenza, the united waters of which form the Black river. The current is very gentle the whole length of the Black river, which in many places does not exceed eighty yards in width. The banks on the lower part of the river present a great luxuriance of vegetation and grass, with red and black oak, ash, pacan, hickory, and some elms.* The soil is black marle, mixed with a moderate proportion of sand, resembling much the soil on the Mississippi banks ; yet the forest trees are not lofty, like those on the margin of the great river, but resemble the growth on the Red river. In latitude 31d. 22m. 46s. N. they observed that canes grew on several parts of the right bank, a proof that the land is not deeply overflowed ; perhaps from one to three feet, the banks have the appearance of stability ; very little willow, or other productions of a newly formed soil being seen on either side. On advancing up the river, the timber becomes larger, in some places rising to the height of forty feet ; yet the land is liable to be inundated, not from the waters of this small river, but from the intrusion of its more powerful neighbour the Mississippi. The lands decline rapidly, as in all alluvial countries, from the margin to the Cypress swamps, where more or less water stagnates all the year round. On the 21st they passed a small, but elevated island, said to be the only one in this river for more than one hundred leagues

*Among the plants growing on the margin of the river is the china root, used in medicine, and the cantac, occasionally used by the hunters for food ; the last has a bulbous root, ten times the size of a man's fist. In preparing it, they first wash it clean from earth, then pound it well, and add water to the mass and stir it up ; after a moment's settlement, the water and fecula is poured off: this operation is repeated until it yields no more fecula, the fibrous part only being left, which is thrown away as useless ; the water is then poured from the sediment, which is dried in the sun and will keep a long time. It is reduced into powder and mixed with Indian meal or flour, and wholesome and agreeable food. The labor is performed by the women whilst they are keeping the camp, and their husbands are in the woods hunting.

---

*Marginal notes:*

paccawn, D, W.

31°. 22′. 46″. W.

cheria root, W.

secula is W, N, *corrected to* secula are DNY;

useless: W.

and makes wholesome W; and wholesome N, *corrected to* and yields wholesome DNY.

### 116

ascending. On the left bank, near this island, a small settlement of a couple of acres has been begun by a man and his wife. The banks are not less than forty feet above the present level of the water in the river, and are but rarely overflowed ; on both sides they are clothed with rich cane brake, pierced by creeks fit to carry boats during the inundation.

They saw many cormorants, and the hooping crane ; geese and ducks are not yet abundant, but are said to arrive in myriads, with the rains and winter's cold. They shot a fowl of the duck kind, whose foot was partially divided, and the body covered with a bluish, or lead coloured plumage. On the morning of the twenty-second, they observed green matter floating on the river, supposed to come from the Catahoola and other lakes and bayaus of stagnant water, which, when raised a little by rain, flow into the Black river; and also many patches of an aquatic plant, resembling small islands, some floating on the surface of the river, and others adhering to, or resting on the shore & logs. On examining this plant, it was found a hollow, jointed stem, with roots of the same form, extremely light, with very narrow willow shaped leaves projecting from the joint, embracing however, the whole of the tube, and extending to the next inferior joint or knot. The extremity of each branch is terminated by a spike of very slender, narrow seminal leaves from one to two inches in length, and one tenth, or less, in breadth, producing its seed on the underside of the leaf, in a double row almost in contact ; the grains alternately placed in perfect regularity ; not being able to find the flower, its class and order could not be determined, although it is not probably new. Towards the upper part of Black river, the shore abounded with muscles and periwinkles. The muscles were of the kind called pearl muscles. The men dressed a quantity of them, considering them as an agreeable food; but Mr. D. found them tough and unpalatable.

On arriving at the mouth of the Ocatahola, they

shore and W.

regularity: W

of the Black W.

Catahoola, D, W; Ocatahola, N, *corrected to* catahola, DNY.

## 117

landed to procure information from a Frenchman settled there.    Having a grant from the Spanish government,  he has made a small  settlement,  and keeps a
ferry-boat for carrying over  men  and horses travelling to and from Natchez, and the settlements on Red
river and on the Washita river.   The country here is
all alluvial.   In process of time, the rivers shutting
up ancient passages and  elevating the banks over
which their waters pass, no longer communicate with
the same facility as formerly ; the consequence is,
that many  larger  tracts formerly subject to inundation, are now entirely exempt from that inconvenience.   Such is the situation of a most valuable tract
upon which this Frenchman is settled.   His house
stands on an Indian mount, with  several others in
view.   There is also a species of rampart surrounding
this place, and one very elevated mount, a view of
which is postponed till the return ; their present situation not allowing of the  requisite delay.   The soil
is equal to the best Mississippi bottoms. *

They obtained from the French settler the follow-
ing list of distances between the mouth of Red river
and the post on the Washita, called fort Miro.
From the mouth of Red river to the mouth of Black
      river, . . . . . . . . . . 10 leagues.
To the mouth of Ocatahola, Washita,
      and Tensaw, . . . . . . 22
To the river Ha-ha, on the right, . . 1

*There is an embankment running from Ocatahola to Black
river (inclofing about two hundred acres of rich land) at present
about ten feet high, and ten feet broad.  This furrounds four
large mounds of earth at the diftance of a bow-fhot from each o-
ther ; each of which may be twenty feet high, one hundred feet
broad, and three hundred feet long at the top, befides a ftupen-
dous turret situate on the back part of the whole, or farthest
from the water, whofe base covers about an acre of ground, ri-
fing by two fteps or ftories tapering  in the afcent, the whole surmounted by a great cone with its  top cut off.  This tower of
earth on admeafurement was found to be eighty feet perpendicular.

view and describe D; view and
description W.

line 25: Catahoola, D, W;
Ocatahola, N, *corrected to*
catahola, DNY.
Tenza, D, W.

line 29: from the Catahoola D, W;
from Ocatahola N, *corrected to*
from catahola DNY.
land), D, W.

25

29

## 113

Continued,  . . . . 33 leagues.

To the Priarie de Villemont, on the
same side, . . . . . . . . 5

To the bayau Louis, on the same side,
rapids here, . . . . . . . 1

To bayau Beauf, on the same side, . 4

To the Priarie Noyu (drowned savanna) . . . . . . . . . 3

To Pine Point on the left, . . . . 4 1-2

To bayau Calumet, . . . . . . 3 1-2

To the Colemine, on the right, and
Gypsum on the opposite shore, . 3

To the first settlement, . . . . . 12

To fort Miro, . . . . . . . 22

——

*Leagues,* 91

From this place they proceeded to the mouth of
Washita, in lat. 31d. 27m. 7s. N. and encamped on
the evening of the 23d.

This river derives its appellation from the name of
an Indian tribe formerly resident on its banks ; the
remnant of which, it is said, went into the great plains
to the westward, and either compose a small tribe
themselves, or are incorporated into some other nation.   The Black river loses its name at the junction
of the Washita, Ocatahola, and Tensaw, although
our maps represent it as taking place of the Washita.
The Tensaw and Ocatahola are also named from Indian tribes now extinct.   The latter is a creek twelve
leagues long, which is the issue of a lake of the same
name, eight leagues in length and about two leagues
in breadth.   It lies west from the mouth of the Ocatahola, and communicates with the Red river during
the great annual inundation.   At the west or north-
west angle of the lake, a creek called Little river,
enters, which preserves a channel of running water
at all seasons, meandering along the bed of the lake ;
but in all other parts, its superficies, during the dry
season from July to November, and often later, is
completely drained, and becomes covered with the

Prairie D, W; Priarie N, *corrected to* prairie DNY.

*line 6*: Bœfs, D, W; Beauf, N, *corrected to* Boeuf, DNY.

*line 7*: Prairie Noyée D; Prairie Noyu, W; Priarie Noyu N, *corrected to* Priarie Noyee DNY.

*line 9*: Point, W.  4 ½ W.

*line 10*: 3 ½ W.

*line 11*: Coal mine D; Coalmine, W.

35° 37′ 7″ W.

into another D, W.

*line 25*: Tenza and the Catahoola D; Catahoola, and Tenza, W; Ocatahola, and Tensaw, N, *corrected to* catahola, and Tensaw, DNY.

*line 27*: Tenza and Catahoola D, W; Tensaw and Ocatahola N; *corrected to* Tensaw and catahola DNY.

*line 31*: Catahoola, D, W; Ocatahola, N; *corrected to* catahola, DNY.

*line 37*: parts its W.

**119**

most luxuriant herbage ; the bed of the lake then becomes the residence of immense herds of deer, of turkies, geese, crane &c. which feed on the grass and grain. Bayau Tensaw serves only to drain off a part of the waters of the inundation from the low lands of the Mississippi, which here communicate with the Black river during the season of high water.

Between the mouth of the Washita, and Villemont's priarie on the right, the current of the river is gentle, and the banks favorable for towing. The lands on both sides have the appearance of being above the inundation ; the timber generally such as high lands produce, being chiefly red, white and black oaks, interspersed with a variety of other trees. The magnolia grandiflora, that infallible sign of the land not being subject to inundation, is not, however, among them. Along the banks a stratum of solid clay, or marle, is observable, apparently of an ancient deposition. It lies in oblique positions, making an angle of nearly thirty degrees, with the horizon, and generally inclined with the descent of the river, although in a few cases the position was contrary. Timber is seen projecting from under the solid bank, which seems indurated, and unquestionably very ancient, presenting a very different appearance from recently formed soil, the river is about 80 yards wide. A league above the mouth of the Washita, the bayau Ha-ha comes in unexpectedly from the right, and is one of the many passages through which the waters of the great inundation penetrate and pervade all the low countries, annihilating, for a time, the currents of the lesser rivers in the neighbourhood of the Mississippi. The vegetation is remarkably vigorous along the alluvial banks, which are covered with a thick shrubbery, and innumerable plants in full blossom at this late season.

Villemont's priarie, is so named in consequence of its being included within a grant under the French government, to a gentleman of that name. Many other parts on the Washita are named after their early

turkeys, W.
Tenza D, W.

prairie D, W.

degrees with W.

soil. The W.

prairie is D, W.

government to W.

**120**

proprietors. The French people projected and began extensive settlements on this river, but the general massacre planned, and in part executed by the Indians against them, and the consequent destruction of the Natchez tribe by the French, broke up all these undertakings, and they were not recommenced under that government. Those priaries are plains, or savannas, without timber; generally very fertile, and producing an exuberance of strong, thick and coarse herbage. When a piece of ground has once got into this state, in an Indian country, it can have no opportunity of re-producing timber, it being an invariable practice to set fire to the dry grass in the fall or winter, to obtain the advantage of attracting game when the young tender grass begins to spring; this destroys the young timber, and the priarie annually gains upon the wood-land. It is probable that the immense plains known to exist in America, may owe their origin to this custom. The plains of the Washita lie chiefly on the east side, and being generally formed like the Mississippi land, sloping from the bank of the river to the great river, they are more or less subject to inundation in the rear; and in certain great floods the water has advanced so far as to be ready to pour over the margin into the Washita. This has now become a very rare thing, and it may be estimated that from a quarter of a mile to a mile in depth, will remain free from inundation during high floods. This is pretty much the case with those lands nearly as high as the post of the Washita, with the exception of certain ridges of primitive high land; the rest being evidently alluvial, although not now subject to be inundated by the Washita river in consequence of the great depth which the bed of the river has acquired by abrasion. On approaching towards the bayau Louis, which empties its waters into the Washita on the right, a little below the rapids, there is a great deal of high land on both sides, which produces pine and other timber, not the growth of inundated lands. At the foot of the rapids the navi-

Q

prairies D, W.

prairie D, W.

**121**

31°. 48′. 57″. 5 W.

appears W.

gation of the river is impeded by beds of gravel formed in it.   The first rapids lie in latitude 31d. 48m.
57s. 5 N. a little above which there is a high ridge
of primitive earth, studded with abundance of fragments of rocks, or stone, which appear to have been
thrown up to the surface in a very irregular manner.
The stone is of a friable nature, some of it having
the appearance of indurated clay; the outside is blackish from exposure to the air, within it is a greyish
white; it is said that in the hill the strata are regular
and that good grindstones may be here obtained.
The last of the rapids, which is formed by a ledge
of rocks crossing the entire bed of the river, was
passed in the evening of the 27th; above it the water
became again like a mill pond and about one hundred
yards wide.   The whole of these first shoals, or rapids, embraced an extent of about a mile and a half;
the obstruction was not continued, but felt at short
intervals in this distance.   On the right, about four
leagues from the rapids, they passed the " Bayau
Aux Boeufs," a little above a rocky hill; high lands
and savanna is seen on the right.   On sounding the
river they found three fathoms water on a bottom of
mud and sand.   The banks of the river, above the
bayau, seem to retain very little alluvial soil; the
highland earth, which is a sandy loam of a light grey
colour, with streaks of red sand and clay, is seen on
the left bank; the soil not rich, bearing pines, interspersed with red oak, hickory and dogwood.   The
river is from sixty to one hundred yards wide here,
but decreases as you advance.   The next rapid is
made by a ledge of rocks traversing the river, and
narrowing the water channel to about thirty yards.
The width between the high banks cannot be less
than one hundred yards, and the banks from thirty to
forty feet high.   In latitude 32d. 10m. 13s. rapids
and shoals again occurred, and the channel was very
narrow; the sand bars, at every point, extended so
far into the bend as to leave little more than the
breadth of the boat of water sufficiently deep for her

32°. 10′. 13″. W.

122

passage, although it spreads over a width of seventy or eighty yards upon the shoal.

In the afternoon of the 31st, they passed a little plantation or settlement on the right, and at night arrived at three others adjoining each other. These settlements are on a plain or priarie, the soil of which we may be assured is alluvial from the regular slope which the land has from the river. The bed of the river is now sufficiently deep to free them from the inconvenience of its inundation ; yet in the rear, the waters of the Mississippi approach, and sometimes leave dry but a narrow stripe along the bank of the river. It is however now more common, that the extent of the fields cultivated (from 1-4 to 1-2 mile) remains dry during the season of inundation ; the soil here is very good, but not equal to the Mississippi bottoms ; it may be esteemed second rate. At a small distance to the east are extensive cypress swamps, over which the waters of the inundation always stand to the depth of from fifteen to twenty-five feet. On the west side, after passing over the valley of the river whose breadth varies from a quarter of a mile to two miles, or more, the land assumes a considerable elevation, from one hundred to three hundred feet, and extends all along to the settlements of the Red river. These high lands are reported to be poor, and badly watered, being chiefly what is termed pine barren. There is here a ferry and road of communication between the post of the Washita, and the Natchez, and a fork of this road passes on to the settlement called the Rapids, on Red river, distant from this place by computation one hundred and fifty miles.

On this part of the river lies a considerable tract of land granted by the Spanish government to the marquis of Maison Rouge, a French emigrant, who bequeathed it with all his property to M. Bouligny, son of the late colonel of the Louisiana regiment, and by him sold to Daniel Clarke. It is said to extend from the post of Washita with a breadth of two leagues,

prairie, D, W.

¼ to ½ W.

**123**

including the river, down to the bayau Calumet ; the computed distance of which along the river is called thirty leagues, but supposed not more than twelve in a direct line.

On the 6th of November, in the afternoon, the party arrived at the post of the Washita, in lat. 32d. 29m. 37s. 25 N. where they were politely received by lieut. Bowmar, who immediately offered the hospitality of his dwelling with all the services in his power.

From the ferry to this place the navigation of the river is, at this season, interrupted by many shoals and rapids. The general width is from eighty to a hundred yards. The water is extremely agreeable to drink, and much clearer than that of the Ohio. In this respect it is very unlike its two neighbours, the Arkansa and Red rivers, whose waters are loaded with earthy matters of a reddish brown color, giving to them a chocolate-like appearance ; and, when those waters are low, are not potable, being brackish from the great number of salt springs which flow into them, and probably from the beds of rock salt over which they may pass. The banks of the river presented very little appearance of alluvial land, but furnished an infinitude of beautiful landscapes, heightened by the vivid coloring they derive from the autumnal changes of the leaf. Mr. Dunbar observes, that the change of color in the leaves of vegetables, which is probably occasioned by the oxygen of the atmosphere acting on the vegetable matter, deprived of the protecting power of the vital principle, may serve as an excellent guide to the naturalist who directs his attention to the discovery of new objects for the use of the dyer. For he has always remarked that the leaves of those trees whose bark or wood are known to produce a dye, are changed in autumn to the same color which is extracted in the dyer's vat from the woods ; more especially by the use of mordants, as allum, &c. which yields oxygen : thus the foliage of the hickory, and oak, which produces the quercitron bark, is changed before its fall into a beau-

32° 29′ 37″. 25 W.

Dyer's D; dyers W.

**124**

tiful yellow ; other oaks assume a fawn color, a liver color, or a blood color, and are known to yield dyes of the same complexion.

In lat. 32d. 18m. N. doct. Hunter discovered a, long the river side a substance nearly resembling mineral coal ; its appearance was that of the carbonated wood described by Kirwan. It does not easily burn; but on being applied to the flame of a candle, it sensibly increased it, and yielded a faint smell, resembling in a slight degree, that of the gum lac of common sealing wax.

Soft friable stone is common, and great quantities of gravel and sand, upon the beaches in this part of the river. A reddish clay appears in the strata, much indurated and blackened by exposure to the light and air.

The position called fort Miro being the property of a private person, who was formerly civil commandant here, the lieutenant has taken post about four hundred yards lower; has built himself some log houses, and inclosed them with a slight stockade.— Upon viewing the country east of the river, it is evidently alluvial; the surface has a gentle slope from the river to the rear of the plantations. The land is of excellent quality, being a rich black mould to the depth of a foot, under which there is a friable loam of a brownish liver color.

At the post of the Washita, they procured a boat of less draught of water than the one in which they ascended the river thus far : at noon, on the 11th of November, they proceeded on the voyage, and in the evening encamped at the plantation of Baron Bastrop.

This small settlement on the Washita, and on some of the creeks falling into it, contains not more than five hundred persons, of all ages and sexes. It is reported, however, that there is a great quantity of excellent land upon these creeks, and that the settlement is capable of great extension, and may be expected, with an accession of population, to become very flourishing. There are three merchants settled

32° 18′ W.

**125**

at the post, who supply, at very exorbitant prices, the inhabitants with their necessaries ; these, with the garrison, two small planters, and a tradesmen or two, constitute the present village. A great proportion of the inhabitants continue the old practice of hunting, during the winter season, and they exchange their peltry for necessaries, with the merchants, at a low rate. During the summer these people content themselves with raising corn, barely sufficient for bread during the year. In this manner they always remain extremely poor ; some few who have conquered that habit of indolence, which is always the consequence of the Indian mode of life, and attend to agriculture, live more comfortably, and taste a little of the sweets of civilized life.

The lands along the river above the post, are not very inviting. being a thin poor soil, and covered with pine wood. To the right, the settlements on the bayau Barthelemi, and Siard, are said to be rich land.

On the morning of the thirteenth, they passed an island and a strong rapid, and arrived at a little settlement below a chain of rocks, which cross the channel between an island and the main land, called Roque Raw. The Spaniard and his family, settled here, a, pear, from their indolence, to live miserably. The river acquires here a more spacious appearance, being about one hundred and fifty yards wide. In the afternoon they passed the bayau Barthelemi on the right, above the last settlement, and about twelve computed leagues from the post. Here commences Baron Bastrop's great grant of land from the Spanish government, being a square of twelve leagues on each side, a little exceeding a million of French acres.— The banks of the river continue about thirty feet high, of which eighteen feet from the water are a clayey loam of a pale ash color, upon which the water has deposited twelve feet of light sandy soil, apparently fertile, and of a dark brown color. This description of land is of small breadth, not exceeding half a mile on each side the river, and may be called

little the D, W.

Bastrops W.

**126**

the valley of the Washita, beyond which there is high land covered with pine.

pines. D, W.

The soil of the " Bayau des Buttes," continues thin, with a growth of small timber. This creek is named from a number of Indian mounts discovered by the hunters along its course. The margin of the river begins to be covered with such timber as usually grows on inundated land, particularly a species of white oak, vulgarly called the over-cup oak ; its timber is remarkably hard, solid, ponderous and durable, and it produces a large acorn in great abundance, upon which the bear feeds, and which is very fattening for hogs.

In lat. 32d. 50m. 8s. N. they passed a long and narrow island. The face of the country begins to change ; the banks are low and steep ; the river deeper and more contracted, from thirty to fifty yards in width. The soil in the neighbourhood of the river is a very sandy loam, and covered with such vegetables as are found on the inundated lands of the Mississippi. The tract presents the appearance of a new soil, very different from what they passed below.— This alluvial tract may be supposed the site of a great lake, drained by a natural channel, from the abrasion of the waters ; since which period the annual inundations have deposited the superior soil : eighteen or twenty feet are wanting to render it habitable for man. It appears, nevertheless, well stocked with the beasts of the forest, several of which were seen.

32° 50′ 8″ W.

is yet wanting D; is wanting W.

Quantities of water fowl are beginning to make their appearance, which are not very numerous here until the cold rains and frost compel them to leave a more northern climate. Fish is not so abundant as might be expected, owing, it is said, to the inundation of the Mississippi, in the year 1799, which dammed up the Washita some distance above the post, and produced a stagnation and consequent corruption of the waters, that destroyed all the fish within its influence.

waters that W.

At noon, on the 15th November, they passed the island of Mallet, and at ninety yards north-east from

**127**

32° 59′ 27″. 5 W.
32½ D (Geom. Survey);
or two seconds and a half W.

the upper point of the island, by a good observation ascertained their latitude to be 32d. 59m. 27s. 5 N. or 32 seconds and a half of latitude south of the dividing line between the territories of Orleans and Louisiana. The bed of the river along this alluvial country, is generally covered with water, and the navigation uninterrupted; but in the afternoon of this day, they passed three contiguous sand bars, or beaches, called " les trois battures," and before evening the " bayau de grand Marais, " or great marsh creek on the right, and " la Cypriere de Chattebrau, " a point

'la Cypriere Chattelrau' D;
"la Cypreri Chattelrau," W.

of high land on the other side, which reaches within half a mile of the river. As they advanced towards the marais de saline, on the right, a stratum of dirty white clay under the alluvial tract, shewed them to be leaving the sunken, and approaching the high land country. The salt lick marsh does not derive its name from any brackishness in the water of the lake or marsh, but from its contiguity to some of the licks, sometimes called " saline " and sometimes "glaise," generally found in a clay, compact enough for potters' ware. The bayau de la Tulipe forms a communication between the lake and the river. Opposite to this place, there is a point of high land, forming a promontory, advancing within a mile of the river, and to which boats resort when the low grounds are under water. A short league above is the mouth of the

Saline (Salt Lick creek). W.
of considerable D; of a considerable
W.

grand bayau de la saline (Salt Lick Creek). This creek is of considerable length, and navigable for small boats. The hunters ascend it, to one hundred of their leagues, in pursuit of game, and all agree that none of the springs which feed this creek are salt. It has obtained its name from the many buffaloe salt licks which have been discovered in its vicinity.— Although most of these licks, by digging, furnish water which holds marine salt in solution, there exists no reason for believing that many of them would produce nitre. Notwithstanding this low and alluvial tract appears in all respects well adapted to the growth of the long moss (tilandsia), none was observ-

**127**

ed since entering it in latitude 32d. 52s. and as the pilot informed them none would be seen in their progress up the river, it is probable that the latitude of thirty-three degrees is about the northern limit of its vegetation. The long-leaf pine, frequently the growth of rich and even inundated land, was here observed in great abundance ; the short-leaved or pitch pine, on the contrary, is always found upon arid lands, and generally in sandy and lofty situations.

This is the season when the poor settlers on the Washita turn out to make their annual hunt. The deer is now fat and the skins in perfection ; the bear is now also in his best state, with regard to the quality of his fur, and the quantity of fat or oil he yields, as he has been feasting luxuriously on the autumnal fruits of the forest. It is here well known that he does not confine himself, as some writers have supposed, to vegetable food ; he is particularly fond of hogs flesh ; sheep and calves are frequently his prey, and no animal escapes him which comes within his power, and which he is able to conquer. He often destroys the fawn, when chance throws it in his way ; he cannot, however, discover it by smelling, notwithstanding the excellence of his scent, for nature has, as if for its protection, denied the fawn the property of leaving any effluvium upon its track, a property so powerful in the old deer.* The bear, unlike most other beasts of prey, does not kill the animal he has seized upon before he eats it ; but regardless of its struggles, cries and lamentations, fastens upon, and if the expression is allowable, devours it alive. The hunters count much on their profits from the oil

---

* It may not be generally known to naturalists, that between the hoof of the deer, &c. there is found a fack, with its mouth inclining upwards, containing more or lefs of musk, and which by escaping over the opening, in proportion to the fecretion, causes the foot to leave a fcent on the ground wherever it paffes. During the rutting feason this musk is fo abundant, particularly in old males, as to be fmelt by the hunters at a considerable distance.

**R**

[margin notes:]

32° 52′, W.

of vegetation D, W.

lands and W.

128

New-Orleans, D; New Orleans, W.

drawn from the bears fat, which, at New-Orleans, is always of ready sale, and much esteemed for its wholesomeness in cooking, being preferred to butter or hogs lard. It is found to keep longer than any other animal oil without becoming rancid; and boiling it, from time to time, upon sweet bay leaves, restores its sweetness, or facilitates its conservation.

In the afternoon of the 17th they passed some sand beaches, and over a few rapids. They had cane brakes on both sides of the river: the canes were small, but demonstrate that the water does not surmount the bank more than a few feet. The river begins to widen as they advance: the banks of the river shew the high land soil, with a stratum of three or four feet of alluvion deposited by the river upon it. This superstratum is greyish, and very sandy, with a small admixture of loam, indicative of the poverty of the mountains and uplands where the river rises. Near this they passed through a new and very narrow channel, in which all the water of the river passes, except in time of freshes, when the interval forms an island. A little above this pass is a small clearing, called " Cache la Tulipe" (Tulip's hiding place); this is the name of a French hunter who here concealed his property. It continues the practice of both the white and red hunters to leave their skins, &c. often suspended to poles, or laid over a pole placed upon two forked posts, In sight of the river, until their return from hunting. These deposits are considered as sacred, and few examples exist of their being plundered. After passing the entrance of a bay, which within must form a great lake during the inundation, great numbers of the long-leaf pine were observed; and the increased size of the canes along the river's bank, denoted a better and more elevated soil; on the left was a high hill (300 feet) covered with lofty pine trees.

The banks of the river present more the appearance of upland soil, the under stratum being a pale yellowish clay, and the alluvial soil of a dirty white, sur-

river; W.

long-leaf D; long leaf W.

### 129

mounted by a thin covering of a brown vegetable earth. The trees improve in appearance, growing to a considerable size and height, though yet inferior to those on the alluvial banks of the Mississippi. After passing the " Bayau de Hachis," on the left, points of high land, not subject to be overflowed, frequently touch the river, and the valley is said to be more than a league in breadth on both sides. On the left are pine hills called " Coe de Champignole." The river is not more than fifty or sixty yards wide. On the morning of the 20th they passed a number of sand beaches, and some rapids, but found good depth of water between them. A creek called " Chemin Convert," which forms a deep ravine in the high lands, here enters the river; almost immediately above this is a rapid where the water in the river is confined to a channel of about forty yards in width; above it they had to quit the main channel, on account of the shallowness and rapidity of the water, and pass along a narrow channel of only sixty feet wide; without a guide a stranger might take this passage for a creek.

Notwithstanding the lateness of the season, and the northern latitude they were in, they this day met with an alligator. The banks of the river are covered with cane or thick under brush, frequently so interwoven with thorns and briars as to be impenetrable. Birch, maple, holly, and two kinds of wood to which names have not yet been given, except " water side wood," are here met with; as also persimons and small black grapes. The margin of the river is fringed with a variety of plants and vines, among which are several species of convolvulus.

On the left they passed a hill and cliff one hundred feet perpendicular, crowned with pines, and called " Cote de Finn" (Fin's hill) from which a chain of high land continues some distance. The cliff presents the appearance of an ash colored clay. A little farther to the right is the Bayau d'Acasia (Locust creek). The river varies here from eighty to an

'Cote D; "Code W.

130

hundred yards in width, presenting frequent indications of iron along its banks, and some thin strata of iron ore. The ore is from half an inch to three inches in thickness.

On the morning of the 22d of November, they arrived at the road of the Caddoques Indian nation, leading to the Arkansa nation: a little beyond this is the Ecor a Fabri (Fabri's cliffs) from 80 to 100 feet high; and a little distance above, a smaller cliff called " Le Petit Ecor a Fabri" (the Little Cliff of Fabri): these cliffs appear chiefly to be composed of ash colored sand, with a sratum of clay at the base, such as runs all along under the banks of the river. Above these cliffs are several rapids; the current is swifter and denotes their ascent into a higher country; the water becomes clear, and equal to any in its very agreeable taste as drinking water. In the river are immense beds of gravel and sand, over which the water passes with great velocity in the season of its floods, carrying with it vast quantities of drift wood, which it piles up, in many places, to the height of twenty feet above the present surface, pointing out the difficulty and danger of navigation in certain times of the flood; accidents, however, are rare with the canoes of the country.

As the party ascended they found the banks of the river less elevated, being only from nine to twelve feet, and probably surmounted by the freshes some feet. The river becomes more obstructed by rapids, and sand and gravel beaches, among which are found fragments of stone of all forms, and a variety of colors, some highly polished and rounded by friction.— The banks of the river in this upper country suffer greatly by abrasion, one side and sometimes both being broken down by every flood.

At a place called " Auges d'Arclon," (Arclon's troughs) is laminated iron ore, and a stratum of black sand, very tenacious, shining with minute chrystals. The breadth of the river is here about eighty yards; in some places, however, it is enlarged by islands, in

Cadadoquis D; Chadadoquis W.

Ecor à Fabri D; Ecor a Frabri W.

cliff of Fabri); D; Cliff of Frabri): W.
stratum W.
this river. D, W.
swifter, W.

taste as a D; taste, and as W.

yards: W.

## 131

others, contracted to eighty or one hundred feet.— Rocks of a greyish color, and rather friable, are here found in many places on the river.* On the banks grow willows of a different form from those found below, and on the margin of the Mississippi; the last are very brittle; these on the contrary, are extremely pliant, resembling the osier, of which they are probably a species.†

At noon on the 24th, they arrived at the confluence of the lesser Missouri with the Washita; the former is a considerable branch, perhaps the fourth of the Washita, and comes in from the left hand. The hunters often ascend the Little Missouri, but are not inclined to penetrate far up, because it reaches near the great plains or priaries upon the Red river, visited by the Osage tribe of Indians, settled on Arkansa; these last frequently carry war into the Caddoques tribe settled on the Red river, about west, southwest from this place, and indeed they are reported not to spare any nation or people. They are prevented from visiting the head waters of the Washita by the steep hills in which they rise. These mountains are so difficult to travel over, that the savages not having an object sufficiently desirable, never attempt to penetrate to this river, and it is supposed to be unknown to the nation. The Caddoques (Cadaux, as the French pronounce the word) may be considered as Spanish Indians; they boast, and it is said with truth, that they never have imbrued their hands in the blood of a white man. It is said that the stream of the Little Missouri, some distance from its mouth flows over a bright splendid bed of mineral of a yellowish white color, (most probably martial pyrites) that thirty years ago, several of the inhabitants, hunters, worked upon this mine, and sent a quantity of

---

\* The banks rise into hills of free ſtone of a very ſharp and fine grit, fit for grind ſtones. The ſtrata irregular, inclining from 20d. to 30d. down the river.

† This is the Salix pentandria of Linæus.

---

prairies upon the red D, W.
the lesser Osage D, W.
Cadadoquis D; Chadadoquis W.

Cadadoquis (or Cadaux, D, W.

mouth, W.

20° to 30° W.

*Not in* D *or* W. *See Textual Introduction.*

**132**

the ore to the government at New-Orleans, and they were prohibited from working any more.

banks: W.

There is a great sameness in the appearance of the river banks ; the islands are skirted with osier, and immediately within, on the banks, grows a range of birch trees and some willows ; the more elevated banks are covered with cane, among which grows

dog wood, D, W.<br>Iron wood D; ironwood, W.

the oak, maple, elm, sycamore, ash, hickory, dog-wood, holly, iron-wood, &c. From the pilot they learned that there is a body of excellent land on the Little Missouri, particularly on the creek called the

"Bayou D; "Bayau W.

"Bayou a terre noire," which falls into it. This land extends to Red river and is connected with the great

prairies D, W. Cadaux D, W.

priaries which form the hunting grounds of the Caddo nation, consisting of about two hundred warriors. They are warlike, but frequently unable to defend themselves against the tribe of Osages, settled on the

Arcansa D, W.<br>prairies, D, W.

Arkansa river, who passing round the mountains at the head of the Washita, and along the priaries, which separate them from the main chain on the west, where

Arcansa D; Acansa W.<br>Cadaux D, W.

the waters of the Red and Arkansas river have their rise, pass into the Caddo country, and rob and plunder them.

The water in the river Washita rising, the party are enabled to pass the numerous rapids and shoals which they meet with in the upper country ; some of which are difficult of ascent. The general height of the main banks of the river is from six to twelve feet above the level of the water ; the land is better in quality, the canes, &c. shewing a more luxuriant vegetation. It is subject to inundation, and shews a brown soil mixed with sand. Near Cache a Macon

'cache à Maçon' (Masons D;<br>Cache Maçon (Maison's W.<br>mine: W.

(Mason's hiding place) on the right, they stopped to examine a supposed coal mine ; doctor Hunter, and the pilot, set out for this purpose, and at about a mile and a half north-west from the boat, in the bed of a creek,* they found a substance similar to what they had before met with under that name, though

Coal-mine W.

* Called Coal mine Creek.

**133**

more advanced towards a state of perfect coal. At the bottom of the creek, in a place then dry, was found detached pieces of from fifty to one hundred pounds weight, adjoining to which lay wood changing into the same substance. A stratum of this coal, six inches thick, lay on both sides of this little creek, over another of yellow clay, and covered by one foot of gravel; on the gravel is eight inches of loam, which bears a few inches of vegetable mould. This stratum of coal is about three feet higher than the water in the creek, and appears manifestly to have been at some period, the surface of the ground. The gravel and loam have been deposited there since, by the waters. Some pieces of this coal were very black and and solid, of a homogenous appearance, much resembling pit coal, but of less specific gravity. It does not appear sufficiently impregnated with bitumen, but may be considered as vegetable matter in the progress of transmutation to coal.

Below the " Bayou de l'eau Froide," which runs into the Washita from the right, the river is one hundred and seventy yards wide, flowing through tolerably good land. They passed a beautiful forest of pines, and on the 28th fell in with an old Dutch hunter and his party, consisting in all of five persons.

This man has resided forty years on the Washita, and before that period, has been up the Arkansa river, the White river, and the river St. Francis; the two last, he informs, are of difficult navigation, similar to the Washita, but the Arkansa river is of great magnitude, having a large and broad channel, and when the water is low, has sand banks, like those in the Mississippi. So far as he has been up it the navigation is safe and commodious, without impediments from rocks, shoals, or rapids; its bed being formed of mud & sand. The soil on it is of the first rate quality. The country is easy of access, being lofty open forests, unembarrassed by canes or under growth. The water is disagreeable to drink, being of a red color and brackish when the river is low.—

homogenous D; homogeneous W.

"Bayau W.

yards broad, flowing D; yards, flowing W.

up the Arcansa D, W.

has great sand D, W.

mud and sand W.

colour D, W.

134

A multitude of creeks which flow into the Arkansa furnish sweet water, which the voyager is obliged to carry with him for the supply of his immediate wants. This man confirms the account of silver being abundant up that river; he has not been so high as to see it himself, but says he received a silver pin from a hunter who assured him that he himself collected the virgin silver from the rock, out of which he made the epinglete by hammering it out. The tribe of the Osage live higher up than this position, but the hunters rarely go so high, being afraid of these savages, who are at war with all the world, and destroy all strangers they meet with. It is reported that the Arkansa nation, with a part of the Choctaws, Chickasaws, Shawneese, &c. have formed a league, and are actually gone; or going, 800 strong, against these depredators, with a view to destroy or drive them entirely off, and possess themselves of their fine priaries, which are most abuudant hunting ground, being plentifully stocked with buffaloe, elk, deer, bear, and every other beast of the chase common to those latitudes in America. This hunter having given information of a saline in their vicinity, from which he frequently supplied himself with salt, by evaporating the water, doctor Hunter, with a party, accompanied him, on the morning of the 29th of November, to the place. They found a saline, about a mile and a half north of the camp from whence they set out, and near a creek which enters the Washita a little above. It is situated in the bottom of the bed of a dry gully. The surrounding land is rich, and well timbered, but subject to inundation, except an Indian mount on the creek side, having a base of eighty or a hundred feet in diameter, and twenty feet high. After digging about three feet, through blue clay, they came to a quick-sand, from which the water flowed in abundance; its taste was salt and bitter, resembling that of water in the Ocean, in a second hole it required them to dig six feet before they reached the quick-sand, in doing which they threw up several

hunter, W.

Arcansa D, W.

prairies, D, W.
abundant W.

informs us of a saline or salt spring D;
information of a small spring in W.
supplied himself with salt by
evaporation D; supplied himself
by evaporating W.

feet diameter, H(o), W.

quicksand H(o), W.
abundance: W.
ocean. In W.

quicksand, H(o), W.

135

broken pieces of Indian pottery. The specific gravity, compared with the river, was, from the first pit, or that three feet deep, 1,02720, from the second pit, or that six feet deep, 1,02104, yielding a saline mass, from the evaporation of ten quarts, which, when dry, weighed eight ounces : this brine is, therefore, about the same strength as that of the ocean on our coast, and twice the strength of the famous licks in Kentucky called Bullet's lick, and Mann's lick, from which so much salt is made.

The "fourche de Cadaux," (Caddoques fork) which they passed on the morning of the 30th, is about one hundred yards wide at its entrance into the Washita, from the left : immediately beyond which, on the same side, the land is high, probably elevated three hundred feet above the water. The shoals and rapids here impede their progress. At noon they deduced their latitude, by observation, to be 34d. 11m. 37s. N. Receiving information of another salt lick, or saline, doctor Hunter landed, with a party, to view it. The pit was found in a low flat place, subject to be overflowed from the river ; it was wet and muddy, the earth on the surface yellow, but on digging through about four feet of blue clay, the salt water oozed from a quicksand. Ten quarts of this water produced, by evaporation, six ounces of a saline mass, which, from taste, was principally marine salt ; to the taste, however, it shewed an admixture of soda, and muriated magnesia, but the marine salt greatly preponderated. The specific gravity was about 1,0176, probably weakened from the rain which had fallen the day before. The ascent of the river becomes more troublesome, from the rapids and currents, particulariy at the " isle du bayau des Roches" (Rocky creek island) where it required great exertions, and was attended with some hazard to pass them. This island is three-fourths of a mile in length. The river presents a series of shoals, rapids, and small cataracts ; and they passed several points of

S

(Cadadoquis D, W.

34° 11′ 37″. D; 30°. 11′. 37″.W.

1.017647. D; 1.076, W.

**136**

high land, full of rocks and stones, much harder and more solid than they had yet met with.

The rocks were all silicious, with their fissures penetrated by sparry matter. Indications of iron were frequent, and fragments of poor ore were common, but no rich ore of that, or any other metal, was found. Some of the hills appear well adapted to the cultivation of the vine ; the soil being a sandy loam, with a considerable proportion of gravel, and a superficial covering of good vegetable black earth. The natural productions are, several varieties of oak, pine, dogwood, holly, &c. with a scattering undergrowth of whortleberry, hawthorn, china briar, and a variety of small vines.

Mellon D (Geom. Survey); Mallon, W.

Above the Isle de Mellon, the country wears another aspect, high lands and rocks frequently approach the river. The rocks in grain, resemble free stone, and are hard enough to be used as hand mill stones, to which purpose they are frequently applied. The quality of the lands improves, the stratum of vegetable earth being from six to twelve inches, of a dark-brown color, with an admixture of loam and sand. Below Deer Island they passed a stratum of free stone, fifty feet thick, under which is a quarry of imperfect slate in perpendicular layers. About a league from the river, and a little above the slate quarry, is

"Prairie D, W.

a considerable plain, called " Priarie de Champignole," often frequented by buffaloe. Some salt licks are found near it, and in many situations on both sides of this river, there are said to be salines which may hereafter be rendered very productive, and from which the future settlements may be abundantly supplied.

34° 21′ 25″. 5. W.

About four miles below the " chuttes," (falls) they, from a good observation, found the latitude 34d. 21m. 25s. 5. The land on either hand continues to improve in quality, with a sufficient stratum of dark earth of a brownish color. Hills frequently rise out of the level country, full of rocks and stones, hard and flinty, and often resembling Turkey oil stones. Of this kind was a promontory which came in from

**137**

the right hand, a little below the chuttes; at a distance it presented the appearance of ruined buildings and fortifications, and several insulated masses of rock, conveyed the idea of redoubts and out-works. This effect was heightened by the rising of a flock of swans which had taken their station in the water, at the foot of these walls. As the voyagers approached, the birds floated about majestically on the glassy surface of the water, and in tremulous accents seemed to consult upon means of safety. The whole was a sublime picture. In the afternoon of the third of December, they reached the chuttes, and found the falls to be occasioned by a chain of rocks of the same hard substance seen below, extending in the direction of north-east and south-west, quite across the river. The water passes through a number of breaches worn by the impetuosity of the torrent where it forms so many cascades. The chain of rock or hill on the left, appears to have been cut down to its present level by the abrasion of the waters. By great exertion, and lightening the boat, they passed the chuttes this evening, and encamped just above the cataracts, and within the hearing of their incessant roar.

breaches, D; branches W.

Immediately above the chuttes, the current of the water is slow, to another ledge of hard free stone; the reach between is spacious, not less than two hundred yards wide, and terminated by a hill, three hundred feet high, covered with beautiful pines: this is a fine situation for building. In latitude 34d. 25m. 48s. they passed a very dangerous rapid, from the number of rocks which obstruct the passage of the water, and break it into foam. On the right of the rapid is a high rocky hill covered with very handsome pine woods. The strata of the rock has an inclination of 30d. to the horizon in the direction of the river descending. This hill may be three hundred or three hundred and fifty feet high: a border or list of green cane skirts the margin of the river, beyond which generally rises a high, and sometimes a barren

34° 25′ 48″ W.

30° W.

**138**

hill. Near another rapid they passed a hill on the left, containing a large body of blue slate. A small distance above the bayau de Saline they had to pass a rapid of one hundred and fifty yards in length, and four feet and a half fall, which, from its velocity, the French have denominated "La Cascade." Below the cascade there are rocky hills on both sides composed of very hard free stone. The stone in the bed of the river, and which has been rolled from the upper country, was of the hardest flint, or of a quality resembling the Turkey oil stone. "Fourche au Tigree," (Tyger's creek) which comes in from the right, a little above the cascade, is said to have many extensive tracts of rich level land upon it. The rocky hills here frequently approach the Washita on both sides; rich bottoms are nevertheless not infrequent, and the upland is sometimes of moderate elevation and tolerably level. The stones and rocks here met with have their fissures filled by sparry and chrystaline matter.

Wild turkies become more abundant and less difficult of approach than below; and the howl of the wolves is heard during the night.

To the "Fourche of Calfat," (Caulker's creek) where the voyage terminates, they found level and good land on the right and high hills on the left hand. After passing over a very precipitous rapid, seemingly divided into four steps or falls, one of which was at least fifteen inches in perpendicular height, and which together could not be less than five and a half feet, they arrived at Ellis's camp, a small distance below the Fourche au Calfat, where they stopped on the sixth of December, as the pilot considered it the most convenient landing from whence to carry their necessary baggage to the hot springs, the distance being about three leagues. There is a creek about two leagues higher up, called "bayau des sources chauds," (hot spring creek) upon the banks of which the hot springs are situated at about two leagues from its mouth. The banks of it are hilly, and the road less eligible than from Ellis's camp.

creek), W.

nevertheless are not infrequent D;
are nevertheless infrequent W.

Ellis's D; Elles's W.

**139**

On ascending the hill, to encamp, they found the land very level and good, some plants in flower, and a great many evergreen vines ; the forest oak with an admixture of other woods. The latitude of this place is 34d. 27m. 32s. 5. The ground on which they encamped was about fifty feet above the water in the river, and supposed to be thirty feet higher than the inundations. Hills of considerable height, and clothed with pine, were in view, but the land around, and extending beyond their view, lies handsomely for cultivation. The superstratum is of a blackish brown color, upon a yellow basis, the whole intermixed with gravel and blue schistus, frequently so far decomposed as to have a strong allumnious taste. From their camp, on the Washita, to the hot springs, a distance of about nine miles, the first six miles of the ro dare in a westward y direction without many sinuosities, and the remainder northwardly, which courses are necesary to avoid some very steep hills. In this distance, they found three principal salt licks, and some inferior ones, which are all frequented by buffaloe, deer, &c. The soil around them is a white, tenacious clay, probably fit for potters' ware ; hence the name of " glaise," which the French hunters have bestowed upon most of the licks, frequented by the beasts of the forest, many of which exhibit no saline impregnation. The first two miles from the river camp is over level land of the second rate quality ; the timber chiefly oak, intermixed with other trees common to the climate, and a few scattering pines. Further on, the lands, on either hand rise into gently swelling hills, covered with handsome pine woods. The road passes along a valley frequently wet by the numerous rills and springs of excellent water which issue from the foot of the hills. Near the hot springs the hills become more elevated, steeper of ascent and rocky. They are here called mountains, although none of them in view exceed four or five hundred feet in altitude. It is said that mountains of more than five times the elevation of these

34° 27′ 31″.5. D, W.

blackish-brown W.

aluminous D; allumnious W.

the first six miles were in a general westerly direction with D; miles of the road is in a westerly direction without W; miles of the road are in a westwardly direction without N.

**140**

hills are to be seen in the north-west, towards the sources of the Washita. One of them is called the glass, chrystal, or shining mountain, from the vast number of hexagonal prisms of very transparent and colourless chrystal which are found on its surface; they are generally surmounted by pyramids at one end, rarely on both. These chrystals do not produce a double refraction of the rays of light. Many searches have been made over these mountains for the precious metals, but it is believed without success.

At the hot springs they found an open log cabbin, and a few huts of split boards, all calculated for summer encampment, and which had been erected by persons resorting to the springs for the recovery of their health.

They slightly repaired these huts, or cabbins, for their accommodation during the time of their detention at the springs, for the purpose of examining them and the surrounding country; and making such astronomical observations as were necessary for ascertaining their geographical position.

It is understood that the hot springs are included within a grant of some hundred acres, granted by the late Spanish commandant of the Washita, to some of his friends, but it is not believed that a regular patent was ever issued for the place; and it cannot be asserted that residence, with improvement here, form a plea to claim the land upon.

On their arrival they immediately tasted the waters of the hot springs, that is, after a few minutes cooling, for it was impossible to approach it with the lips when first taken up, without scalding; the taste does not differ from that of good water rendered hot by culinary fire.

On the 10th they visited all the hot springs. They issue on the east side of a brook at the base of a hill, except one spring, which rises on the west bank of the brook where the huts are. From the small quantity of calcarious matter yet deposited, the west

*lines 36–39*:
They issue from the side and foot of a hill placed on the east side of the narrow valley where we are hutted, one small spring only rises out of the face of the west bank of the creek; D; They issue on the east side of the valley, where the huts are, except one spring, which rises on the west bank of the creek, from the sides and foot of a hill. W.

36

**141**

ern spring does not appear to be of long standing; a natural conduit probably passes under the bed of the creek, and supplies it. There are four principal springs rising immediately on the east bank of the creek, one of which may be rather said to spring out of the gravel bed of the run ; a fifth, a smaller one than that above mentioned, as rising on the west side of the creek ; and a sixth, of the same magnitude, the most northwardly, and rising near the bank of the creek ; these are all the sources that merit the name of springs, near the huts; but there is a considerable one below, and all along, at intervals, the warm water oozes out, or drops from the bank into the creek, as appears from the condensed vapours floating along the margin of the creek where the drippings occur.

vapor D; vapour W.

The hill from which the hot springs issue is of a conical form, terminating at the top with a few loose fragments of rock, covering a flat space twenty-five feet in diameter. Although the figure of the hill is conical it is not entirely insulated, but connected with the neighbouring hills by a very narrow ridge. The primitive rock of this hill, above the base, is principally silicious, some part of it being of the hardest flint, others a freestone extremely compact and solid, and of various colors. The base of the hill, and for a considerable extent, is composed of a blackish blue schistus, which divides into perpendicular laminæ like blue slate. The water of the hot springs is, therefore, delivered from the silicious rock, generally invisible at the surface, from the mass of calcarious matter with which it is incrusted, or rather buried, and which is perpetually precipitating from the water of the springs : a small proportion of iron, in the form of red calx, is also deposited ; the color of which is frequently distinguishable in the lime.

laminæ D; lamina W.

of a red D, W. colour D, W.

In ascending the hill several patches of rich black earth are found, which appear to be formed by the decomposition of the calcarious matter; in other situations the superficial earth is penetrated or encrusted, by limestone, with fine laminæ, or minute fragments of iron ore.

penetrated, W.
laminæ D; lamina, W.

142

must formerly D, W.

The water of the hot springs must frequently have issued at a greater elevation in the hill, and run over the surface, having formed a mass of calcarious rock one hundred feet perpendicular, by its deposition. In this high situation they found a spring, whose temperature was 140d. of Fahrenheit's thermometer.

140° of Farenheight's W.

After passing the calcarious region they found the primitive hill covered by a forest of not very large trees, consisting chiefly of oak, pine, cedar, holly, hawthorn, and others common to the climate, with a great variety of vines, some said to produce black, and others yellow grapes, both excellent in their kinds. The soil is rocky, interspersed with gravel, sand, and fine vegetable mould. On reaching the height of two hundred feet perpendicular, a considerable change in the soil was observable ; it was stony and gravelly, with a superficial coat of black earth, but immediately under it lies a stratum of fat, tenacious, soapy, red clay,

colour D, W.

inclining to the color of bright Spanish snuff, homogeneous, with scarcely any admixture of sand, no saline, but rather a soft agreeable taste ; the timber diminishes, and the rocks increase in size to the summit. The whole height is estimated at three hundred feet above the level of the valley.

On examining the four principal springs, those which yield the greatest quantity of water, are of the highest temperature, No. 1 was found to raise the

line 28: degree signs in W. }
N°. 2 145°- D; No. 2 to 154°. W. }
Farenheit's W.

mercury to 150d. No. 2 to 145d. No. 3 to 136d. and No. 4 to 132 degrees of Fahrenheit's thermometer; the last is on the west side of the creek ; No. 3 is a small bason in which there is a considerable quantity of green matter, having much the appearance of a vegetable body, but detached from the bottom, yet connected with it by something like a stem, which rests in calcarious matter. The body of one of these pseudo plants was from four to five inches in diameter ; the bottom a smooth film of some tenacity, and the upper surface divided into ascending fibres of half

28

three fourths W.

or three-fourths of an inch long, resembling the gills of a fish, in transverse rows. A little further on was

**143**

another small muddy basin, in which the water was warm to the finger : in it was a vermes about half an inch long, moving with a serpentine or vermicular motion. It was invariably observed, that the green matter forming on the stones and leaves covered a stratum of calcarious earth, sometimes a little hard, or brittle, at others soft and imperfect. From the bottom of one of the hot springs a frequent ebulliti- | ebulition D, W.
on of gas was observed, which not having the means of collecting, they could not ascertain its nature ; it | nature: W.
was not inflammable, and there is little doubt of its being carbonic acid, from the quantity of lime, and the iron, held in solution by the water.

They made the following rough estimate of the quantity of water delivered by the springs. There are four principal springs, two of inferior note ; one rising out of the gravel, and a number of drippings and drainings, all issuing from the margin, or from under the rock which overhangs the creek. Of the four first mentioned, three deliver nearly equal quan- tities, but No. 1, the most considerable, delivers a- bout five times as much as one of the other three ; the two of inferior note may, together, be equal to one ; and all the droppings, and small springs, are probably underrated at double the quantity of one of the three ; that is, all together, they will deliver a quantity equal to eleven times the water issuing from the one most commodiously situated for measure- ment. This spring filled a vessel of eleven quarts in eleven seconds, hence the whole quantity of hot wa- ter delivered from the springs at the base of the hill is 165 gallons in a minute, or 3771 1-2 hogsheads | 3771½ D, W.
in 24 hours, which is equal to a handsome brook, and might work an overshot mill. In cool weather condensed vapour is seen rising out of the gravel bed of the creek, from springs which cannot be taken into account. During the summer and fall the creek receives little or no water but what is supplied by the hot springs ; at that season itself is a hot bath, too hot, indeed, near the springs ; so that a person may

T

**144**

choose the temperature most agreeable to himself, by selecting a natural basin near to, or farther from, the principal springs.   At three or four miles below the springs the water is tepid and unpleasant to drink.

From the western mountain, estimated to be of equal height with that from which the hot springs flow, there are several fine prospects.   The valley of the Washita, comprehended between the hills on either side, seemed a perfect flat, and about twelve miles wide.   On all hands were seen the hills, or mountains, as they are here called, rising behind each other.   In the direction of north, the most distant were estimated to be fifty miles off, and are supposed to be those of the Arkansa river, or the rugged mountains which divide the waters of the Arkansa from those of the Washita, and prevent the Osage Indians from visiting the latter, of which they are supposed ignorant ; otherwise their excursions here would prevent this place from being visited by white persons, or other Indians.   In a southwest direction, at about forty miles distance, is seen a perfectly level ridge, supposed to be the high priaries of the Red river.

Notwithstanding the severity of the weather, a considerable number, and some variety of plants were in flower, and others retained their verdure ; indeed the ridge was more temperate than the valley below ; there it was cold, damp, and penetrating ; here dry, and the atmosphere mild.   Of the vegetables growing here was a species of cabbage ; the plants grow with expanded leaves, spreading on the ground, of a deep green, with a shade of purple : the taste of the cabbage was plainly predominant, with an agreeable warmth inclining to that of the radish ; several tap-roots penetrated into the soil, of a white color, having the taste of horse-radish, but much milder. A quantity of them taken to the camp and dressed, proved palatable and mild.   It is not probable that cabbage seed has been scattered on this ridge ; the hunters ascending this river have always had different objects. Until further elucidation, this cabbage must

of whose existence D; of whom W.

prairies D, W.

cabbage: W.

**145**

be considered as indigenous to this sequestered quarter, and may be denominated the radish cabbage with purple flowers, of the Washita.     They found a plant, then green, called by the French "racine rouge," (red root) which is said to be a specific in female obstructions; it has also been used, combined with the China root, to dye red, the last probably acting as a mordant.     The top of this ridge is covered with rocks of a flinty kind, and so very hard as to be improper for gun flints, for when applied to that use the stone soon digs cavities in the hammer of the lock. This hard stone is generally white, but frequently clouded with red, brown, black, and other colors. Here and there fragments of iron stone were met with, and where a tree had been overturned, its roots brought to view fragments of schistus, which were suffering decomposition from exposure to the atmosphere.     On digging where the slope of the hill was precipitous, they found the second stratum to be a reddish clay, resembling that found on the conical hill, east of the camp.     At two-thirds down the hill, the rock was a hard freestone, intermixed with fragments of flint, which had probably rolled from above. Still lower was found a blue schistus, in a state tending to decomposition where exposed to the atmosphere, but hard and resembling coarse slate in the interior.     Many stones had the appearance of Turkey oil stones; the foot of the hill expands into good farming lands.

Dr. Hunter, upon examining the waters of the hot springs, obtained the following results;

It differed nothing from the hot water in smell or taste, but caused a slight eructation shortly after drinking it.

Its specific gravity is equal to rain or distilled water.

It gave to litmus paper, a slight degree of redness, evincing the presence of the carbonic acid, or fixed air, sulphuric acid threw down a few detached particles.     Oxalat of ammoniac caused a deposition and white cloud, shewing the presence of a small portion

cabbage radish D, W.

gun flints; D; gun-flints W. use it soon D, W.

oil stones: at the foot of the hill it expands W.

Litmus H; litamus W.
or fixed air.- H; or fixed air sulphuric, and threw W.
Oxalat H; Oxylat W.

## 146

of lime. Prusiat of potash produced a slight and scarcely perceptible tinge of blue, designating the presence of a small quantity of iron.

Sixteen pounds of water evaporated to dryness left ten grains of a grey powder, which proved to be lime.

The myrtle wax tree grows in the vicinity of the springs. At the season in which the voyagers were there, the wax was no longer green, but had changed its colour to a greyish-white, from its long exposure to the weather. The berry is less than the smallest garden pea, approaching to an oval in form. The nucleus, or real seed, is the size of the seed of a radish, and is covered with a number of kidney shaped glands, of a brown color and sweet taste ; these glands secrete the wax which completely envelopes them, and, at this season, gives to the whole the appearance of an imperfectly white berry. This is a valuable plant and merits attention ; its favorite position is a dry soil, rather poor, and looking down upon the water. It is well adapted to ornament the margins of canals, lakes or rivulets. The cassina yapon, is equally beautiful, and proper for the same purpose ; it grows here along the banks of this stony creek, intermingled with the myrtle, and bears a beautiful little red berry, very much resembling the red currant.

The rock through which the hot springs either pass or trickle over, appears undermined by the waters of the creek. The hot water is continually depositing calcarious, and, perhaps, some silicious matter, forming new rocks, always augmenting and projecting their promontories over the running water of the creek, which prevents its formation below the surface. Wherever this calcarious crust is seen spreading over the bank and margin of the creek, there, most certainly, the hot water will be found, either running over the surface, or through some channel, perhaps below the new rock, or dripping from the edges of the overhanging precipice. The progress of nature in the formation of this new rock is curious, and worthy the attention of the mineralogist. When

*line 10*: examined the berries with the microscope; D; berry when examined by a microscope, is W. nucleus D; nuclus, W.

cultivation; D; attention: W.

purpose: W.

10

**147**

the hot water issues from the fountain, it frequently spreads over a superficies of some extent ; so far as it reaches, on either hand, there is a deposition of, or growth of green matter.   Several laminæ of this green matter will be found lying over each other, and immediately under, and in contact with the inferior lamina, which is not thicker than paper, is found a whitish substance resembling a coagulum ; when viewed with a microscope, this last is also found to consist of several, sometimes a good number of la-minæ, of which that next the green is the finest and thinnest, being the last formed ; those below increas-ing in thickness and tenacity until the last terminates in a soft, earthy matter, which reposes on the more solid rock.   Each lamina of the coagulum is pene-trated in all its parts by calcarious grains, extremely minute, and divided in the more recent web, but much larger and occupying the whole of the inferior lamina.   The under stratum is continually consoli-dating, and adding bulk and height to the rock. When this acquires such an elevation as to stop the passage of the water, it finds another course over the rock, hill, or margin of the creek, forming, in turn, accumulations of matter over the whole of the adja-cent space.   When the water has found itself a new channel, the green matter, which sometimes acquires a thickness of half an inch, is speedily converted into a rich vegetable earth, and becomes the food of plants. The surface of the calcarious rock also decomposes and forms the richest black mould intimately mixed with a considerable portion of soil ; plants and trees vegetate luxuriantly on it.

On examining a piece of ground upon which the snow dissolved as it fell, and which was covered with herbage, they found, in some places, a calcarious crust on the surface; but in general a depth of from five inches to a foot of the richest black mould. The surface was sensibly warm to the touch.   In the air the mercury in the thermometer stood at 44d ; when placed four inches under the surface, and covered

laminæ D, N; lamina W.

lamina D, W, N.

laminæ, D, N; lamina W.

the last reposing on D; which reposes in W.

under stratum D; understratum W.

44°; W.

**148**

68°; W.

8o°. W.

130°. W.

gradually became whiter D;
became gradually whiter W.

formed a flat superficies of silicious
lime stone; D, W.

perpendr.; from that division D;
perpendicular; in this region W.

with earth, it rose rapidly to 68d. ; and upon the calcarious rock, eight inches beneath the surface, it rose to 80 degrees. This result was uniform over the whole surface, which was about a quarter of an acre.

On searching they found a spring, about fifteen inches under the surface, in the water of which the thermometer shewed a temperature of 130d. Beneath the black mould was found a brown mixture of lime and silex, very loose and divisible, apparently in a state of decomposition, and progressing towards the formation of black mould; under this brownish mass it became whiter and harder, to the depth of from six to twelve inches, where it was a calcarious sparkling stone. It was evident that the water had passed over this place, and forms a flat superficies of lime stone; and that its position, nearly level, had facilitated the accumulation of earth, in proportion as the decomposition advanced. Similar spots of ground were found higher up the hill, resembling little savannas, near which hot springs were always discovered, which had once flowed over them. It appears probable that the hot water of the springs, at an early period, had all issued from its grand reservoir in the hill, at a much greater elevation than at present. The calcarious crust may be traced up, in most situations on the west side of the hill facing the creek and valley, to a certain height, perhaps one hundred feet perpendicular; above the calcarious region the hill rises precipitously, and is studded with hard silicious stones; below, the descent is more gradual, and the soil is calcarious black earth. It is easy to discriminate the primitive hill from that which has accumulated, by precipitation, from the water of the springs; this last is entirely confined to the west side of the hill, and washed at its base by the waters of the creek, no hot springs being visible in any other part of its circumference. By actual measurement along the base of the hill the influence of the springs is found to extend seventy perches, in a direction a

**149**

little to the east of north; along the whole of this space the springs have deposited stony matter, calcarious, with perhaps an addition of silex. The accumulation of calcarious matter is more considerable at the north end of the hill than at the south; the first may be above a hundred feet perpendicular, but sloping much more gradually than the primitive hill above, until it approaches the creek, where not unfrequently it terminates in a precipice of from six to twenty feet. The difference between the primitive and secondary hill is so striking that a superficial observer must notice it; the first is regularly very steep and studded with rock and stone of the hardest flint, and other silicious compounds, and a superficies of two or three inches of good mould covers a red clay; below, on the secondary hill, which carries evident marks of recent formation, no flint, or silicious stone is found; the calcarious rock conceals all from view, and is, itself, frequently covered by much fine rich earth. It would seem that this compound, precipitated from the hot waters, yields easily to the influence of the atmosphere; for where the waters cease to flow over any portion of the rock, it speedily decomposes; probably more rapidly from the heat communicated from the interior of the hill, as insulated masses of the rock are observed to remain without change.

The cedar, the wax myrtle, and the cassina yapon, all evergreens, attached themselves particularly to the calcarious region, and seem to grow and thrive even in the clefts of the rock.

A spring, enjoying a freedom of position, proceeds with great regularity in depositing the matter it holds in solution; the border or rim of its basin forms an elevated ridge, from whence proceeds a glasis all around; when the waters have flowed for some time over one part of the brim, this becomes more elevated, and the water has to seek a passage where there is less resistance; thus forming, in miniature, a crater, resembling in shape the conical summit of a

north: W.

silex, or chrystalized lime. D, W.

than the south; W.

steep, W.

attach D, W.

the solid rock. D, W.

glacis D, W;
around; when D; around, where W.
brim, D; brim; W.

150

above, the progress D;
above the progress W.

into the run D; in the run W.

130°. W.

examination by W.
*line 26*: was spread upon D; ⎱
spreads itself on W. ⎰
rise W.

microscope it W.

belief in W.

color D; colour W.

volcano. The hill being steep above, the progress of petrifaction is stopped on that side, and the waters continue to flow and spread abroad, incrusting the whole face of the hill below. The last formed calcarious border of the circular basin is soft, and easily divided ; at a small depth it is more compact ; and at the depth of six inches it is generally hard white stone. If the bottom of the basin is stirred up, a quantity of the red calx of iron rises, and escapes over the summit of the crater.

Visitants to the hot springs having observed shrubs and trees with their roots in the hot water, have been induced to try experiments, by thrusting branches of trees into the run of hot water. Some branches of the wax myrtle were found thrust into the bottom of a spring run, the water of which was 130d. by Fahrenheit's thermometer ; the foliage and fruit of the branch were not only sound and healthy, but at the surface of the water roots were actually sprouting from it : on pulling it up the part which had penetrated the hot mud was found decayed.

The green substance discoverable at the bottom of the hot springs, and which at first sight have the appearance of plush, on examination with the microscope, was found to be a vegetable production. A film of green matter spreads itself over on the calcarious base, from which rises fibres more than half an inch in length, forming a beautiful vegetation. Before the microscope, it sparkled with innumerable nodules of lime, some part of which was beautifully chrystalized. This circumstance might cause a doubt of its being a true vegetable, but its great resemblance to some of the mosses, particularly the byssi, and the discovery which Mr. Dunbar made of its being the residence of animal life, confirmed his belief of its being a true moss. After a diligent search he discovered a very minute shell fish, of the bivalve kind, inhabiting this moss ; its shape nearly that of the fresh water muscle : the color of the shell a greyish brown, with spots of a purplish color. When the

26

**151**

animal is undisturbed it opens the shell, and thrusts out four legs, very transparent, and articulated like those of a quadruped ; the extremities of the fore legs are very slender and sharp, but those of the hind legs somewhat broader, apparently armed with minute toes : from the extremity of each shell issues three or four forked hairs, which the animal seems to possess the power of moving ; the fore legs are probably formed for making incisions into the moss for the purpose of procuring access to the juices of the living plant, upon which, no doubt, it feeds : it may be provided with a probosis, although it did not appear while the animal was under examination : the hind legs are well adapted for propelling it in its progress over the moss, or through the water ; the largest did not exceed one fiftieth of an inch in length.

It would be desirable to ascertain the cause of that perpetual fire which keeps up the high temperature of so many springs as flow from this hill, at a considerable distance from each other : upon looking around, however, sufficient data for the solution of the difficulty are not discoverable. Nothing of a volcanic nature is to be seen in this country ; neither could they learn that any evidence in favor of such a supposition was to be found in the mountains connected with this river. An immense bed of dark blue schistus appears to form the base of the hot spring hill, and of all those in its neighborhood ; the bottom of the creek is formed of it ; and pieces are frequently met with rendered soft by decomposition, and possessing a strong alumnious taste, requiring nothing but lixiviation and chrystalization to complete the manufacture of alum. As bodies undergoing chemical changes generally produce an alteration of temperature, the heat of these springs may be owing to the disengagement of chaloric, caused by the decomposition of the schistus : another, and perhaps a more satisfactory cause may be assigned ; it is well known, that within the circle of the waters of this river vast beds of martial pyrites exist ; they have not yet,

U

water. *end of paragraph,* W (*last sentence of paragraph in* N *substantially from* D).

produce D; produced W.

chaloric, or the decomposition W.

assigned: W.

**152**

however, been discovered in the vicinage of the hot springs, but may, nevertheless, form immense beds under the bases of these hills ; and as in one place at least, there is evidence of the presence of bitumen,* the union of these agents will, in the progress of de-composition, by the admission of air and moisture, produce degrees of heat capable of supporting the phenomena of the hot springs. No sulphuric acid is present in this water ; the springs may be supplied by the vapor of heated water, ascending from caverns where the heat is generated, or the heat may be im-mediately applied to the bottom of an immense natu-ral caldron of rock, contained in the bowels of the hill, from which as a reservoir the springs may be supplied.

A series of accurate observations determined the latitude of the hot springs to be 34d. 31m. 4s. 16 N. and long. 6h. 11m. 25s. or 92d. 50m. 45s. west from the meridian of Greenwich.

While Mr. Dunbar was making arrangements for transporting the baggage back to the river camp, doc-tor Hunter, with a small party, went on an excur-sion into the country. He left the hot springs on the morning of the 27th, and after travelling sometimes over hills and steep craggy mountains with narrow valleys between them, then up the valleys and gene-rally by the side of a branch emptying into the Wash-ita, they reached the main branch of the Calfat in the evening, about twelve miles from the springs. The stones they met with during the first part of the day were silicious, of a whitish-grey, with flints, white, cream-colored, red, &c. The beds of the rivulets, and often a considerable way up the hills, shewed immense bodies of schistus, both blue and grey, some of it efflorescing and tasting strongly of alum. The latter part of the day, they travelled over and

34° 31′ 4″, 16 N. and long 6h. 11′ 25″, or 92° 50′ 45″ west W.

* Having thrust a stick down into the crater of one of the springs, at some distance up the hill, several drops of petroleum, or naptha, rose and spread upon the surface ; it ceased to rise after three or four attempts.

**153**

between hills of black, hard and compact flint in shapeless masses, with schist as before. On ascending these high grounds you distinctly perceive the commencement of the piney region, beginning at the height of sixty or seventy feet and extending to the top. The soil in these narrow valleys is thin and full of stones. The next day, which was stormy, they reached a branch of the bayau de saline, which stretches towards the Arkansa, and empties into the Washita many leagues below, having gone about twelve miles. The mountains they had passed being of the primitive kind which seldom produce metals, and having hitherto seen nothing of a metallic kind, a little poor iron ore excepted, and the face of the country, as far as they could see, presenting the same aspect; they returned to the camp, at the hot springs, on the evening of the thirtieth, by another route, in which they met with nothing worthy notice.

    In consequence of the rains which had fallen, Mr. Dunbar, and those who were transporting the baggage to the river camp, found the road watry. The soil on the flat lands under the stratum of vegetable mould is yellowish, and consists of decomposed schistus, of which there are immense beds in every stage of dissolution, from the hard stone recently uncovered and partially decomposed to the yellow and apparently homogenous earth. The covering of vegetable earth between the hills and the river is, in most places, sufficiently thick to constitute a good soil, being from four to six inches; and it is the opinion of the people upon the Washita, that wheat will grow here to great perfection. Although the higher hills, three hundred to six hundred feet in height, are very rocky, yet the inferior hills, and the sloping bases of the first, are generally covered with a soil of a middling quality. The natural productions are sufficiently luxuriant, consisting chiefly of black and red oak, intermixed with a variety of other woods, and a considerable undergrowth. Even on these rocky hills are three or four species of vines, said to produce annually an

minerals or metals H.
of a mineral kind W.

homogenious D; homogeneous W.

**154**

abundance of excellent grapes. A great variety of plants which grow here, some of which in their season are said to produce flowers highly ornamental, would probably reward the researches of the botanist.

On the morning of the 8th January, 1805, the party left Ellis's on the river camp, where they had been detained for several days, waiting for such a rise in the waters of the river, as would carry their boat in safety over the numerous rapids below. A rise of about six feet, which had taken place the evening before, determined them to move this morning; and they passed the chuttes about one o'clock. They stopped to examine the rocky promontory below these falls, and took some specimens of the stone which so much resembles the Turkey oil stone. It appears too hard. The strata of this chain were observed to run perpendicularly nearly east and west, crossed by fissures at right angles from five to eight feet apart: the laminæ from one fourth of an inch to five inches in thickness. About a league below, they landed at Whetstone hill and took several specimens. This projecting hill is a mass of greyish blue schistus of considerable hardness, and about twenty feet perpendicular, not regularly so; and the laminæ are from a quarter to two inches in thickness, but do not split with an even surface.

They landed again on the morning of the 9th, in sight of the bayou de la priarie de champignole, to examine and take specimens of some free stone and blue slate. The slate is a blue schistus, hard, brittle, and unfit for the covering of a house: none proper for that purpose have been discovered, except on the Calfat, which Dr. Hunter met with in one of his excursions.

On the evening of the 10th they encamped near Arclon's Troughs, having been only three days in descending the distance which took them thirteen to ascend. They stopped some time at the camp of a Mr. Le Fevre. He is an intelligent man, a native of the Illinois, but now residing at the Arkansas. He came

promontory D; promontary W.

laminæ D; lamina W.

so, and from a quarter W.
does not W.

Bayou de la Prairie D; bayau de
la prairie W.

**155**

here with some Delaware and other Indians, whom he had fitted out with goods, and receives their peltry, fur, &c. at a stipulated price, as it is brought in by the hunters. Mr. Le Fevre-possesses considerable knowledge of the interior of the country; he confirms the accounts before obtained, that the hills or mountains which give rise to this little river are in a manner insulated; that is, they are entirely shut in and inclosed by the immense plains or priaries which extend beyond the Red river, to the south, and beyond the Missouri, or at least some of the branches, to the north, and range along the eastern base of the great chain, or dividing ridge, commonly known by the name of the sand hills, which separate the waters of the Mississippi from those which fall into the Pacific ocean. The breadth of this great plain is not well ascertained. It is said by some to be at certain parts, or in certain directions, not less than two hundred leagues; but it is agreed by all who have a knowledge of the western country, that the mean breadth is at least two thirds of that quantity. A branch of the Missouri called river Platte, or Shallow river, is said to take its rise so far south as to derive its first waters from the neighbourhood of the sources of the Red and Arkansa rivers. By the expression plains or priaries in this place is not to be understood a dead flat, resembling certain savannas, whose soil is stiff and impenetrable, often under water, and bearing only a coarse grass resembling reeds; very different are the western priaries, which expression signifies only a country without timber. These priaries are neither flat nor hilly, but undulating into gently swelling lawns, and expanding into spacious valleys, in the middle of which is always found a little timber growing on the banks of brooks and rivulets of the finest waters. The whole of these priaries are represented to be composed of the richest and most fertile soil; the most luxuriant and succulent herbage covers the surface of the earth, interspersed with millions of flowers and flowering shrubs,

prairies D, W.

its branches, D, W.

of this quantity; D; of that distance, W.

prairies D, W.

prairies, D, W.

prairies D, W.

in the center of D, W.
of brooks D; of the brooks W.

prairies D, W.

## 156

kinds. D, W.
prairies, W.
it was only W.

landscape W.

*line 12*: savages and by immense D; ⎱
savages, and by the immense W. ⎰
(Bison) which people those
countries; D; (bison) which people
these countries. W.
mountains; W.
retrograde D; retrogade W.

subjected W.

territory, W.

together: W.
mountains D; mountain W.

comparatively D, W.

so extremely abundant, D, W.

Nacokdoches D; Nacogdoches W.

of the most ornamental kind.    Those who have viewed only a skirt of these priaries, speak of them with enthusiasm, as if it were only there that nature was to
be found truly perfect ; they declare, that the fertility
and beauty of the rising grounds, the extreme richness of the vales,  the coolness and excellent quality
of  the  water found in every  valley,  the  salubrity
of the atmosphere,  and above all  the grandeur of
the  enchanting  landscape,  which this country presents, inspire the soul  with sensations not to be felt
in any other region of the globe.    This paradise is
now very thinly inhabited by a few tribes of savages,
but immense herds of wild cattle, (bison) are spread
over  those  countries.    The  cattle  perform  regular
migrations,  according  to  the  seasons,  from south to
north, and from the plains to the mountains : and in
due time, taught by their instincts, take a retrogade
direction.    These  tribes  move  in  the  rear  of  the
herds, and pick up stragglers, and such as lag behind,
which  they  kill  with the bow and  arrow,  for  their
subsistence.    This  country  is  not subject  to  those
sudden deluges of  rain which in most hot countries
and even in the Mississippi Territory, tear up and
sweep  away  with  irresistible  fury,  the  crop and soil
together ;  on  the  contrary,  rain  is  said  to  become
more rare in proportion as the great chain of mountains is approached ;  and  it  would  seem  that within
the sphere of  the  attraction  of these elevated ridges,
little or no rain falls on the adjoining  plains.    This
relation  is  the  more  credible,  as in  that respect our
new country may resemble other flat or comparitive-
ly  low  countries,  similarly  situated :  such  as  the
country lying between the Andes and the western Pacific ;  the  plains  are  supplied  with  nightly dews so
abundant, as to have the effect of refreshing showers
of rain ; and the spacious valleys, which are extremely level,  may with facility,  be  watered by  the rills
and brooks which are never absent from these situations.    Such  is  the  description of the  better known
country lying to the south of Red river, from Naga-

12

**157**

doches towards St. Antoine, in the province of Texas ; the richest crops are said to be produced there
without rain ; but agriculture in that quarter is at a
low ebb ; the small quantities of maize furnished by
the country, is said to be raised without cultivation.
A rude opening is made in the earth, sufficient to deposit the grain, at the distance of four or five feet, in
irregular squares, and the rest is left to nature. The
soil is tender, spongy and rich, and seems always to
retain humidity sufficient, with the bounteous dews
of Heaven, to bring the crops to maturity.

The Red and Arkansa rivers, whose courses are
very long, pass through portions of this fine country.
They are both navigable to an unknown distance by
boats of proper construction ; the Arkansa river is,
however, understood to have greatly the advantage
with respect to the facility of navigation. Some difficult passages are met with on the Red river below
the Natchitoches, after which it is good for fifty or
sixty leagues, (probably computed leagues of the
country, about two miles each); there the voyager
meets with a very serious obstacle, the commencement of the " raft," as it is called ; that is, a natural
covering which conceals the whole river for an extent of 30 or 35 leagues at irregular intervals, continually augmenting by the drift-wood brought down
by every considerable fresh. This covering, which
for a considerable time was only drift-wood, now
supports a vegetation of every thing abounding in the
neighboring forest, not excepting trees of a considerable size ; and the river may be frequently passed
without any knowledge of its existence. It is said
that the annual inundation is opening for itself a new
passage through the low grounds and lakes ; but it
must be long before nature, unaided, will excavate a
passage sufficient for the waters of Red river. About
fifty leagues above the natural bridge, is the residence
of the Caddo or Caddoques nation, whose good qualities are already mentioned. The inhabitants represent the post of Natchitoches to be half way between

---

{ *line 1*: St. Antonio, D, W.
{ Texas: D; Taxus: W.
produced there D; procured there W.

Arcansa D, W.

Arcansa D, W.

difficult places D, W.

Nakitosh, D, W. good for one
  hundred fifty leagues, D, W.

extent of seventeen leagues, continually D, W.

which, W.

grounds near the hills; D, W.

the natural D; this natural W.
Cadeaux or Cadadoquis D, W.

Nakitosh D, W.

**158**

New Orleans D, W. Cadeaux D, W.

Arcansa D, W.
safe, W.

spacious Vales D; spacious vallies W.
forests consist D, W.

river, until it ascends to the
prairie country, D, W.
Arcansa D, W.
prairie; D, W.

Arcansa D, W;

Arcansa, D, W.

Arcansa, D, W.

New-Orleans and the Caddo nation. Above this point the navigation of Red river is said to be embarrassed by many rapids, falls and shallows. The Arkansa river is said to present a safe agreeable and uninterrupted navigation as high as it is known. The lands on each side are of the best quality, and well watered with springs, brooks and rivulets, affording many situations for mill-seats. From description it would seem that along this river there is a regular gradation of hill and dale, presenting their extremities to the river; the hills are gently swelling eminences, and the dales, spacious vallies with living water meandering through them ; the forest consists of handsome trees, chiefly what is called open woods. The quality of the land is supposed superior to that on Red river, below the priarie country, where the lands on both rivers are probably similar. About two hundred leagues up the Arkansa is an interesting place called the Salt priarie ; there is a considerable fork of the river at that place, and a kind of savanna where the salt water is continually oozing out and spreading over the surface of a plain. During the dry summer season the salt may be raked up in large heaps ; a natural crust of a hand breadth in thickness is formed at this season. This place is not often frequented, on account of the danger from the Osage Indians ; much less dare the white hunters venture to ascend higher, where it is generally believed that silver is to be found. It is further said, that high up the Arkansa river salt is found in form of a solid rock, and may be dug out with the crow-bar. The waters of the Arkansa, like those of Red river, are not potable during the dry season, being both charged highly with a reddish earth or mould, and extremely brackish. This inconvenience is not greatly felt upon the Arkansa, where springs and brooks of fresh water are frequent ; the Red river is understood not to be so highly favored. Every account seems to prove that immense natural magazines of salt must exist in the great chain of mountains to the westward ; as all

**159**

the rivers in the summer season, which flow from them, are strongly impregnated with that mineral, and are only rendered palatable after receiving the numerous streams of fresh water which join them in their course. The great western priaries, besides the herds of wild cattle, (bison, commonly called buffaloe) are also stocked with vast numbers of wild goat (not resembling the domestic goat) extremely swift footed. As the description given of this goat is not perfect, it may from its swiftness prove to be the antelope, or it possibly may be a goat which has escaped from the Spanish settlements of New Mexico. A Canadian, who had been much with the Indians to the westward, speaks of a wool bearing animal larger than a sheep, the wool much mixed with hair, which he had seen in large flocks. He pretends also to have seen a unicorn, the single horn of which, he says, rises out of the forehead and curls back, conveying the idea of the fossil cornu ammonis. This man says he has travelled beyond the great dividing ridge, so far as to have seen a large river flowing to the westward. The great dividing mountain is so lofty that it requires two days to ascend from the base to its top; other ranges of inferior mountains lie before and behind it; they are all rocky and sandy. Large lakes and valleys lie between the mountains. Some of the lakes are so large as to contain considerable islands; and rivers flow from some of them. Great numbers of fossil bones, of very large dimensions, are seen among the mountains, which the Canadian supposes to be the elephant. He does not pretend to have seen any of the precious metals, but has seen a mineral which he supposes might yield copper. From the top of the high mountain the view is bounded by a curve as upon the ocean, and extends over the most beautiful priaries, which seem to be unbounded, particularly towards the east.— The finest of the lands he has seen are on the Missouri; no other can compare in richnes and fertility with them. This Canadian, as well as Mr. Le Fe-
V

prairies, D, W;

perfect, D, N; pefect, W.

wool-bearing D, W.

vallies D, W.

prairies, D, W.

M. Le Fevre D; Le Fever, W.

**160**

unprincipled: W.

destruction. D, W.

lower upon this D; below upon this
W.

33° 40' W.

(Tilandsia) D; (Telandsia) W.
33°, W.
*line 17*: 
M. Le fevre D; Mr. Le Fever, W.
existence at the Arcansa D;
exisence on the Arcansa W.
*line 18*:
known to be not far beyond 33° of
Latitude; D; known to lie in about
the same parallel; W; known to lie
to the north of this parallel; N.
*line 25*:
Congress D; congress, W.
*line 29*:
rowing down . . . in each 24 hours
we gain upon the Current 6½
miles; D; In ascending the river,
they found their rate of going to
exceed that of the current about
six miles and a half in twenty-four
hours; and that on the 12th, W;
On the 12th, N.
*line 30*:
descending D; decending W.

vre, speak of the Osages of the tribe of Whitehairs, as lawless and unprincipled ; and the other Indian tribes hold them in abhorrence as a barbarous and uncivilized race ; and the different nations who hunt in their neighbourhood, have their concerting plans for ther destrution.  On the morning of the 11th, the party passed the petit ecor a Fabri.  The osier which grows on the beaches above, is not seen below on this river ; and here they began to meet with the small tree called ' charnier' which grows only on the water side, and is met with all the way down the Washita.  The latitude of 33d. 40m. seems the northern boundary of the one, and the southern boundary of the other of those vegetables.  Having noticed the limit set to the long moss, (Tilandsia) on the ascent of the river, in latitude 33d. Mr. Dunbar made enquiry of Mr. Le Fevre, as to its existence in the Arkansa settlement, which is known to lie to the north of this parallel ; he said, that its growth is limited about ten miles south of the settlement, and that as remarkably, as if a line had been drawn east and west for that purpose ; as it ceases all at once, and not by degrees.  Hence it appears, that nature has marked with a distinguishing feature, the line established by Congress, between the Orleans and Louisiana territories.  The cypress is not found on the Washita higher than thirty-four degrees of north latitude.

On the 12th, they had passed the apex of the tide or wave, occasioned by the fresh, and were descending along an inclined plane ; as they encamped at night, they found themselves in deeper water the next morning, and on a more elevated part of the inclined plane than they had been in the preceding evening, from the progress of the apex of the tide during their repose.

At noon on the 16th, they reached the post of the Washita.

Mr. Dunbar being anxious to reach the Natchez as early as possible, and being unable to procure hor-

17
18

25

29
30

## 161

ses at the post, took a canoe with one soldier and his own domestic, to push down to the Ocatahola, from whence to Concord there is a road of thirty miles across the low ground. He set off early on the morning of the 20th. and at night reached the settlement of an old hunter with whom he had conversed on his way up the river. This man informed him, that at the place called the mine, on the Little Missouri, there is a smoke which ascends perpetually from a particular place, and that the vapour is sometimes insupportable. The river, or a branch of it, passes over a bed of mineral, which from the description given is, no doubt, martial pyrites. In a creek, or branch of the Fourch a' Luke, * there is found on the beaches, and in the cliffs, a great number of globular bodies, some as large, or larger, than a man's head, which when broken exhibit the appearance of gold, silver and precious stones; most probably pyrites and chrystalized spar. And at the Fourche des Glaises a' Paul (higher up the river than Fourche a' Luke), near the river there is a cliff full of hexagonal prisms, terminated by pyramids, which appear to grow out of the rock; they are from six to eight inches in length, and some of them are an inch in diameter. There are beds of pyrites found in several small creeks communicating with the Washita, but it appears that the mineral indications are greatest on the Little Missouri, because, as before noted, some of the hunters actually worked on them, and sent a parcel of the ore to New-Orleans. It is the belief here, that the mineral contains precious metal, but that the Spanish government did not choose a mine should be opened so near to the British settlements. An express prohibition was issued against working these mines.

At this place, Mr. Dunbar obtained one or two slips of the " bois de arc" (bow wood) or yellow wood), from the Missouri. The fruit of which had

* Three leagues above Fllis's camp.

down to Catahoola, D; down to the Catahoola, W.
grounds. W.

hunter, D, W.

Fourche D, W.

New Oreleans D; New Orleans. W.

(bow wood) or yellow wood, D; (bow wood) or yellow wood), W.

Ellis's W.

## 162

fallen before maturity, lay upon the ground. Some were of the size of a small orange, with a rind full of tubercles; the color, though it appeared faded, still retained a resemblance to pale gold.

The tree in its native soil, when laden with its golden fruit, (nearly as large as the egg of an ostrich), presents the most splendid appearance; its foliage is of a deep green, resembling the varnished leaf of the orange tree, and, upon the whole, no forest tree can compare with it in ornamental grandeur. The bark of the young tree resembles, in texture, the dog-wood bark; the appearance of the wood recommends it for trial as an article which may yield a yellow dye. It is deciduous; the branches are numerous, and full of short thorns or prickles, which seem to point it out as proper for hedges or live fences. This tree is known to exist near the Natchitoches (perhaps in latitude 32d.), and upon the river Arkansa, high up (perhaps in latitude 36d.); it is therefore probable that it may thrive from latitude 30d. to 40d. and will be a great acquisition to the United States if it possess no other merit than that of being ornamental.

In descending the river, both Mr. Dunbar and Dr. Hunter searched for the place said to yield gypsum, or plaister of Paris, but failed. The former gentleman states, that he has no doubt of its existence, having noted two places where it has been found: one of which is the first hill, or high land which touches the river on the west, above the bayau Calumet, and the other is the second high land on the same side. As these are two points of the same continued ridge, it is probable that an immense body of gypsum will be found in the bowels of the hill which connects the points, and perhaps extending far beyond them.

On the evening of the 22d, Mr. Dunbar arrived at the Ocatahola, where a Frenchman of the name of Heberard, who keeps the ferry across Black river, is settled. Here the road from the Washita forks, one branch of it leading to the settlement on Red river, and the other up to the post on the Washita. The

Dogwood D; dog wood W.

Nakitosh D, W.
32°) W. Arcansa, D, W.
36°) W.
38° to 40° W.

*line 33*: hill connecting those two points and perhaps D; hills where they meet, and perhaps W.
22d D, W.
Catahoola, D, W.
Hebrard, D, W.

33

163

proprietor of this place has been a hunter and a great traveller up the Washita and into the western country ; he confirms generally the accounts received from others.   It appears, from what they say, that in the neighbourhood of the hot springs, but higher up among the mountains, and upon the Little Missouri, during the summer season, explosions are very frequently heard, proceeding from under the ground ; and not rarely a curious phenomenon is seen, which is termed the blowing of the mountains ; it is confined elastic gas forcing a passage through the side or top of a hill, driving before it a great quantity of earth and mineral matter.   During the winter season the explosions and blowing from the mountains entirely cease, from whence we may conclude, that the cause is comparatively superficial, being brought into action by the increased heat of the more direct rays of the summer sun.

The confluence of the Washita, Ocatahola and Tensaw, is an interesting place.   The last of these communicates with the Mississippi low lands, by the intervention of other creeks and lakes, and by one in particular, called "Bayau d' Argent," which empties into the Mississippi, about fourteen miles above Natchez.   During high water there is a navigation for batteaux of any burthen along the bayau.   A large lake, called St. John's, occupies a considerable part of the passage between the Mississippi and the Tensaw ; it is in a horse shoe form, and has at some former period, been the bed of the Mississippi ; the nearest part of it is about one mile removed from the river at the present time.   This lake, possessing elevated banks, similar to those of the river, has been lately occupied and improved.   The Ocatahola bayau is the third navigable stream ; during the time of the inundation there is an excellent communication by the lake of that name, and from thence, by large creeks, to the Red river.   The country around the point of union of these three rivers is altogether alluvial, but the place of Mr. Heberard's residence is no

up among D; up, among W.

blowing of D, W.
cease, D; ceases, W.

Catahoola D, W.
Tenza, D, W.

St. John's lake, D, W.
Tenza; D, W.
has, W.
Mississippi: W.

Catahoola D, W.
stream: W.

Hebrard's D, W.

164

longer subject to inundation. There is no doubt, that as the country augments in population and riches, this place will become the site of a commercial inland town, which will keep pace with the progress and prosperity of the country. One of the Indian mounts here is of a considerable elevation, with a species of rampart surrounding a large space, which was, no doubt, the position of a fortified town.

While here, Mr. Dunbar met with an American who pretended to have been up the Arkansa river three hundred leagues. The navigation of this river he says is good for that distance, for boats drawing three or four feet water. Implicit faith, perhaps, ought not to be given to his relation, respecting the quantity of silver he pretends to have collected there. He says he has found silver on the Washita, thirty leagues above the hot springs, so rich, that three pounds of it yielded one pound of silver, and that this was found in a cave. He asserts, also, that the ore of the mine upon the Little Missouri, was carried to Kentucky, by a person of the name of Boon, where it was found to yield largely in silver. This man says he has been up the Red river likewise, and that there is a great rapid just below the raft, or natural bridge, and several others above it; that the Caddo nation is about fifty leagues above the raft, and near to their villages commences the country of the great priaries, which extend four or five hundred miles to the west of the sand mountains, as they are termed. These great plains reach far beyond the Red river to the south, and northward over the Arkansa river, and among the numerous branches of the Missouri. He confirms the account of the beauty and fertility of the western country.

On the morning of the 25th, Mr Dunbar set out, on horseback, from the Ocatahola to Natchez. And Dr. Hunter and the remainder of the party descended the Washita, with the boat in which they ascended the river, and, ascending the Mississippi, reached St. Catharine's landing on the morning of the 31st January, 1805.

---

**Marginal notes (left column):**

good to that D, W.

little D, W.

Cadaux D; Caddo W.

prairies, D, W.

Catahoola D, W. *See Appendix A4 for text missing in N, giving more details of Dunbar's return journey, and the original botanical list. See Textual Introduction, "Copy for the Natchez Edition" and "The Botanical Notes."*

*Not in* W.

# EXTRACTS

## FROM THE APPENDIX

## To Mr. Dunbar's Journal.

*List of Stages and Distances, on the Red and Wash-*
*ita rivers, in French computed Leagues.*

|  | LEAGUES. |  |
|---|---|---|
| From the Mouth of RED RIVER, |  |  |
| To the confluence of Red and Black rivers, . . . | 10 |  |
| To the confluence of Washita, Catahoola and Tensaw, | 22 |  |
| Bayou Haha, . . , | 1 | E. side. |
| Priarie Villemont, . . | 5 | E. |
| Bayou Louis and Rapids, - | 1 | E. |
| Buffalo River, . . . | 4 | E. |
| Drowned Priarie, . . | 3 | E. |
| Pine Point, . . . | 4 1-2 | W. |
| Bayou Calumet, . . . | 3 1-2 | W. |
| Coal or carbonated wood, ⎱ | 3 | E. |
| Gypsum or Plaister of Paris, ⎰ |  | W. |
| Olivot 1st settlement, . . | 12 | E. |
| Mallet's Cliffs, . . . | 3 | W. |
| Priarie de Mannoir, . . | 2 | E. |
| Belle Cote, . . . | 2 1-2 | W. |
| Bayou de la belle Cheniere, . | 1 | W. |
| Priarie des bois, . . | 4 | E. |
| Bayou de la Cheniere au tondre, | 3 | W. |
| Post of Washita, or Fort Miro, | 5 | E. |

Total distance to Fort Miro, 90 1-2

| To Bayou Siard, . . | 2 | E. |
|---|---|---|
| Bayou d'Arbonne, . . | 1 | W. |
| Petite Cheniere, . . | 1 | W. |

4

94 1-2

166

*Not in* W.

| | | LEAGUES. | 94 1-2 |
|---|---|---|---|
| *Brought forward,* | | | |
| To Egg Point, | . . | 1 | E. |
| Black water bayou, | . . | 2 | E. |
| Grand Roque-rau, | . . | 1 | W. |
| Otter Bayou, | . . | 1 | W. |
| Bayou Barthelemi, | . . | 3 | E. |
| Papaw Bayou, | . . | 1 | E. |
| Bayou Mercier, | . . | 1 | W. |
| Bayou des buttes, | . . | 2 | E. |
| Bayou de la batture aux pierres, | | 2 | W. |
| Bayou Franqueure, | . . | 1 1-2 | W. |
| Bayou de la longue vue, | . | 1 1-2 | E. |
| Isle de Mallet, lat. 33d. N. | | 1 1-2 | E. |
| Trois Battures, | . . | 1 1-2 | |
| Bayou de la Pille, | . . | 3 | W. |
| Bayou de la Saline, | . . | 2 1-2 | E. |
| Marrais de Cannes, | . . | 5 | E. |
| L'Aigle, (the Eagle's nest) | | 4 | E. |
| Cache la Tulipe, | . . | 3 | W. |
| Bay Morrau, | . . | 2 | E. |
| Fritter Camp, | . . | 7 | E. |
| Chemin Couvert, | . . | 5 | W. |
| La Piniere, | . . | 2 | E. |
| Vieille Abattas, | - - - | 2 | W. |
| Petite baye, | - - - | 2 | E. |
| Cote á faine (Beech-mast hill) | | 3 | W. |
| Locust Bayou, | - - - | 1 | E. |
| Petite pointe Coupée, | . . | 5 | W. 5 |
| Les deux bayous, | . . | 1 1-2 | E. & W. |
| Grand Ecor à Fabri, | . . | 1 1-2 | W. |
| Petit Ecor á Fabri, | . . | 1 1-2 | W. |
| Grosse batture, | . . | 3 | E. |
| Isles Soulardes (drunken islands) | | 2 | |
| Ecor á Sofrion, | . . | 1 | W. |
| Grande Pointe Coupèe, | . | 1 | E. |
| Arclon's Troughs, | . . | 2 | W. |
| Little Missouri, | . . | 3 | W. |
| | | | ——— |
| | | | 83 |
| | | | ——— |
| | | | 177 1-2 |

*Not in* W.

## 159

| | | | |
|---|---|---|---|
| Cypress Bayau, | . . | 5 | W. |
| Cache à Macon, | . . | 5 | E. |
| Bayau de l'eau froide | . . | 3 | E. |
| Grand Glaise | . . | 3 | W. |
| Ecor á Chicots, | . . | 2 | W. |
| Fourche des Cadaux, | . | 3 | W. |
| Bayau des Roches, | . . | 1 | W. |
| Mellon Island, | . . | 4 | W. |
| Bayau de la prairie de Champignole | | 4 | W. |
| Grande Chute, | . . | 4 | W. |
| Fourche au Tigre, | . . | 2 | E. |
| Ellis' Camp, | . . | 2 | E. |
| By land to the Hot-Springs | | 3 | |
| | | —— | |
| | | | 62 1-2 |

Total from the mouth of the Red
river to the HOT SPRINGS,          221 1-2
By the geographical survey, the whole distance
from the mouth of the Red river to the Hot-Springs,
is about 508 miles, from whence it appears that the
French computed league is not quite 2 miles and a
quarter.

——

*Recapitulation of the principal distances.*

| From the CITY of NEW-ORLEANS, | *Eng. miles.* |
|---|---|
| To the mouth of Red river, . | 225 |
| To the mouth of Black river, . | 27 |
| To the mouth of Washita, . | 51 |
| To Fort Miro, . . . | 119 |
| To the Little Missouri, . | 212 |
| To the Hot Springs, . . | 100 |
| | —— |
| Total distance from New-Orleans to the HOT SPRINGS, | 734 |

MILES.

| | |
|---|---|
| Distance from Natchez by the way of Concord to Catahoola, by land, | 30 |
| From Natchez by water from Catahoola to Fort Miro, | 149 |

W

*Not in* W.

## 160

From Natchez to the Hot Springs,    461

List of Stages on the great Saline Bayau, a navigable stream for boats, falling into the Washita about 30 computed leagues or 67 miles above Fort Miro.

| From the mouth of the Bayau | *Leagues.* | |
|---|---|---|
| To Bayau de la Tulipe, | 2 | W. |
| Prudhomme's Camp, | 4 | W. |
| Mocasin Camp, | 2 | E. |
| Petit abattis, | 4 | W. |
| Beaver Swamp, | 4 | W. |
| Bayau de la Tete, | 1 | E. |
| Grand Ecor, | 4 | E. |
| Bayau de l'abattis, | 3 | E. |
| Saline Noire, | 3 | W. |
| Petite Glaise, | 4 | E. |
| Patruillage, | 4 | W. |
| Grande Glaise, | 3 | E. |
| Cote Plage, | 3 | E. |
| Campement de la Baye, | 3 | W. |
| Arcansa Path, | 4 | W. |
| High Road, | 3 | E. |
| Old Field Camp, | 6 | E. |
| Petite Cote, | 3 | E. |
| Beau Campement, | 7 | W. |
| Lower end of the Great *Island, | 4 | |
| Gallien's Camp on the Island, | 3 1-2 | |
| Great raft at the upper end of the Island, | 3 1-2 | |
| Grand Abattis on both sides, | 4 | |
| Black water Creek, | 4 | W. |
| Marignon's Lick, | 5 | E. |
| Channel's Hill, | 3 | E. |
| Campement de la Verdure, | 15 | E. |
| Total, | 111 | |

This Bayau is not generally navigable higher, and the last stage is about East of the Bayau of the Prairie de Champignole on the Washita.

* This Island lies about 50 miles East of Cache à Macon on the Washita.

. Stages on the little Missouri falling into the West

## 161

*Not in* W.

side of the Washita, about 87 computed leagues, or 212 miles above Fort Miro.

From the mouth of the little Missouri, *Leagues.*

| | | |
|---|---|---|
| To the Alumn-mine, | 1-2 | *South side.* |
| To the Bayau de la terre noire, | 1-2 | N. |
| The Troughs,    . | 5 | S. |
| Cliff on the right hand,    . | 5 | N. |
| Red Cliff,    . | 4 | S. |
| Small Hill,    . | 5 | S. |
| Cabane des Chefs,    . | 1 | S. |
| Camp at the Prairie of Han, | 1 | S. |
| The Eagle,    . | 2 | S. |
| *The three Pine-trees,    . | 3 | N. |
| Anthony's Fork,    . | 5 | N. |
| The Blue Hill,    . | 5 | N. |
| The Bayau of Ausane's little Prairies, | 4 | S. |
| Saline one mile from the River, | 4 | N. |
| Several Islands and to the Mine, | 2 | N. |
| The little Prairie, | 6 | N. |
| The two forks, | 5 | |
| | ── | |
| | 58 | |

This river is navigable considerably higher, but not much frequented, because of the danger from the visits of the tribes of the Grand Osages living upon the Arcansa river.

* *No Cypress grows above this place.*

───── ─ ─────

Short lists of the most obvious vegetable productions of the WASHITA COUNTRY, which are indigeneous or growing without cultivation.

### FOREST TREES.

| LINNAEN NAMES. | POPULAR NAMES. |
|---|---|
| Quercus Alba, | White oak, 4 species. |
| rubra, | Red oak 5 or 6 species. |
| nigra, | Black oak, 4 species. |
| Juglans alba, | Hickory, 4 species. |
| | Paccan. |
| nigra, | Black walnut. |
| Fraxinus, | Aſh, 3 species. |
| Tanthoxylum fraxinifolium, | Prickly aſh. |

*Not in* W.

## 162

| | |
|---|---|
| ————clavaherculis, | Tooth-ache tree. |
| Ulmus, | Elm, 3 species. |
| Acer, | Maple, 2 species. |
| | Do. Sugar, not productive. |
| Pinus, | Pine, short leaf on high arid land. |
| | ————Long leaf on rich land. |
| Ilex, | Holly. |
| Magnolia grandiflora, | Laurel leaved tulip tree. |
| acuminata, | Cucumber tree. |
| tripetala, | Umbrella tree. |
| accriculata, | Ear leaved magnolia, with several other species of this family. |
| Laurus, | Bay, several species. |
| Laurus saffafras, | Saffafras. |
| Liquidamber, | Sweet gum. |
| Juniperus, | Red cedar. |
| Tilia, | Linn or Linden. |
| Sideroxylon, | Iron wood. |
| Salix diandra, | Common willow. |
| pentadra, | Osier. |
| Platanus occidentalis, | Plane tree, button wood. |
| Fagus Sylvatica, | Beech. |
| Castanea, | Chesnut. |
| Pumila, | Chinquapin. |
| Diospyros, | Persimon. |
| Annona trilaba, | Papaw—custard apple. |
| Morus nigra, | Black mulberry. |
| Prunus, | Wild plum, 3 species. |
| virginiana, | Wild cherry. |
| Robinia, | Locust. |
| Gledisia, | 3 thorned do. honey locust. |
| Cornus, | Dogwood, 2 species. |
| Liriodendron tulipifera, | Tulip tree, improperly called Poplar. |
| Populus deltoides, | Cotton wood—water pop. |
| Cercis, | Judas tree—red bud. |
| Cupressus disticha, | Cypress. |
| Elœagnus, | Wild Olive. |
| Nyssa, | Tupelo tree. |
| Betula nigra. | Black birch. |
| Bignonia catalpa, | Catalpa. |
| Juniperus sabina, | Sabin tree. |
| Pyrus coronaria, | Crab-appie, |

## 163

*Not in* W.

### LESSER TREES, SHRUBS AND VINES.

| | |
|---|---|
| Myrcia cerifera, | Wax bearing myrtle. |
| Ricinus, | Palma chrifti. |
| Corylus avellana, | Harel—Filbert. |
| Vitis, | Grape vine—varieties. |
| Ilex vomitoria, [Hiton.] | Evergreen caffina yapon. |
| Vaccinium, | Whortleberry, 4 fpecies, 3 ripe in May and June and one in the fall. |
| Laurus Æftivalis, | Spice wood. |
| Smilax, | China root. |
| | Falfe do.—Cantae. |
| Rofa carolina, | Wild rofe, fingle. |
| Roffa, | Hep tree. |
| Sam bucus, | Elder. |
| Chiananthus, | Snow drop tree, |
| Celtis, | *Lotus or Lote tree. |
| Viburnum, | Hawthorn with black fruit |
| | Do. with red fruit. |
| | Do. with larger red fruit. |
| Melaftoma, | Wild Goofeberry with fmall dark red fruit. |
| Rhus, | Sumack, 2 fpecies. |
| Æfculus fpicata of Bartram, | Dwarf Buck eye or horfe chefnut. |
| Hamamelis, | Witch—hazel—bois *a* Ca. bane. |
| Berberis, | Barberry. |
| Hypericum, | St. John's wort. |
| Vifcum, | Mifletoe. |
| Gelfeminum nitidum, | Carolina yellow. |
| | Jeffamine ; evergreen. |
| Ipomœa, | Cyprefs vine—Indian creeper. |
| Erythrins, | Coral tree. |

---

### HERBACEOUS PLANTS, CREEPERS, &c.

| | |
|---|---|
| Podophylum peltatum, | May-apple. |
| Trifolium, | Wild clover. |
| Glycine, | Wild liquorice. |
| Gnaphalium, | Life everlafting. |
| Calendula, | Marigold. |
| Mimofa pudica, | Senfitive humble plant. |
| Nymphœa nilumbo, | Water lily. |
| Amomum filveftre, | Wild ginger. |

*Called Alifier by the French hunters, it bears no fruit, the Indians make arrows of it.

164

*Not in* W.

| | |
|---|---|
| Iris, | Flag. |
| Plantago, | Plantain, 2 species. |
| Potamogiton natans, | Pond weed. |
| Hyrophylum, | Water leaf. |
| Verbafcum, | Mullein. |
| Datura ftramonium, | Thorn-apple. |
| Thefium, | Flax weed |
| Portulaca, | Purflane. |
| Fragaria, | Strawberry. |
| Syfymbricum, | Water crefs. |
| Solidago, | Golden rod. |
| Helenium, | Wild fmall fun-flower. |
| Alfine, | Chickweed. |
| Carduus, | Thiftle. |
| Sonchus, | Sow thiftle. |
| Preanthes alba, | Wild lettuce, commonly called gall of the earth, a fpecific for the cure of the bite of the rattle fnake &c. |
| Juncus, | Rufh, fome varieties |
| Origanum, | Dittany. |
| Rumex, | Dock. |
| Patientia, | Patience. |
| Papaver, | Wild poppy white & red. |
| Phytolacca decandra, | Poke, |
| Polypodium, | Fern |
| Adiantum, | Capilair-maiden hair, two fpecies |
| Euonimus Qu:? | Bears grafs-ever green Spindle tree. |
| Azalea, | American honey fuckle. |
| Saururus, | Lizard's tail. |
| Tillanffa ufneoides, | Long mofs. |
| Polygonum fagittatum, | Arfmart. |
| Humulus lupulus, | Hop. |
| Artemifia, | Wormword. |
| Spirea trifoliata, } | Falfe Ipecacuana or |
| Trioftoeum, } | Fever-root. |
| Afelepias decumbens, | Pleurify root. |
| Paffiflora. | Paffion flower. |
| Diofcorea. | Indian potatoe. |
| Arum triphyllum, | Indian turnip. |
| Ranumculus fcaleratus, | Crow-foot an acrid plant. |
| Rhus radicans, | Poifon vine. |
| Daucus filveftris, | Wild carrot. |
| Braffica Wafhita, | Mountain dwarf cabbage |

## 165

|  | with crimſon flowers, new. |
|---|---|
| Lupinus perennis, | Lupine-peavine. |
| Dolichos, | Wild pea. |
| Vicia ſilvatica, | Vetch-peavine. |
| Allium Silveſtre, | Wild onion. |
|  | Wild Shallot. |
| Cucumis, | Coloquintida. |
| Mentha, | Wild mint. |
| Nepeta, | Cat-mint. |
| Cichorium, | Wild endive. |
| Prinos, | Winter berry. |
| Pyrola, | Winter green. |
| Arbutus viridis, | Partrige berry. |
| Spigelia marilandica, | Carolina pink-root. |
| Mentha pulegium, | Penny royal. |
| Punctuata, | Horſe mint. |
| Gentiana, | Centaury, leſſer. |
| Marubium, | Horehound. |
| Glycyrrhira glabra, | Liquorice. |
| Utrica, | Nettle, 2 ſpecies. |
| Chenopodium, | Jeruſalem oak. |
| Calycanthus floridus, | Sweet ſcented ſhrub. |
| Viburnum, | Snow-ball. |
| Solidago, | Golden-rod. |
| Polygala ſenega, | Snake root—milk wort. |
| Chiropa angularis, | American centaury. |
| Viola inordorata, | Wild violet. |
| Leontodon, | Dandelion. |
| Malva rotundifolia, | Mallow. |
| Trillium, | True love of Canada. |
| Cherophylum, | Wild charvil. |
| Chamœrops, | Palmeto. |
| Frantinalis, | Water-moſs. |
| Oxalis, | Wood-ſorrel. |
| Aſeyrum, | St. Peter's wort. |
| Serratula ſpecioſa, | Saw-wort. |
| Aſter, | Star-wort, ſeveral ſpecies. |

Not in W.

### GRASSES.

| Callitriche, | Star-graſs. |
|---|---|
| Anthoxanthum, | Spring-graſs. |
| Scirpus, | Ruſh-graſs. |
| Alopecurus, | Fox tail. |
| Daƈylis | Cocks foot-graſs |
| Feſtuca | Feſcue, 2 ſpecies. |
| Stipa, | Feather graſs. |

## 166

*Not in* W.

| | |
|---|---|
| Avena Ipicata, | Wild oats. |
| Poa, | Meadow grafs. |
| Galium, | Goofe-grafs. |
| Panicum, | Panic-grafs. |
| Agaricus, | Mufhroom, a great variety, fome rooted in the earth, others parafites attached to living & to dead trees. |

Notice of certain vegetables, of which a part is perhaps new.

Bois d'Arc, Bow-wood-yellow wood, an ornamental tree bearing large gold-colored fruit.

Medecine de chaine—Jointed root—Cathartic.

Wild hemp.

A very ftrong faw-briar.

Cantac, refembling fmilax with an efculent root.

Wild ginger.

Herbe *a* Jofeph—Jofeph's herb—a vulnary of fpeedy effect.

Herbe au Crocodile—Aligator plant, a vulnerary of great power.

Racine rouge—Red root, a fpecific in femal obftructions and a good dye.

Racine au Chevreuil—deer's root, an efculent farinaceous globular body from 2 to 8 inches in diameter without ftem or leaf above ground.

Patate au Chevreuil—Deer's potatoe, a very fweet, juicy, fibrous root, from 3 to 8 inches in length, fupporting a fhort ftragling vine, bearing abundance of ftriped or fpeckled peas.

Silk plant—perhaps periploca.

Charnier—a tree of fmall fize found only along the river bank.

Bois de bord de l'eau—Water fide wood—This is alfo a tree of fmall growth, found only by the river fide.

Yellow root—This is a fibrous root, yielding a remarkable fine yellow dye.

Another fmall root which is probably a fpecies of Madder yields a good red dye.

Of the medical properties of the Hot-Springs.

Thofe fprings have already acquired confiderable celebrity in Louifiana, for the remedy of a variety of difeafes : many cafes of fuccefsful cure might be related, of which feveral are narrated in a manner to border a little upon the marvelous, and feem from the very fpeedy effects faid to have been produced in certain cafes, to refemble the reported influence of Mefmerifm, Perkinifm, &c. and as thefe are now fufficiently underftood to depend totally upon the

**167**

powerful operation of the imagination upon the phyſical ſyſtem, we may be permitted to aſcribe at leaſt ſome part of the pretended virtues of the Hot-Springs to a ſimilar cauſe. So high an opinion is entertained by many, of the certain efficacy of theſe waters, that patients do often repair to the Hot-Springs with the fulleſt aſſurance of a moſt ſpeedy and complete cure : it is well known to the gentlemen of the faculty, what happy effects are generally conſequent upon ſuch a pre-exiſting ſtate of the mind.

It is not however intended to deny that the Hot-Springs may be poſſeſſed of certain virtues ; for who can doubt of the powerful agency of hot ſteam ? but in order to underſtand this ſubject, it will be proper to explain the manner in which the waters are adminiſtered, and alſo to know what are the mineral impregnations of the ſprings.

It appears that the cures aſcribed to the Hot-Springs, depend neither upon the drinking of, nor the bathing in the waters, but upon the uſe of the Balnea Laconica or vapour bath ; for which purpoſe rude ſcaffoldings of round poles are placed immediately over the moſt convenient baſons of the Hot-Springs ; the patient is extended upon this rough ſtage covered with a blanket, and ſo near to the hot water, that the heat of the ſteam is ſometimes born with a degree of torture which nothing but a ſpecies of enthuſiaſm could enable him to ſupport, being fully perſuaded that the certainty of a ſpeedy cure depends upon the magnitude of his ſufferings : when the patient is thus brought to perſpire very profuſely, he is removed from the grid-iron and laid upon a temporary couch covered ſufficiently to prevent catching cold and ſuffered to cool gradually ; after which he is replaced upon his ſcaffold until a ſecond copious perſpiration comes on, which requires a ſhorter time than the firſt, and this operation of alternate heating and cooling is continued, the intervals becoming continually ſhorter, until the patient nearly exhauſted, petitions for a reſpite of his ſufferings, and is permitted to repoſe the remainder of the day : many of the patients drink or rather ſip of the hot water conſtantly, during the uſe of the ſteam bath. In this manner the waters are adminiſtered by the white people, and by ſuch procedure patients are ſaid to have been radically cured of Rhumatiſm, Palſy, Cramp, Aſthma, Dropſy, Old ulcers, Obſtinate head-ache and Colic, Diarrhœa, St. Anthony's fire, Gonorrhœa, Creticular diſorders, &c. The Indians proceed in a manner ſomewhat different and more analogous to their hardy mode of life : After being brought into a ſtate of copious perſpiration, they ſpring from the ſcaffold and walk about in the open air almoſt naked, and continually fanned by their attendants, by which means they are ſpeedily cooled, and are immediately replaced upon the ſcaffolding, undergoing a ſeries of alternate heating and cooling, of which the alternations continually diminiſh as before, and in order to cloſe the ſcene for the day, the man of nature plunges into a pool

X

*Not in* W.

**168**

*Not in* W.

a little below the springs where the heat of the water is just tolerable; from whence he retires to cool and repose himself.

Such are the usual modes of administering the Hot-Spring waters and which are continued daily until the patient is either cured or disappointed.

From the above account it is evident, that whatever mineral impregnations the waters may contain, if they are not of a volatile nature, they cannot bestow any properties upon the hot vapor, superior to that of common water. From the first inspection of the hot springs, the most superficial observer discovers, that they are continually depositing stoney matter, which is carbonate of lime (soft limestone) and a small portion of red calx of Iron, neither of which are volatile at the temperature of the hot springs, and by analysis it does not appear, that they contain any thing else, a little free carbonic acid (fixed air) excepted. Altho' the mass of calcareous matter deposited on the face of the hill be immensely great, yet the quantity held in solution by the water of the hot-springs is very inconsiderable: it is known that water dissolves only one seven hundredth part of its weight of caustic lime, for which it has a great attraction, the quantity of carbonate of lime must be much less, as by a very careful and rigorous trial, the specific gravity of the water of the hot-springs was not found sensibly greater than that of rain water, and the portion of iron was still more minute; it was probably precipitated before its water flowed from the bason of the fountain head, as the presence of iron was not detected in the water by the application of the Prussian lixivium, but the sediment or red calx which was found in all the fountains was turned instantly blue by the action of the lixivium. Dr. Fordyce remarks that he has never found any metal dissolved in mineral waters but by the aid of the sulphuric acid, and that when the metallic salt is diffused thro' a great proportion of water, it is speedily decomposed, the metallic calx being precipitated and the acid disappearing; which accounts satisfactorily for no evidence of iron appearing in the waters, altho' the red calx of that metal is found in the sediment of all the fountains: hence it appears that no new property can be imparted to the vapor by the mineral impregnations of the hot-springs, and it is highly improbable that the medical virtues of the water itself are in any degree superior to those of common springs issuing from hills containing limestone.

If therefore the steam bath of the hot-springs is found to be really beneficial in certain diseases of the human body, we have no reason to doubt that the same advantage may be obtained more commodiously and with equal effect at our own homes.

This powerful remedy which is perhaps too much neglected both in Europe and the United States, was known from the most remote antiquity in the countries of the east, and Egypt preserves to the present day, the pleasure and salubrity of its hot baths. Those of Grand Cairo are magnificent and commodious: " The Bath is a

### 169

"spacious and vaulted apartment, paved and lined with fine mar-
"ble ; the bathers are extended on a fine carpet, the head support-
"ed on a small cushion, turning themselves freely in every posture,
"whilst they are wrapped up in a cloud of odoriferous vapors,
"which penetrate into all their pores. After reposing some time,
"until there is a gentle moisture over the whole body, an attendant
"comes and presses gently the bather, turns him over, and when
"his limbs are become supple and flexible, he makes all the joints
"crack without difficulty ; he seems to knead the flesh, without
"causing the smallest pain, on the contrary producing a luxurious
"sensation.

"This operation finished, he puts on a stuff glove and rubs the
"body detaching from it, while running with sweat, a sort of small
"scales, and removes the imperceptible matter which stops the
"pores ; the skin becomes soft and smooth like satin, and lastly he
"pours the lather of perfumed soap upon the head of the bather
"and retires.

"The bather returns slowly by several passages, the heat gradu-
"ally diminishing until he arrives at a spacious apartment commu-
"nicating with the external air by which he entered ; here he re-
"poses himself, the breast expands and he breaths with voluptuous-
"ness, the blood circulates with freedom, he feels as if regenerated,
"in short both mind and body experience a sentiment of univer-
"sal delight."*

The ancients treated their guests in a more voluptuous manner.
Whilst Telemachus was at the court of Nestor, "The beautiful Po-
"lycasta, the handsomest of the daughters of the King of Pylos, led
"the son of Ulysses to the bath, washed him with her own hands,
"and after anointing his body with precious oils, covered him with
"rich habits and a splendid cloak."† Pisistratus and Telemachus
were equally well treated in the palace of Menelaus. "When they
"had admired its beauties, they were conducted to basons of mar-
"ble where a bath was prepared. Beautiful female slaves washed
"them, and after anointing them with oil, covered them with rich
"tunicks and precious furs."‡

It would be improper to dissuade any person possessed of an high
opinion of the virtues of the hot-springs from visiting them for
the recovery of his health. It is well known that many persons
have enjoyed perfect health, on parties of pleasure or employment,
living in the open air with the occasional protection of a tent, who
have been little better than valetudinarians when in the possession
of the refined accommodations of a city : change of air, new scenes,
privation of usual luxuries, and above all the emancipation of the
mind from the pressure of the anxieties of a life of business, hustle
and perplexity cannot fail to produce the most salutary effects,
especially if the patient be accompanied by a select few, agreeable
and accommodating companions.

* *Savary.*      † *Odyssey, book 3d.*      ‡ *Odyssey, book 4th.*

*Not in* W.

For alternative text in W, see Appendix A5.

170

## METEOROLOGICAL observations made by Mr. Dunbar and doctor Hunter, in their voyage up the Red and Washita rivers, in the year 1804.

| Latitude. | Days. | THERMOMETER. | | | Wind. | STATE OF THE WEATHER. |
|---|---|---|---|---|---|---|
| | | In Air. | | River water. | | |
| | | Greatest. | Least. | | | |
| 31° 23 | October 20 | 80 | 47 | | s. s. E. | Cloudy. |
| | 21 | 83 | 60 | | s. s. E. | Light rain. |
| | 22 | 79 | 65 | | w. NW. | Clear. |
| 31 36 | 23 | 73 | 68 | | | Cloudy. |
| 31 42 | 24 | 65 | 54 | 71 | N. | Cloudy. |
| | 25 | 56 | 49 | 68 | N. | Cloudy. |
| 31 49 | 26 | 70 | 40 | | N. | Clear. |
| | 27 | 73 | 32 | 64 | N. | Clear. |
| 31 54 | 28 | 78 | 40 | 63 | NW. | Clear. |
| 31 58 | 29 | 62 | 41 | 62 | NW. | Clear. |
| 32 5 | 30 | 83 | 47 | 60 | N. NW. | Clear. |
| 32 10 | 31 | 84 | 44 | 62 | N. NW. | Clear. |

**171**

## CONTINUED.

| Latitude. | Days. | THERMOMETER. | | | Wind. | State of the weather. |
|---|---|---|---|---|---|---|
| | | In Air. | | River water. | | |
| | | Greatest. | Least. | | | |
| 32o 17' | Novem. 1 | 85 | 48 | 62 | Calm. | Clear. |
| 32 21 | — 2 | 84 | 48 | 62 | s. se. | Light clouds. |
| | — 3 | 86 | 52 | 64 | | Do. |
| | — 4 | 70 | 54 | 64 | | Clear. |
| | — 5 | 68 | 52 | 62 | | Foggy. |
| | — 6 | 59 | 45 | 64 | w. | Thick fog. |
| 32 30 | — 9 | 72 | 42 | 61 | | Cloudy. |
| | — 10 | 70 | 40 | 60 | | Cloudy. |
| | — 11 | 58 | 24 | | | |
| 32 34 | — 12 | 64 | 36 | 54 | Calm. | Clear. |
| | — 13 | 62 | 33 | 55 | Do. | Fog and rain. |
| 32 50 | — 14 | 72 | 44 | 55 | Do. | Clear. |
| | — 15 | 60 | 33 | 55 | Do. | Hoar frost and |
| 33 | — 16 | 51 | 38 | 54 | Do. | Cloudy. |

## CONTINUED.

172

| Latitude. | Days. | THERMOMETER. | | | Wind. | State of the weather. |
|---|---|---|---|---|---|---|
| | | In Air. | | River water. | | |
| | | Greatest. | Least. | | | |
| 33° 13' | Novem. 17 | 51 | 40 | 54 | Calm. | Foggy. |
| 33 17 | — 18 | 57 | 32 | 52 | Do. | Serene. |
| | — 19 | 62 | 54 | 54 | Do. | Cloudy. |
| | — 20 | 62 | 59 | 54 | Do. | Cloudy. |
| 33 29 | — 21 | 72 | 43 | 54 | Do. | Foggy. |
| | — 22 | 68 | 40 | 54 | Do. | Light clouds. |
| 33 42 | — 23 | 72 | 48 | 53 | Do. | Do. |
| | — 24 | 65 | 48 | 54 | Do, | Do. |
| | — 25 | 70 | 54 | | Do. | Rain during the whole day. |
| 33 54 | — 26 | 68 | 50 | 57 | Do. | Clear. |
| | — 27 | 71 | 54 | 58 | Do. | Cloudy. |
| | — 28 | 78 | 68 | 60 | Do. | Cloudy. |
| | — 29 | 76 | 52 | 62 | s. | Cloudy. |
| 34 12 | — 30 | 57 | 38 | 60 | Calm. | Clear. |

**CONTINUED.**

**173**

| Latitude. | Days. | THERMOMETER. | | | Wind. | State of the weather. |
|---|---|---|---|---|---|---|
| | | In Air. | | River water. | | |
| | | Greatest. | Least. | | | |
| | Decem. 1 | 58 | 32 | 54 | Calm. | Clear. |
| |    - 2 | 59 | 30 | 50 | Do. | Clear. |
| 34o 21' |    - 3 | 59 | 38 | 48 | Do. | Do. |
| 34 26 |    - 4 | 50 | 36 | 48 | Do. | Do. |
| |    - 5 | 56 | 23 | 47 | Do. | Serene and fine. |
| |    - 6 | 67 | 45 | 48 | sw. | Cloudy. |
| 34 27 ½ |    - 7 | 56 | 38 | 47 | nw. | Cloudy. |
| |    - 8 | 47 | 10 | 43 | nw. | Very Serene. |
| |    - 9 | 42 | 19 | 41 | nw. | Do. |
| | **At the Hot-Springs.** | | | | | |
| 34 31 |    - 10 | 40 | 26 | | nw. | Do. |
| |    - 11 | 59 | 48 | | se. | Cloudy and dark. |
| |    - 12 | 50 | 36 | | n. | Do. |

**CONTINUED.**

174

| Latitude | Days | THERMOMETER. In Air. | | Wind | State of the weather |
|---|---|---|---|---|---|
| | | Greatest. | Least. | | |
| 34° 31′ | Decem. 13 | 40 | 26 | N. | Cloudy and dark. |
| | 14 | 40 | 28 | NE. | Cloudy, with sleet. |
| | 15 | 32 | 26 | NW. | Cloudy, strong wind. |
| | 16 | 34 | 21 | NW. | Clearing up. |
| | 17 | 42 | 26 | NW. | Clear. |
| | 18 | 36 | 32 | N. | Cloudy, damp. |
| | 19 | 30 | 28 | W. | Four inches of snow. |
| | 20 | 36 | 30 | NW. | Snow. |
| | 21 | 36 | 30 | N. | Cloudy, dark, and snow. |
| | 22 | 36 | 31 | N. | Do. |
| | 23 | 44 | 30 | NW. | Cloudy. |
| | 24 | 45 | 32 | NW. | Clearing up. |
| | 25 | 51 | 34 | NW. | Cloudy. |
| | 26 | 50 | 34 | NW. | Clear. |

At the Hot-Springs.

**175**

**CONTINUED.**

| Latitude. | Days. | THERMOMETER. | | | Wnd. | State of the weather. |
|---|---|---|---|---|---|---|
| | | **In Air.** Greatest. | Least. | River water. | | |
| 34° 31' | Decem. 27 | 45 | 26 | | | Fine. |
| | 28 | 34 | 30 | | | Cloudy. |
| | 29 | | 24 | | sw. | Snow. |
| | 30 | 38 | 9 | 36 | nw. | Very serene. |
| | 31 | 32 | 29 | 36 | se. | General dark cloud. |
| 34 27½ | 1805. January. 1 | 32 | 18 | 32 | nw. | Twelve inches of snow. |
| | 2 | 45 | 6 | 34 | nw. | Very Serene. |
| | 3 | 48 | 22 | 36 | nw. | Clear. |
| | 4 | 50 | 22 | 36 | Calm. | Very serene. |
| | 5 | 55 | 22 | 38 | nw. | Clear. |
| | 6 | 50 | 28 | 44 | | Cloudy with light rain. |
| | 7 | 75 | 38 | 46 | | Rain. |
| | 8 | 37 | 28 | | n. | Cloudy. |

## CONTINUED.

176

| Latitude. | Days. | THERMOMETER. | | | Wind. | STATE OF THE WEATHER. |
| --- | --- | --- | --- | --- | --- | --- |
| | | In Air. | | River water. | | |
| | | Greatest. | Least. | | | |
| 34o 27½' | January. 9 | 42 | 24 | 44 | NE. | Light rain. |
| 34 | 10 | 32 | 19 | 42 | N. | Dark and cloudy. |
| 33 40 | 11 | 32 | 11 | 39 | N. | Fine. |
| 34 29½' | 12 | 43 | 20 | 40 | | Cloudy. |
| 33 21 | 13 | 55 | 27 | 40 | Calm. | Very fine. |
| 33 12 | 14 | 53 | 23 | 40 | NW. | Clear. |
| 32 49 | 15 | 63 | 30 | 40 | | Cloudy. |
| 32 30 | 16 | 65 | 36 | 41 | SE. | Thick fog. |
| | 17 | 60 | 53 | 44 | SW. | Cloudy. |
| | 18 | | | | | |
| | 19 | | | | | |
| | 20 | | | | | |
| | 21 | | | | | |
| | 22 | | | | | |

**177**

## CONTINUED.

| Latitude. | Days. | THERMOMETER. | | | Wind. | STATE OF THE WEATHER. |
|---|---|---|---|---|---|---|
| | | In Air. | | River water. | | |
| | | Greatest. | Least. | | | |
| | January. 23 | | | | | |
| | - 24 | | | | | |
| | - 25 | | | | | |
| | - 26 | | | | | |
| | MISSISSIPPI. | | | | | |
| 31o 1' | - 27 | 50 | 32 | 34 | E. | Clear. |
| | - 28 | 56 | 26 | 33 | NW. | Clear. |
| 31 6 | - 29 | 56 | 34 | 34 | N. | Fine. |
| 31 | - 30 | 55 | 36 | 34 | NE. | Cloudy. |
| | - 31 | 60 | 56 | 38 | SE. | Cloudy. |

*Appendix A*
## Pages in A. & G. Way
## Not Included in Natchez 1806

*Appendix A1: folding chart omitted from the Natchez edition. Size reduced. See page 74.*

**A. SIOUX PROPER.** — **DARCOTAR.**

| B. | C. | D. | E. | F. | G. | H. | I. | J. | K. |
|---|---|---|---|---|---|---|---|---|---|
| Wâh´-pa-tone. | La Soo. | *Darcotar or Sioux. | One. | 80 | 200 | 700 | On the north side of the river St. Peters, 18 leagues from its mouth. | Messrs. Campbell, Dickson and others, who trade to Michilimackinac. | On the Mississippi and St. Peters rivers, at sundry places not stationary. |
| Min´-da, wâr´-câr-ton. | Gens de Lake. | Do. | Do. | 120 | 300 | 1,200 | On the Mississippi, at the mouth of the river St. Peters. | Ditto. | Ditto. |
| Wâh´-pa-coo-ta. | La Soo. | Do. | | 60 | 150 | 400 | On the south-west side of the river St. Peters, 30 leagues above its mouth, in Arrow Stone Prairies. | Ditto. | Ditto. |
| Sis-sa-toné, | La Soo. | Do. | | 80 | 200 | 800 | On the heads of the river St. Peters and Red river of Lake Winnipie. | Mr. Cammaron, a merchant who trades extensively to Michilimackinac. | An establishment at the head of St. Peters river, about 130 leagues from its mouth. |
| Yank´-ton, (of the north or plains). | La Soo. | Do. | | 200 | 500 | 1,600 | From the heads of the river St. Peters and Red river to the Missouri, about the *great bend.* | Ditto. | Ditto. |
| Yank´-ton âh-nâh´. | La Soo. | Do. | | 80 | 200 | 700 | From the river All Jacque eastwardly, on the lower portion of the river Sioux and heads of Foids river, Little, Sioux and Demoin rivers. | Principally with Mr. Crawford, of the river Demoin, | On the river Demoin at their hunting camps, and sometimes at the Ayauwais village Prairie de Chien. |
| Té-ton. | Bois brûlé. | Do. | | 120 | 300 | 900 | On the east side of the Missouri, from the mouth of White river to Teton river. | Mr. Loisell and Co. of St. Louis. | At the Cedar Island, and near the mouth of the Chyenne river, on the Missouri. |
| Té-ton,-o-kan-dan-das. | La Soo. | Do. | | 50 | 120 | 360 | On each side of the Missouri, from the mouth of Teton river to the mouth of the Chyenne river. | Ditto. | Ditto, and at the Rickaras. |
| Té-ton,-min-na-kine-az´-zo. | La Soo. | Do. | | 100 | 250 | 750 | From the mouth of the Chyenne river on each side of the Missouri as high as the Rickaras. | Ditto. | Ditto. |
| Té-ton,-sâh-o-né. | La Soo. | Do. | | 120 | 300 | 900 | On each side of the Missouri from the Rickaras to the mouth of Warrecoonne river. | Ditto. | Ditto. |

CONTINUED.

| | B. | L. | M. | N. | O. | P. | Q. | R. |
|---|---|---|---|---|---|---|---|---|
| | Wáh´-pa-tone. | 10.000 | 18.000 | Deer skins principally, skins of the black bear, otter, fisher, marten, rackoon, grey foxes, muskrats, and minks. | Skins of the small deer black bear, otter, beaver, fisher, marten, racoon, grey fox, muskrat, and mink; also, elk and deers, tallow and bears oil. | On the west side of the Mississippi, about the mouth of St. Peters river, or falls of St. Anthony. | Principally with the Chippeways, La Follovoine, those of Leach and Sandy lakes; defensive with the Saukees, Renars and Ayauwais. | With the Sioux bands and all the nations east of the Mississippi, and south of the Chippeways, who never wage war against the nations on the Missouri. |
| | Min-da-wár´-cár-ton. | 8.700 | 16.000 | Ditto. | Ditto. | Ditto. | Ditto. | Ditto. |
| | Wáh´-pa-coo-ta. | 3.800 | 6.000 | Ditto, with a much larger proportion of otter. | Ditto. | Ditto. | With the Chippeways generally, and sometimes an offensive war on the nations most convenient to them on the Missouri. | Ditto. |
| **DARCOTAR.** | Sis-sa-toné. | 17.000 | 30.000 | Ditto, with a much larger proportion of beaver, otter, and black bear. | Ditto. | About the head of the river St. Peters, at the portage between that river and the Red river, of lake Winnipie. | With the Chippeways generally, the Assinniboins, Christenois, Mandans, Minetares, Ahwahbaways and Chyennes. | Ditto, and partially with the Ricaras. |
| | Yank-ton, (of the north or plains.) | 1.800 | 3.000 | Buffaloe robes and wolf skins. | Ditto, and buffaloe robes, tallow, dried meat and grease in addition. | Ditto, and on the Missouri, near the mouth of Chyenne river. | Ditto. | With the other Sioux bands and partially with the Ricaras. |
| | Yank-ton áh-náh´. | 3.000 | 5.000 | Deer and racoon principally, some black bear, beaver, and otter, | Buffaloe robes, tallow, dryed meat and grease, skins of the small deer, black bear, wolves, elk, rackoon, elk and deers, tallow and bears oil. | At the Council Bluff, or mouth of river Chyenne. | With the Ricaras and the nations on the lower portion of the Missouri and west of it within their reach, except the Mahas and Poncars, also with the Chippeways. | Mahas, Poncaras, Saukees, Renars, Ayauwais and the nations east of the Mississippi and south of the Chippeways; also, with the other bands of Sioux. |
| | Té-ton. | 5.000 | 7.000 | Buffaloe robes, grease & tallow, dressed buffaloe skins, and some dried meat. | Buffaloe robes, tallow, grease and dried meat, skins of the beaver, small and large foxes, small and large wolf, antelope, elk, and deer in great abundance; also, tallow and deers tallow, and a few grissly bears. | At or near the mouth of the Chyenne river. | With all the nations on the lower portion of the Missouri, and west of it within their reach; also, the Mandans, Ahwahhaways, the Minatares, Assinniboins, Christenois and Chippeways. | With all the other bands of Sioux, and with none else except partially with the Ricaras, whom they keep in perpetual dread of them, and plunder without reserve. |
| | Té-ton,-o-kan-dan-das. | 1.500 | 2.500 | Ditto. | | | | |
| | Té-ton,-min-na-kine-az´-zo. | 2.000 | 3.000 | Ditto. | | | | |
| | Té-ton,-sáh-o-né. | 2.300 | 3.500 | Ditto. | | | | |

**A. SIOUXS PROPER.**

*To follow page 30.*

*Appendix A2: folding chart omitted from the Natchez edition. See page 74.*

*The subdivisions of the Darcotar or Sioux nation, with the names of the principal chiefs of each band and subdivision.*

| NAMES OF THE BANDS. | NAMES OF THE SUBDIVISIONS. | NAMES OF THE CHIEFS. | REMARKS. |
|---|---|---|---|
| Mindawarcarton. | Mindawarcarton. Kee-uke-sah. Tin-tah-ton. Mah-tah-ton. | * Ne-co-hun-dah. Tar-tong-gar-mah-nee. Cha-tong-do-tah. | Those marked with a star are the principal chiefs of their respective bands, as well as their own subdivisions. |
| Walhpatone. | Wah-pa-tone. O-ta-har-ton. | * Tar-car-ray. War-bo-sen-dat-ta. | |
| Wahpacoota. | Wah-pa-coo-ta. Mi-ah-kee-jack-sah. | * War-cah-to. Chit-tah-wock-kun-de-pe. | |
| Sissatone. | Sissatone. Caw-ree. | * Wack-he-en-do-tar. Tar-tung-gan-naz-a. | |
| Yankton, (of the north.) | Kee-uke-sah. Sah-own. Hone-ta-par-teen. Hah-har-tones. Hone-ta-par-teen-waz. Za-ar-tar. | * Mah-to-wy-ank-ka. . . . . Arsh-kane. Pit-ta-sah. Mah-pe-on-do-tak. Tat-tung-gar-weet-e-co. | Said individually to be very friendly to the whites. He possesses great influence in his band and nation. |

| | | | Remarks. |
|---|---|---|---|
| Yankton ahnah. | Yank-ton,-sa-char-hoo. | *Nap-pash-scan-na-mah-na. | Accepted a medal and flag of the United States. |
| | Tar-co-im-bo-to. | War-ha-zing ga. . . . . . | Do. a medal. |
| Teton, (Bois brûlé.) | E-sah-a-te-ake-tar-par. War-chink-tar-he. Choke-tar-to-womb. Oz-ash. Me-ne-sharne. | *Tar-tong-gar-sar-par. . . Man-da-tong-gar. . . . . . Tar-tang-gar-war-har. Mah-zo-mar-nee. Wah-pah-zing-gar. | Do. do. & flag of U. S. A great scoundrel; we gave him a medal before we were acquainted with his character. |
| Teton,O-kan-dan-das. | She-o. O-kan-dan-das. | *O-ase-se-char. Wah-tar-pa. | |
| Teton,min-na-kine-az-zo. | Min-na-kine-az-zo. Wan-nee-wack-a-ta-o-ne-lar Tar-co-eh-parh. | *Wock-ke-a-chauk-in-dish-kah. Chan-te-wah-nee-jah. | |
| Teton,sah-o-ne. | Sah-o-ne. Tack-chan-de-see-char. Sah-o-ne-hont-a-par-par. | *Ar-kee-che-tar. War-min-de-o-pe-in-doo-tar Sharh-ka-has-car. | |

*To follow page 34.*

*Appendix A3: See page 74.*

64

A. Pania Piqûe⟩.
B.
C. La Paunee Piqûe⟩.
D. Pania Proper.
E.    F.    G.    H.    I.    J.    K.    L.
M.    N.    O.    P.    Q.    R.
S. These people have no intercourse with the inhabitants of the Illinois ; the information, therefore,
   which I have been enabled to obtain, with respect
   to them, is very imperfect.    They were formerly
   known by the name of the *White* Panias, and
   are of the same family with the Panias of the
   river Platte.    They are said to be a well disposed
   people, and inhabit a very fertile country ; certain it is that they enjoy a delightful climate.

A. Paducas.
B.
C. La Paddo.
D. *
E.    F.    G.    H.    I.    J.    K.    L.
M.    N.    O.    P.    Q.    R.
S. This once powerful nation has, apparently, entirely disappeared ; every inquiry I have made
   after them has proved ineffectual.    In the year
   1724, they resided in several villages on the
   heads of the Kansas river, and could, at that
   time, bring upwards of two thousand men into
   the field (see Monsr. Dupratz history of Louisiana, page 71, and the map attached to that
   work).    The information that I have received is,
   that being oppressed by the nations residing on
   the Missouri, they removed to the upper part of
   the river Platte, where they afterwards had but
   little intercourse with the whites.    They seem
   to have given name to the northern branch of that
   river, which is still called the Paducas fork.    The

### 65

most probable conjecture is, that being still further reduced, they have divided into small wandering bands, which assumed the names of the
subdivisions of the Paducas nation, and are
known to us at present under the appellation of
Wetepahatoes, Kiawas, Kanenavish, Katteka,
Dotame, &c. who still inhabit the country to
which the Paducas are said to have removed.
The majority of my information led me to believe
that those people spoke different languages, but
other and subsequent information has induced me
to doubt the fact.

9

*Appendix A4: See page 74–75.*

169

of a considerable elevation, with a species of rampart surrounding a large space, which was, no doubt, the position of a fortified town.

While here, Mr. Dunbar met with an American who pretended to have been up the Arkansa river three hundred leagues. The navigation of this river he says is good to that distance, for boats drawing three or four feet water. Implicit faith, perhaps, ought not to be given to his relation, respecting the quantity of silver he pretends to have collected there. He says he has found silver on the Washita, thirty leagues above the hot springs, so rich, that three pounds of it yielded one pound of silver, and that this was found in a cave. He asserts, also, that the ore of the mine upon the little Missouri, was carried to Kentucky, by a person of the name of Boon, where it was found to yield largely in silver. This man says he has been up the Red river likewise, and that there is a great rapid just below the raft, or natural bridge, and several others above it; that the Caddo nation is about fifty leagues above the raft, and near to their village commences the country of the great prairies, which extend four or five hundred miles to the west of the sand mountains, as they are termed. These great plains reach far beyond the Red river to the south, and northward over the Arkansa river, and among the numerous branches of the Missouri. He confirms the account of the beauty and fertility of the western country.

On the morning of the 25th Mr. Dunbar set out, on horseback, from the Catahoola to Natchez. The rain which had fallen on the preceding days rendered the roads wet and muddy, and it was two in the afternoon before he reached the Bayau Crocodile, which is considered half way between the Black river and the Mississippi. It is one of the numerous creeks in the low grounds which assist in venting the waters of the inundation. On the margins of the water courses the lands are highest, and produce canes; they fall

22

170

off, in the rear, into cypress swamps and lakes. The waters of the Mississippi were rising, and it was with some difficulty that they reached a house near Concord that evening. This settlement was begun since the cession of Louisiana to the United States, by citizens of the Mississippi territory, who have established their residence altogether upon newly acquired lands, taken up under the authority of the Spanish commandant, and have gone to the expense of improvement either in the names of themselves or others, before the 20th of December, 1803, hoping thereby to hold their new possessions under the sanction of the law.

Exclusive of the few actual residents on the banks of the Mississippi, there are two very handsome lakes in the interior, on the banks of which similar settlements have been made. He crossed at the ferry, and at mid-day of the 26th reached his own house.

Dr. Hunter, and the remainder of the party, followed Mr. Dunbar, down the Washita, with the boat in which they ascended the river, and, ascending the Mississippi, reached St. Catharine's landing on the morning of the 31st January, 1805.

*Common names of some of the trees, shrubs and plants growing in the vicinity of the Washita.*

THREE kinds of white oak, four kinds of red oak, black oak, three kinds of hickory, one of which has an oblong nut, white and good, chinkapin, three kinds of ash, one of which is the prickly, three kinds of elm, two kinds of maple, two kinds of pine, red cedar, sweet gum, black gum, linden, two kinds of iron wood, growing on high and low lands, sycamore, box elder, holly, sweet bay, laurel, magnolia accuminata, black walnut, filbert, buckeye, dogwood,

### 171

three kinds of locust, the three thorned and honey locust, hazle, beech, wild plumb, the fruit red, but not good, bois d'arc (bow wood) called also bois jaune (yellow wood) a famous yellow dye, three kinds of hawthorn, with berries, red, scarlet and black, lote tree, for Indian arrows, bois de carbane, a small growth, and proper for hoops, two kinds of osier, myrtle, tooth ache tree and magnolia.

A vine, bearing large good black grapes in bunches, black grape, hill grape, yellow grape, muscadine, or fox grape, and a variety of other vines. The saw briar, single rose briar, and china root briar, wild gooseberry, with a dark red fruit, three kinds of whortle berry, wild pomgranate, passion flower, two sorts of sumach, winter's berry, winter's green, a small red farinaceous berry like a haw, on a plant one inch high, which grows under the snow, and is eaten by the Indians, the silk plant, wild endive, wild olive, pink root, snake root, wild mint of three kinds, coloquintida (bitter apple) growing along the river side, clover, sheeps clover, life everlasting, wild liquorice, marygold, missletoe, thistle, wild hemp, bull rush, dittany, white and red poppy, yellow jessamine, poke, fern, capillaire, honeysuckle, mosses, petu to make ropes with, wormwood, hops, ipecacuanha, persicaria, Indian turnip, wild carrot, wild onion, ginger, wild cabbage, and bastard indigo.

*Appendix A5: the Meteorological Tables as published in W. See Textual Introduction, "Meteorological Tables," pages 76–77.*

*METEOROLOGICAL observations made by Mr. Dunbar and doctor Hunter, in their voyage up the Red and Washita rivers, in the year 1804.*

| Time of observ. | | | | | | |
|---|---|---|---|---|---|---|
| Day of the month. | THERMOMETER. | | | In river water. | Wind. | Weather and Meteorological phenomena, &c. |
| | Sun's rise. | 3 P. M. | 8 P. M. | | | |
| 1804. October 20 | 40° | 80° | ° | 73° | | Light clouds. |
| 21 | 60 | 83 | . | . | s. s. e. | Cloudy. |
| 22 | 65 | 79 | . | . | s. s. e. | |
| 23 | 67 | 73 | . | . | | |
| 24 | 54 | 68 | . | 71 | n. nnw. | Cloudy in morning; evening clear. |
| 25 | 49 | 60 | . | 68 | North. | Cloudy morn; clear evening. |
| 26 | 40 | 70 | . | 65 | n. w. | Light clouds. |
| 27 | 32 | 73 | . | 64 | North. | Hoar frost; fog on river; clear above. |
| 28 | 40 | 73 | 56 | 63 | | |
| 29 | 41 | 85 | 62 | 62 | nw. sw. | Fog on river. |
| 30 | 47 | 83 | 60 | 60 | w. n. w. | Fog on river; clear above. |
| 31 | 44 | 84 | . | 62 | nnw. | Ditto,                   ditto. |

| November | | | | | | |
|---|---|---|---|---|---|---|
| 1 | 48 | 85 | 64 | 62 | . | Calm and clear above. |
| 2 | 48 | 84 | 78 | 62 | s. s. e. | |
| 3 | 52 | 86 | 72 | 64 | . | Some light clouds. |
| 4 | 54 | 83 | 63 | 64 | . | Clear. |
| 5 | 52 | 68 | 58 | 62 | n. w. | Heavy fog and damp air. |
| 6 | 45 | 79 | . | 64 | West. | Heavy fog. |
| 7 | 52 | 80 | 67 | 64 | . | Clear. Lat. 32° 29' N. |
| 8 | 53 | 61 | 56 | 58 | . | Cloudy. A disagreeable damp day. |
| 9 | 42 | 72 | . | 61 | . | Cloudy, damp and cold. |
| 10 | 40 | 72 | 34 | 58 | . | Clear and calm. |
| 11 | 24 | . | . | 53 | | Do.    ditto. |
| 12 | 36 | . | 54 | 54 | . | Clear and calm; cloudy in evening. |
| 13 | 33 | 66 | 62 | 55 | South. | Fog on river; calm; evening cloudy. |
| 14 | 44 | 58 | 44 | 55 | . | Clear and calm. |
| 15 | 38 | 60 | 50 | 54 | . | Clear and calm. |
| 16 | 38 | 51 | 42 | 54 | North. | Morning calm; afternoon cloudy, damp and disagreeable. |
| 17 | 40 | 41 | 44 | 54 | . | Calm, fog on river. Lat. 33° 13' N. |
| 18 | 32 | . | 57 | 52 | . | Serene morning; cloudy evening. |
| 19 | 54 | 67 | 62 | 54 | . | Cloudy; calm. |
| 20 | 59 | 62 | 54 | 54 | . | Cloudy; calm. |

## CONTINUED.

| Time of observ. | THERMOMETER. | | | | Wind. | Weather and meteorological phenomena, &c. |
|---|---|---|---|---|---|---|
| Day of the month. | Sun's rise. | 3 P.M. | 8 P.M. | In river water. | | |
| **1804.** | | | | | | |
| November 21 | 43° | 72° | 58° | 54° | . | Calm; a little fog. |
| 22 | 40 | 68 | . | . | . | |
| 23 | 48 | 72 | 54 | 54 | . | Light clouds; calm. |
| 24 | 48 | 72 | 59 | 54 | . | Light clouds; calm. |
| 25 | . | . | . | . | . | Rainy. |
| 26 | 50 | 68 | 62 | 57 | . | Clear. |
| 27 | 54 | 71 | 66 | 58 | . | Cloudy. |
| 28 | 68 | 78 | 73 | 60 | . | Cloudy; calm. |
| 29 | 72 | 76 | 52 | 62 | South. | Cloudy and strong wind; rain 9 A. M. clear at noon. |
| 30 | 32 | 57 | . | 60 | . | Cloudy and calm. |
| December 1 | 32 | 58 | 35 | 54 | . | Clear and calm. |
| 2 | 30 | 59 | 38 | 50 | . | Clear and calm. |

| | | | | | |
|---|---|---|---|---|---|
| 3 | 38 | 59 | 44 | 48 | . | Clear and calm. |
| 4 | 36 | 50 | 36 | 48 | . | Clear and calm. |
| 5 | 23 | 56 | 38 | 47 | . | Serene and calm. |
| 6 | 45 | 67 | 56 | 48 | s. w. | Cloudy; light wind. |
| 7 | 38 | 50 | 24 | 47 | n. w. | Cloudy. Lat. 34° 27' 31" |
| 8 | 10 | 47 | . | 43 | n. w. | High wind; very serene. |
| 9 | 19 | 42 | 28 | 41 | n. w. | Very serene; wind moderate. |
| 10 | 26 | 50 | 28 | . | n. w. | Very serene; wind moderate. Lat. 34° 31' N. at Hot Springs. |
| 11 | 48 | 59 | 50 | . | s. e. | Cloudy, damp, and penetrating. |
| 12 | 36 | 44 | 32 | . | North. | Cloudy, damp, and disagreeable. |
| 13 | 26 | 40 | 30 | . | North. | Cloudy, dark, and disagreeable. |
| 14 | 28 | 40 | 32 | . | n. e. | Cloudy, dark and cold, with sleet. |
| 15 | 26 | 32 | 30 | . | n. w. | Wind strong; cloudy. |
| 16 | 21 | 32 | 22 | . | n. w. | Wind moderate. |
| 17 | 26 | 42 | 28 | . | n. w. | Wind moderate; bright morn; fine day; rain in the night. |
| 18 | 34 | 36 | 32 | . | North. | Cold and damp; dark and cloudy; rain at noon; hail and snow in evening. |
| 19 | 30 | 30 | 23 | . | West. | Snowing. Ground covered 4 inch. with snow. |
| 20 | 30 | 36 | 32 | . | West. | Light driving clouds from N. W. |

## CONTINUED.

| Time of observ. | THERMOMETER. | | | | Wind. | Weather and meteorological phenomena, &c. |
|---|---|---|---|---|---|---|
| Day of the month. | Sun's rise. | 3 P.M. | 8 P.M. | In river water. | | |
| 1804. | | | | | | |
| December 21 | 32° | .° | 31° | .° | North. | Cloudy and damp; snow on ground. |
| 22 | 31 | 36 | 34 | . | North. | Dark and cloudy; rain early in the day; snow in evening. |
| 23 | 30 | 40 | 33 | . | N. W. | Clouds begin to dissipate. |
| 24 | 32 | 45 | 34 | . | N. W. | Wind moderate. |
| 25 | 34 | 50 | 44 | . | N. W. | Cloudy. |
| 26 | 34 | 50 | 34 | . | N. W. | Clear and windy. |
| 27 | 26 | 45 | 38 | . | N. E. | Clear and cold. |
| 28 | 34 | 32 | 30 | . | S. W. | Cloudy in morning; snow in afternoon. |
| 29 | 25 | . | 24 | . | N. W. | Strong wind; stormy afternoon; calm night. |
| 30 | 9 | 38 | 21 | 36 | N. W. | High wind; last night very cold. |
| 31 | 29 | 32 | . | 36 | S. ·E. | Snow. Lat. 34° 28' N. |

| 1805. January | | | | | Wind | |
|---|---|---|---|---|---|---|
| 1 | 26 | 32 | 18 | · | · | Snow. |
| 2 | 6 | 45 | 32 | 32 | · | Calm. |
| 3 | 22 | 48 | 30 | 34 | N. W. | Wind moderate. |
| 4 | 22 | 50 | 32 | 36 | | |
| 5 | 22 | 55 | 28 | 36 | N.W. S.E. | Clear. |
| 6 | 28 | 50 | 44 | 38 | · | Cloudy and a little rain. |
| 7 | 64 | 78 | 38 | 44 | · | Night cloudy, cold and moist. |
| 8 | 28 | 37 | 37 | 46 | | Rain in evening and night. |
| 9 | 42 | 36 | 24 | 44 | North. | Dark, cloudy and cold, with hail. |
| 10 | 23 | 32 | 19 | 42 | North. | Cold and damp.  Lat. 34° N. |
| 11 | 11 | 32 | 26 | 89 | | Fine morning, and very cold. |
| 12 | 20 | 43 | 30 | 40 | · | The air damp and penetrating. |
| 13 | 27 | 53 | 30 | 40 | · | Morning fine and dry; evening moist. |
| 14 | 23 | 53 | 32 | 40 | N. E. | Light wind; atmosphere dry. |
| 15 | 30 | 63 | 43 | 40 | N. W. | Cloudy; wind light. |
| 16 | 36 | 65 | 60 | 41 | s. E. | At fort Miro. Lat. 32° 30' N. |
| 17 | 60 | | | 44 | | Cloudy. |
| 18 | · | | · | | S. W. | |
| 19 | | 58 | 50 | 43 | s. w. | Clear. |
| 20 | 56 | 51 | 40 | 43 | · | Cloudy, and drizzly rain. |

## CONTINUED.

| Time of observ. | THERMOMETER. | | | | Wind. | Weather and meteorological phenomena, &c. |
|---|---|---|---|---|---|---|
| Day of the month. | Sun's rise. | 3 P.M. | 8 P.M | In river water. | | |
| 1805. | | | | | | |
| January 21 | 21° | 36° | 26° | 40° | East. | Wind variable. |
| " 22 | 21 | 48 | 40 | 39 | N. E. | Weather raw and cold. |
| " 23 | 49 | 64 | 54 | 42 | s. E. | Clouds and drizzly raw. |
| " 24 | 55 | 50 | 46 | 43 | | Rain. Lat. 31° 37' N. |
| " 25 | 36 | 40 | 40 | 40 | · | Windy ; cold and raw. |
| " 26 | 32 | 36 | 33 | 42 | N. E. | Stormy and snow. |
| " 27 | 24 | 50 | 32 | 44 | East. | Lat. 31° N. |
| " 28 | 26 | 56 | 40 | 34 | North. | On Mississippi river; clear and moderate. |
| " 29 | 34 | 56 | · | 33 | North. | Fine weather. |
| " 30 | 36 | 55 | 53 | 34 | N. E. | Raw and cloudy. |
| " 31 | 56 | · | · | 38 | s. E. | Cloudy and moderate. |

## ❧ *Appendix B*
# John Sibley Correspondence

This appendix contains transcriptions of five manuscripts by John Sibley now at the Library of Congress among the Thomas Jefferson Papers, and one letter from Jefferson to Sibley. In chronological order, they are:

B1  John Sibley to Governor Claiborne, October 10, 1803.

B2  John Sibley to Thomas Jefferson, March 20, 1804.

B3  John Sibley, "1804 Account of the Indians," written 1805 and sent to General Dearborn.

B4  John Sibley, "on the country between Misipi and Rio Bravo," written 1805 and sent to General Dearborn.

B5  Sibley's account of Red River, the second part of item B4.

B6  Thomas Jefferson to John Sibley, Washington, May 27, 1805.

Two other published letters of Sibley dealing with Louisiana are not reprinted here. They are "A Letter from John Sibley . . . to J. Gales, December 13, 1803,"[1] and John Sibley to William Dunbar, April 2, 1805.[2] Both of these letters provide interesting parallels to the accounts printed in the *Message* to Congress.

---

❧ B1 Letter of John Sibley to Gov. William C. C. Claiborne, governor of Mississippi Territory, and later governor of Orleans Territory. A description of Louisiana, including a map "Sketched out in the Night, for I am obliged to be Cautious." In a letter to Jefferson of August 24, 1803,[3] Claiborne commented that he was expecting this information.

[1] White, *News of the Plains and Rockies*, item A1.
[2] Rowland, 162–74.
[3] Quoted by Brandt, 369.

Natchitoches 10th. Octobr. 1803

Dear Sir,

I Recd. yesterday your letter of the 30th Ult. and the News Papers Accompanying it, No Cordial Balm could have been so gratefull, in proportion to the anxiety, doubts and fears that kept my mind in torment, so was their Receipt agreable, not like an Anodyne producing a stupid sleepiness, for my spirits were so exhilarated that I thought I should not want to sleep any more I have for sometime wish'd I had wings that I could fly to the City of Washington, by way of the Town of Washington. But you assure me that no part of Louissiana is to be disposed of, & that you expect to be in Orleans in December, and that you beleive West Florida is included in the Cession; I have known a Long time that Louissiana used to comprehend it but reposed some article in the treaty excluding it from Govr. Salcedo's Proclamation, if not it will Answer all the immediate purposes, by opening a Rt to the Tombeebee Settlement, which is all that Suffice, for Back of East Florida we have no settlements, & it will Secure the whol of both banks of the Missisippi, and I think the acquisition of Batton rouge of importance, it is the Best Situation for a large Town between the Balize & Chickesaw Bluff. My fancy has anticipated many Circumstances that must Occur—This Post or Near it is an important Point, the Great Road towards Mexico here takes off, it is an Out Post to the Westward, Stores &c can Come here by Water, & I have Already look'd round for a Suitable place of deposit, a Situation high, Surrounded with bountifull springs, timber and of easy Ascent &c; And I find an excellent Road may be made between this And Natchez & Nearly always passable, and that Natchez is but Verry little out of a right line from this place to New Orleans, particularly by the Lake Ponchartrain & it will forever be the *best* road that Can be found, the Coarse of Red River & the course of Missisippi from Red River downwards is Nearly the same, from the Mouth of Red River upwards Missisippi bears much to the East, to get a good Road from here to Natchez is a great Point, for there will then be a fine Road all the way from Orleans to Mexico.

I am Sorry I cant Send you a Map that will afford you some information, there is none in this Country, & I believe in no other, there has been none taken Since the Country belong'd to Spain if there are any they must be old French Ones; but I Never Saw One, I have Often seen good Charts of the Coast of the Gulph of Mexico, taken by order of the English Governmt. but none of the Interior Country. I have from much inquiry Learned the Names of the Rivers between Missisippi and River Grand, and without any pretentions to Accuracy sketch'd them down on a piece of paper in the order they are, the first River west of Red River is the *Quelqueshoe* it heads fifteen or 20 miles from this Post, runs So. Eastwardly and falls into a Lake or sound that communicates with the Gulph of Mexico by an Inlet of twelve feet Water, it is about 150 Miles long & I believe is not of much account for its Navigation, it affords some beautifull Bodies of Pararie Lands; & Low down will do for Sugar, there are some Settlements on it, it is under the government of Louissiana and no one pretends otherwise. The Next in Order is the *Sabine,* it is Sixty Miles West of Red River & heads About one hundred & fifty Miles N. Westwardly of this post, it is Near three hundred Miles Long, empties into the Same lake or Sound the Quelqueshoe does, but a few Miles west of It is a Shallow River fordable at Low Water, Low Banks & Low grounds five or six miles Wide, and Subject to overflow, Except in a few Places. Low down the Country is generally Flat and wet, there are some handsome Bluffs on the River, it might be used for Boats in high water, there is Much good land on it & on the Smaller Streams that empty into it, is a remarkable fine Stock Country, no Settlements on it Except a few families on & Near where the Great Road crosses it, this River for 200 Miles is Said to have been the antient Limits of Louissiana.

The Next River is the Angalena or Snow River it passes by Natchidoches a small distance to the West, is less and Shorter than the Sabine, is about 70 or 80 Miles from it and the Country between these two Rivers is the Beauty of all these Countries, it is Excessively Rich well Laying & well Watered. The Next is Trinity River, the Next the Braces, then The Colerado or Red River, then the little River St. Antoine on which the Town or Station of St. Antoine is Situated, then a little River called Gaudelope, then the Nuces or Walnut River which is a Branch of River Grand, it is a fine Country all the way from Natchidoches to St. Antoine, the distance is about four hundred Miles, the Braces is Nearly half way, from Natchidoches to St. Anthoine; River Grand is about 160 miles beyond, in all this Extensive Country there is no settlements, except about 100 families in and About Natchidoches, 2 or 300 at St. Anthoine and below St. Anthoine 120 Miles & 60 Miles from the Sea on the Same River is a Small Settlement of Christianis'd Indians. The place is called Lauerdee.[4] but all these Countries have Numerous tribes of Indians. beyond River Grand the Country is full of Towns & People and Mines, all the way to Old Mexico—New Mexico is on River Grand high up, Santa Fee the Capital is on the East Side of River Grand amongst Mountains & Towns. The head of Red River which is understood to be in Louissiana, Rises it is believed in the same Mountains that River Grand does, which is the dividing ridge that Separates

[4]Laberdee S4; Labahie W page 70, S1 (Appendix B3).

the Waters of the Atlantic from those that fall into the Western Ocean and the Gulph of California.

The length of Red River is not known, it is Six or seven hundred Miles to the Pawnie or Towiash Indians, and it is a Large Navigable River thus far, and they Say is so a thousand Miles beyond them, and all the Way a Beautifull Rich & well Watered Country, abounding with fine Pararies Stocked with Buffelo &c—as Red River and its Branches extend very far to the Westward, and Missisippi bends Eastward the Province of Louissiana about the Mouth of Missouri in that fine Climate is not less than fifteen hundred Miles wide; its form is Triangular.

In one of the papers you was so good as to Send me there is a pretty long piece on Louisiana, taken from the Charter City Gazette of Freneau & Williams, which I attribute to Judge Bay, I am well Acquainted with him, & know his Stile and his Connection with that press. he once lived in Pensacola and Acted as Secretary to the Governor, is no doubt well informed about the Antient Limits of Louisiana. To the eastward, I should be disposed to respect his Opinion thus far; he has correctly Stated the History of the transfer of the East side of the Missisippi, from which it appears Clearly, that West Florida must be Included in the Cession; but it is Laughable to hear him propose that all the Inhabitants Should be Withdrawn from the West Side, and make the River the Boundary, he would find it difficult Removing an hundred Thousand People and a Million or two of cattle &c. but if the Judge could disswade the government into that Measure perhaps he might then be able to Sell some Land on Second & Wills Creeks, and his famous Walnut Hill Tract he has likewise committed a Gross Mistake in Calling the distance from Batton Rouge to the Mouth of Red River 200 miles—And Another when he Says that from the Mouth of Red River to Natchitoches is another hundred & that, that, is the first high land on Red River that will do to Settle—from the mouth of Red River to Natchatoch is 247 Miles, and the beautifull Settlement of Izavial [Avoyall?] where is 300 families is 165 Miles below Natchitoch as the River runs, and Izavial 72 Miles above the Mouth, but Black River 31 Miles up Red River may be Settled, and it is Dead Water to Ascend insted of the Judges Strong Current, The Common Passage with a Large Loaded Barge, from New Orleans to Natchitoches is 25 or 28 days; but at times it is done in less.—And when you Arrive at Natchitoch Such is the beauty and conveniency of the Banks that Boats are unloaded by Laying a Plank from the Boat to the Bank, at the warehouse door, I look upon the Conveniency of the Loading & unloading, as much greater than at Natchez as to fully Compensate the difference in distance to Ascend the River, at any rate Natchitoch is more Convenient to Market & trade than the Walnut Hills.

There are on Red River four or five & Twenty Cotton Gins and Several More building—there went down the River last year upwards of three Thousand Bales of Cotton, a Large quantity of Tobacco & Peltry which is Calculated to be equal in Amt. to the Cotton—And Last year an Estimate was made of 7300 Horses that went out of, & pass'd through this Country; and from Apalousa & Tuckepa at Least double the quantity of Cotton, these Exports from New Orleans will Cut some figure from the Country that the Judge would have abandoned to the Indians; besides a quantity of Beef and Pork that might be Purchased & Exported from this country almost incalculable, In this devoted Country to the Indians there may be made at Least a Thousand Sugar Plantations, there are upward of an hundred already on the West Side of the River, Including Tuckepa And both Banks of La Fosh for 70 Miles; Good Part of Tuckepa & Quelqueshoe is capable of being turn'd into sugar plantations. Red River alone below Natchitoches is Capable of being turned into Sugar Plantations—Red River Alone below Natchitoches is Capable of making more Tobacco than is made at present in all the United States, of a Superior quality, and at one fourth Part of the Labour, for in this Country it is always made without raising any Hill, they only make a hole and Set the plant, & they find the Overflow'd ground is the Best for Tobacco, the water is always off time enough, & there is no grass nor weeds, and the Land is so Strong they Generally Cut it three times, the Common Calculation is 2000 pounds to the Acre and a hand Can easily manage five Acres, and make Corn besides, but their way of making it up into Carrots is very troublesome, and they Loose very much in weight by throwing away the Stems; I know a field in the Neighbourhood of this Village that from a Calculation, it appears, it has been planted every year in either Corn or Tobacco for 97 years which is the date of the first establishment of this post, and it produc'd this year as fine Tobacco as I ever Saw; and the Owner suposes as well as it Ever did, it Never had any Manure for no Such thing is known here, not even the gardens.

The King of the Caddos is now here, a very fine Looking Man, he comes to see me half a dozen times a day and deposits with me all his goods and finery. he travel'd all around the Neighbourhood yesterday to find an Interpreter, at last found a Frenchman who spoke Caddo, he came with him he wanted to know about the Americans coming, I did not think Proper to tell him much at present; but told him to go home and wait three Moons; he said the Chickesaws had told him how the

Americans let them have a three Point Blanket for five Skins, & other goods as Cheap, and how they had got a Cotton Gin, Spinning Whee-les & Looms, and a Blacksmiths shop but they did not beleive the Chickesaws; I told him it was true I believed,—I likewise told him the great Man the President had heard of the Caddos, that they were good people & Never kill'd ye white Men, he said they Never did, and Lov'd the English—he then made a Long Speech, discribing what a fine Country they had, and Mark'd out a place which the Interpreter told me he wanted Lay'd off for them, and all the rest was for the Ameri-cans—he said after three Moons I Should see him again, he would come down. This Nation is but Small; the Small Pox destroy'd a Great Many of them lately; but they Boast of their Never having shed white Mans Blood; they I think might with Proper management be made good Citizens, at any rate usefull, on the frontier as a protection against any other Indians, I should think myselfe as Safe in their towns as in the City of Natchez.

There is lately considerable talk about the Spaniard resuming Again their Old Post 21 miles from here call'd the Izard I. or Z.I. Calle'd some-times Adaize, Forty Miles this Side of Sabine, which there is no doubt of its being in Louissiana, it is Clearly my Opinion that the United States should immediately establish a Post on the East Bank of the Sabine, the Country is all Open as Hostile Interpretation can be put upon it, 'tis true the Jurisdiction of the Governor General of the five interior Provinces who resides at Coaguila, has at present Jurisdiction this Side the Sabine, and so he has at Bayou Pierre on Red River; but that is only an Arangement between two Commandants Since the Country has all been Spanish the United States are in no Condition to give up to Spain at Present an Inch of Territory that belongs to them; but if they Get Possession of 40 Miles of Louissiana it may be not so easy to get them away.

On the head of Quelqueshoe, between that and Sabine on a creek Called by the Spaniards Yan a Cookoo, which runs through a Parairie of the Same Name, which in English would be Called the Cookoos Meadow, the word Yan in Spanish is Meadow in English & Parairie in French—the Bird Cookoo is the same in both Spanish and French, this place has been describ'd to me by a Gentleman who has several times been through it, he says the Parairie he thinks comprehends irregularly as much as an hundred Square Miles, but it is all Over it Interspersed with the most beautifull trees Consisting of Lofty Oaks & Pacans that are so handsome they Look as though they had been trim'd, all under these Clumps, fine beautifull Grass without a Single Bush and the woods round about the Parairie are of the same discription, the Soil very Rich and well watered with Mill Seats &c. he says once in the Parairie he found a Number of old Peach trees; probably planted by some Frenchman before Louissiana was ceted to Spain. He thinks Two hundred families might be as well Setled there as any place he knows.

The Same Gentleman has describ'd to me Another place Call'd the Three Parairies, they begin about 30 Miles from here North of the Great Western road and not far from it, they are Only seperated by a small Open wood, he thinks they Contain Two hundred Square Miles, and are but very little inferior in beauty, Richness and Water to Yan a Cookoo: but from these last mentioned pararies it is all a Rich beauti- full Country for More than a Thousand Miles, Bayou Pierre where are 20 or 30 good families settled part of it, it is a water of Red River Large Boats go from [blank] into the heart of the settlement at all seasons. a beautifull Parairie Country Sixty Miles by Land from here, about halfe way to the first Caddo Towns on the West Side the River, and at pres- ent under the Jurisdiction of the Province of Taxus (or Tachus as it is spoken) in the district of Natchidoches, though 140 Miles from it, and no Settlements between except a few families on Sabine.

The Inclosed Map I send you which I Sketched out in the Night, for I am obliged to be Cautious, at Least I think it best to be so at present. I have no pretentions to its Accuracy; but I believe those the best Acquainted with the Country Cannot say it is very inaccurate, if you Should with to make any other use of it than in your own Closet, I wish you would have it Coppied and Scal'd which may be done by right lines from known Points of Latitude on the Missisippi, and have Natchitoch Lay'd down not quite so far North for it is not half a degree North of Natchez—it is impossible to Lay down for the Rivers any thing more than Crooked lines resembling a River near where we know the Rivers are and their General Course and heads, but the particular Bends of a River is an unimportant Circumstance in forming a General Geo- graphical Idea of a Country. The upper Forks of Red River are to appearance much larger than the whol Lower Down United; for from this to its Mouth is very deep Several Large Vessels have been built here, and the Country above Abounds in Cedar equal to those of Lebanos, Enough to build a Navy, the Real Red Cedar, Loggs of it every Fresh come down, and Thousands of them as sound as when they were Growing are Now lodged in the Great Raft which begins about 30 Miles above this place and Extends for Near an hundred Miles up, Compleatly Choaking up the Old River, which in One place a Soil has formed over the Raft with trees growing on it, over which a person might ride a horseback without suspecting there was any River under him; but by holding the Ear to the Surface the water may be heard running through amongst the Logs: but there is a Passage by Water around the Raft, and a little Labour will make it much better than through the River was Opined, for it will Pass through Lake Bisteno, which is Near 50 Miles long and Water deep enough for a Ship at all times and from 3 to 6 Miles wide, the Passage from the upper end of this Lake Communicates with the River above the Raft and is Open and fine, the Lower end of the Lake is within about 3 Miles of Bayau Channo which is Open & deep allways into the River below the Raft, at high water or Bastard, they go through now; but a little Diging would make it good at all Seasons.

I am Exceedingly Obliged to you for the care you took of me in writing to the Consul at Orleans I shall long remember it, I believe all is Safe Now, I am Inform'd Our Commedant here who is a good Man but no Solomon and was Never out of Louissiana, and has from his Infancy belong'd to the King of Spain, wrote a Letter about it to the New Commedant of Natchadoches as there was a Man Out there by the name of Bird who Came here with me, who might be a spy to the Commedant who is an European, and more liberal, took No Notice of it only Laugh'd at the Nonsence. Mr. Tredo our Commedant and Our priest and a number of others are now at Natchidoches.—What kind of government would at first be most Suitable and proper God Only knows, it would be farcical to see a Lawyer in a Court of Justice addressing a Jury of them at present, with a few exceptions they have no Other Idea of any kind of Government than a Commedant with both Civil & Military Jurisdiction, they have been accustomed to Such Ill Luck in any attempt to Obtain Justice, they Seldom apply, and Submit to any thing that hapens quietly.

There is in the office of Mr. Tredo here Nearly a Cart Load of Old Records about Lands & Intestate Estates Wills &c that belong only to the Country which Should be Safely kept, all the Public Property I know of here is an Old Log Jail but belonging to the Church or Religious Society is a Large Church, a Pretty Good Parsonage House with Out Houses and a Large Garden there. All the Houses Occupied by the Commedant, with the Stores and Barracks are his private property I believe.

Accept my best Wishes
Your Obt. Servt.
John Sibley

Governor Claiborne

❧ B2 John Sibley to Thomas Jefferson, March 20, 1804, presenting specimens of dyes from Osage orange wood. The letter was received on July 12.

Thomas Jefferson Esq
President of the United States

Sir,

I reside at present at Natchitoches on Red River in Louissiana am a Native of Massachusetts, have liv'd some years in Fayetteville North Carolina, was bred a Physician, the Practise as such I now Persue. Since I have been on Red River which is about ten Months, amongst a Variety of Botanical observations have found here in almost exhaustless quantities a yellow wood the French call it *Boi d arc*, or Bow wood I have heard it Call'd Saphira, it has a beautiful fine grain, takes a polish like a Varnish when it is Nearly the Patent yellow Colour it is more elastic than any other wood; the Indians use it for Bows, and the Inhabitants sometimes for Ax helves and handles for other Tools, I think it would be highly esteem'd by Cabinet makers for Inlaying & Fineering, and by Turners. But probably would be more Valuable as a dye wood; a few days ago I had some experiments made in colouring with it and have taken the Liberty of Inclosing to you some samples of colours it produs'd. N$^{os}$. 1–2 & 3 are what a decoction of the wood made without anything else being added, the difference in the Shades are from the article remaining a little longer or Shorter time in the dye. No. 2 is Sheeps wool. all the other colours from 3 to 12 were made by the addition of Salt of Tartar, Blue Vitriol or Logwood in small quantities and a Variation of proportions. I have no doubt by a person skill'd in dying a very numerous Variety of Colours might be produc'd from this wood as the Basis; from an experiment I believe the Colours will Neither wash out; nor fade by washing; I have not seen the Tree in foliage therefore can give no account of it in that respect, some of them grow to the size of two or three feet in diameter, not tall, but somewhat resembling an Appletree

Many other woods, Shrubs & herbs grow here that I have never seen in any of the United States, their particular uses will no doubt be found out—did I not with almost every body else look up to you as the Patron of arts and usefull discoveries I should not have address'd you on this Subject, I hope you will have the goodness to pardon my presumption. and while I intreat you to accept of my best wishes in your private as well as public capacity, beg Leave to make you a tender of my services in whatever manner you may think proper to command them

In the mean time

I am Sir with the
Greatest respect & Esteem
Your Most Hble Servt.

John Sibley.

Natchitoches March 20th 1804

---

### ॐ B3 John Sibley "1804" Account of the Indians

Catalogued by Library of Congress as 1804, but written in 1805, after March 5, as internal references indicate.[5] There are indications, for example the mileage calculation in the first sentence, that this is a draft, not a copy. These notes were expanded (presumably by Sibley, since the expansions required detailed knowledge), and the full text sent to General Dearborn on April 5, 1805. Dearborn acknowledged receipt of the full document on May 25, calling it "very satisfactory."[6] The document may then have received light editing by Nicholas King. The misreading "Oufotu" on the last page of the text printed in W and N is clearly a misreading of Sibley's "Ousotu" but from a copy where the 's' was written long, unlike the present manuscript, where it is short.

#### SIBLEY'S ACCT OF THE INDIANS

pa. [paragraph] 1. the French while possessing Louisiana had a fort & some souldiers 375 + 120 = 495 miles above Natchitoches on the Red river, at the antient settlement of the Caddos. their present settlemt 120 mi. N.W. from Natchitoches the Caddos, Yattassees, Nandakoes, Nabedaches, Inies or Tachies, Nacogdoches, Keychies, Adais, & Natchitoches, all speak the Caddo language. the Caddo country hilly, and rich they raise corn, beans, pumpkins, &c.

pa. 2. the Yattassees, live on Bayou Pierre, branch of Red river 50. mi. above Natchitoches. their village surrounded by a settlem$^t$ of French families, under the Spanish govmt, where there is a Spanish guard of a noncomm$^d$. officer & 8 souldiers. the rights to land of these French

[5]See for example, paragraph 3, referring to the journal for March 5, 1805, and paragraph 10, where 1707 is given as "98. years ago." While the first of these may be a writing error for "March 5, 1803" (the date of Sibley's journey up the Red River), the second is unusually precise.

[6]Brandt, p. 370 and n.30.

families were granted to them by the French govmt of Louisiana. the French had formerly a station & factory there, & another on Sabine river near 100. miles N.W. of the Bayou Pierre settlement. the original language of the Yattassees was not the Caddo but they have adopted that. 40. men. 25. women. agricultural

pa. 3. Nandakoes on Sabine river 60. or 70. mi. W. of Yattassees where the former French station & factory were. 40. men.

Adais 20. men. 40. mi from Natchitoches & 20. mi. North from where the Spanish post Fort or mission of Adais was ~~Nobody~~ now at the old port of Adais, it is grown up. Sibley's Ent[ry] of Mar 5. 05.

Aliche, pronounced Ayeish. 25. souls. near Nacogdoches. their native language different, but now speak Caddo.

4. Keyes or Keychies. 60. men. live on E. bank of Trinity river a little above where the road from Natchidoches to S[t]. Antoine crosses it. have a peculiar native language, but speak Caddo. agricultural

Inies or Tachies, from whom the province of Techas is called. 80. men. 25. mi. W. of Natchidoches, on a small branch of Sabine calld Naches. their language is the Caddo. excellent land. agricultural.

Nabidaches on W. side of same river, 15 mi. above the Tachies. 80. men. same language. excellent land. agricultural.

Bedies on Trinity river 60. mi. S. of Nacogdoches. 100. men. language different from all others, but speak Caddo. they are hunters.

Accokesaws on the W. side of the Colorado or Riv. Rouge 200 mi. S.W. of Nacogdoches. a fine country. have a language of their own, but communicate by the language of signs which they all understand. 80. men. the Spaniards 30. or 40. y. ago had a mission there, which they broke up and removed to Nacogdoches. they talk of resettling it. they are hunters.

pa. 5. Maies on large creek S[t]. Gabriel, on bay of S[t]. Bernard, near the mouth of Guadaloupe river. 200 men. always at war with Spaniards, much attach[d] to French ever since La Salle landed in their neighborhood. Mattagordo is near them where the Spaniards talk of opening a new post & making a settlement, and where they say are the remnants of a French blockhouse. the cannon now at Labahie were brought from that place, & are known by the engravings now on them. have a language of their own, but speak Attacapa. converse by signs.

Carankouas, on an island or Peninsula in the bay of S[t]. Bernard, 10 mi.

long 5. mi. wide. very rich. a bluff adjacent is of coal which has been afire many years, affording light by night and smoke by day. coast continues shoaling out of sight of land. irreconcileable enemies to Spaniards, kind to French. 500. men. speak Attacapa.

pa. 6. Cances. a very numerous nation, consisting of a great many tribes, occupying from the bay of S[t]. Bernard across the Rio Grande towards La vera cruz. hostile to Spaniards, friendly to French, are hunters ad use the bow chiefly. the Spaniards used to make slaves of them. many were sold to the Fr. inhab. at Natchitoches @ 40. or 50. D. a number still there, but free. 20. y. ago the k. of Spain forbade making any more of them slaves, & emancipated those there. the women brought up there married natives & now have families. they have a peculiar language. speak by signs. in friendship with all other Indians except the Hietans.

Tankaways or Tanks. have no land nor fixed residence. they occupy alternately the country watered by the Trinity, Braces, & Colorado, towards S[ta]. Fé. 200. men. hunters. have the best breed of horses.

7. Tawakenoes, or Three Canes. on W. side of the Braces 200. mi. W. of Nacogdoches towards S[ta]. Fé. 200. men. hunters. have guns, but hunt principally with the bow. they trade at Nacogdoches. the[y] speak the same language with the Panis or Towiaches.

Panis or Towiaches. the latter their proper name; the former their French appelation. they live on the South bank of the Red river 800 mi. above Natchitoches by the meanders of the river, but only 340. mi. by ~~straight line~~. the nearest path. they have 2 towns near together. the lower where their chief, called the great bear, lives is Witcheta [1806 *Message:* Niteheta] town, & the the other Called Tawaahach. at war with Spaniards. friendly to French & Americans. at war with Osages. a rich country of prairies for many hundred miles round them. many horses & mules. they raise corn, pumpkins, beans, tob[o]. to spare, which they sell to the Hietans for rugs, horses & mules. have but few guns, little ammunition, which they keep for war, & hunt with the bow. they have some white hares and white bears. their language peculiar. 400. men.

8. Hietans or Comanches. wanderers, no villages, divided into numerous hordes unknown to one another. no estimate of their numbers. they have tents of dressed skins, conical, s[u]ff[icien]t for a family of 10. or 12. persons. they have 2. horses for every tent, besides which they travel on horseback. the horses never at large, but tethered. vast droves of wild horses among them. generally at war with the Spaniards, but friendly to French & Americans. they commit depred[atio]ns in S[ta]. Fé & S[t]

Antoine. cleanly and dressy. never remain long enough in any place to plant any thing. Cayenne pepper spontaneous among them. they wander over all the country from the Trinity & Braces, crossing Red river to the heads of Arcansa, Rio grande & Missouri & even to the waters of the Western Ocean, where they say they have seen ships. language peculiar. have that of signs.

[pa]ra. 10. Natchitoches. formerly lived at Natchitoches which took it's name from them, & was settled by the French 98. years ago (1707) the remains of the Natchez nation, after their massacre of the French in 1728. fled and encamped on Red river 6. mi. below Natchitoches, & created a mound still remaining. S$^t$. Deny, a Canadian, then Command$^t$ of Natchitoches with a few souldiers & militia & the Natchitoches attacked & exterminated the Natchez of this settlem$^t$. the lake on which they encamped still called the Natchez lake. the Natchitoches now live 25. mi. by land above the town of Natchitoches near Lake de Muire. there remain of them but 12. men and 19. women. their original language the same as the Yattassee, but they speak Caddo, & French. they only claim the small part of land they live on, for which they have a title from the former govmt. agricultural.

11. Boluxas, emigrants from near Pensacola, about 42. years since. they live at the mouth of Rigolet de Bondieu, a division of Red river 50. mi. below Natchitoch, are catholics—30. in number. peculiar language, but speak Mobilian which is spoken by all the Ind$^{ns}$. from the E. side of Misipi

Appalaches, emigrants from W. Florida from the river Apalachy. came over about the time the Beloxas did, & live on the river above Bayou Rapide. 14. men. have their own language, but speak Mobilian & French.

Alibamis, from the Alibama river in W. Florida about the same time with the Biloxas and Appalachies. live up Red R. near the Caddos. they speak Creek, Choctaw, Mobilian, French & some of them English. about 30. men. there is another party of them of 40. men on a small creek in Appalousa district 30. mi. N.W. from the church of Appalousa. agricultural.

12. Conchattas. are almost the same people as the Alibamas, but came over only 10. y. ago. on E. bank of Sabine river 80. mi. nearly S. from Natchitoches. 160. men. hunters, particularly of bears. a bear generally yields from 8. to 12. gall$^s$. oil, worth 1 D. a gallon, & the skin sells for 1. D. they say the Carankouas are 80. mi. S. of them, on the bay, which is

the nearest point of the sea from Natchitoch, a few families of Choctaws have lately settled near the Conchattas. these last speak Creek, which is their native language.

Pacanas. 30 men. on the Quelqueshose river which falls into the bay between Attacapa & Sabine, about 40 mi. S.W. of Natchitoch. they emigrated from W. Florida 40. y. ago. their village 50. S.E. of the Conchattas. have peculiar language, but speak Mobilian.

13. Attacapas (means Man-eaters) 20. mi. W. of Attacapa church towards Quelqueshoe. with some Tunicas & Humas married among them they are about 80. men. agricultural, & aboriginal of the part they live in. their language and the Carankouas the same.

Appalousas. (means Black head) aboriginal of their place which is 15. mi. W. from Appalousa church. 40. men. language peculiar, but understand Attacapa & French. agricultural.

Tunicas. formerly lived on the Bayou Tunica above point Coupé on the E. side of Misipi. now at Avoyall. 25. men. language peculiar, but speak Mobilian. agricultural.

Pascagoulas, emigrants from Pascagoula river. now on Red R. 60. mi. below Natchitoches. 25. men. language peculiar, but speak Mobilian & French. agricult[l]

14. Tenisaws, emigrants from Tensaw R. which falls into the bay of Mobile, 40. y. ago now removing to Bayou Boeuf, 25. mi. S. from Pascagoulas. speak Mobilian and French. agricultural.

Choctaws aboriginal of their canton on Bayou boeuf 2. mi. S. of Bayou Rapide on Red R. towards Appalousa. 30. men. language peculiar but speak Mobilian. delightful lands. Bayou boeuf falls into the Chaffalaya & discharges thro' Appalousa and Attacapa into Vermilion bay.

Washas. they were inhab. of Barritaria when the French first came. only 2. men & 3. women living in French families, extinct as a nation & their language lost.

Chactaws. there is one village of about 30. men 12. mi. above the post on Washita & on that river who have not been home for several years. & another village of 50 men on Bayou chico, in the Northern part of the district of Apelousa, who have been there about 9. years, having as they say the permission of the Gov[r]. of Louisiana to settle there. they are liked neither by the red nor white people.

15. Arkensaws on the S side the Arkansa, in 3. villages, about 12. mi.

above the post or station. the 1^st. village called Tawanima, 2^d. Ousotu. 3^d. Ocapa. 100. men. Aboriginal proprietors of the country on that river which they claim for about 300. miles above them to the Junction of the river Cadwa with Arkansa. above that fork the Osages claim. they are at war with the Osages, but peace with all other people white & red. their language is Osage.

The preceding is a list of all the Indians South of Arkansa between the rivers Misipi & Grande. the Avoyals and Humas are extinct.

The following should have been at the head of the list, page 1^st.

Caddoquis. 35. mi. W. of the main branch of Red R. on Bayou Sodo, navigable in rainy seasons within 6. mi. of their village. 120. mi. N.W. from Natchitoches. they have lived there but 5 years. their aboriginal settlem^t. was 375. mi. higher up the Red R. 100. men. very brave. boast that they never shed white man's blood. have great influence over the other Indian tribes. hostile to Choctaws, & Osages. most of them have guns.

---

❧ B4 John Sibley, "on the country between Misipi and Rio Bravo."

Notes for the materials sent April 10, 1805, to General Dearborn with the Red River account (the following item, B5), but not included in the 1806 *Message*.

## SIBLEY, ON THE COUNTRY BETWEEN MISIPI & RIO BRAVO

on the Sabine are Salines.
rich low grounds about 3. miles wide
in dry weather but a creek

from Bayou Patron to Nacogdoches to a great extent is the handsomest country in the world. gentle hills with pleasant rich vallies & meadows.
continues to Trinity river. beyond y^t more prairie.

from the river Nueces (Walnuts) to Rio bravo, poorer, abounds with Prickly pear 10. or 12. f. high. cochineal
on the Trinity many wild cattle, & millions of horses.

Nacogdoches 100. families
25. soldiers. all cavalry

S^t. Antonio 250. houses mostly of stone.

the country round rich prairie, gently hilly, beautiful clear gravelly streams of water, little timber
river heads 20. mi. above the city. used for irrigation.
sugar cane grows well here.
residence of the Gov^r. of Texas & a bishop.
60. or 70. souldiers.

from the river S. Antonio to Nueces very rich.
no settlements. silver ore.

Labahie 100. below S^t. Antonio, on same river, 120 houses
60. or 70. souldiers.

Rio Bravo or Grande.
on E. bank a town La Rado. 110. families
a company of souldiers.
here is the cross^g. place fr^m. S^t. Antonio or Labahie to Mexico.
this is the only town on the E. bank of Rio Bravo below the settlem^ts
of S^ta. Fé which are 1000 mi. above
from La Rado to the mouth of Rio bravo 100. leagues
on the W. side of Rio Bravo, about 60. mi. above La Rado is a town
Placido Riogrande, the mor[e] common cross^g. place from S^t. Antonio
to Mexico.
Ravillia, a handsome town a few leagues below La Rado, on W. bank.
no troops. much & fine cochineal.
West of Rio grande the country hilly, full of towns in the vallies
amongst the mines of silver ore
Valecillo is the 1^st. mine worked, 50. mi. from river on the road to
Mexico.
country full of sheep. some individual 20, or 30,000
Montelrey, Montclova, Cua[d]ereta, Santander, are towns of 3. to
5000 inhab. build^gs. stone, streets pav^d.
at Montelrey 100. coaches.
raise much chocolate.
150. mi. N. from S^t. Antonio tow^ds. Red river, a mine of Platine not
worked.
Santa fé half the size of N. Orleans 5. or 6000. inhab.
rich place. considble miltary. many small towns of 1. to 300 families in
vicinity.
Santa fé is a considble distance N.E. from river surrounded by high
mountains, & rich silver mines the silver carried on mules to Mexico.
surrounded by Appaches, Hietans, & Cances.
Rio grande near as large as Misipi, curr^t. not stronger clear water, does
not overflow

Nacogdoches, S[t]. Antonio, Labahie, & La Rado are the only settlem[ts]. in the province of Techas

3. companies of souldiers among them all.

their whole militia 7. or 800. most of them metiso, i.e. married Indian & Spanish.

Mattagordo, a small distance E. of the mouth of S[t]. Antonio water for large vessels. settlem[t]. proposed there.

The Accokesas near the mouth of Trinity. beautiful country. the Spaniards had a mission there 40. y. ago, which was broke up when Nacogdoches was established.

[Table of distances omitted.]

B5  Sibley's account of the Red River. The second part of the manuscript (previous item, B4) headed "Sibley, on the country between Misipi & Rio Bravo." Written at the same time, and sent in expanded form to Dearborn on April 10, 1805. The account based on these notes was printed as the second of the two reports to Dearborn in the 1806 *Message.*

### SIBLEY'S ACCOUNT OF RED RIVER.

the mouth of Red river, follow[s] Misipi, 220. mi. from N. Orl
water red, brackish. curr[t] 2. mi. an hour.

Avoyelles, at high water, is an island, ab[t] 30. or 40. ab[ve] high water. the settlement is round a prairie 40. mi. in circumference.

Hoomes's is on a bluff 120. above mouth of river.
adjoining are lowgrounds 40. mi. sq. extends to Appalousa rich. drained & watered by Bayou Robert & Bayou Boeuf, two streams of clear water, rising in the highlands between Red R. & Sabine, & falling into Chaffelya. well timbered

Bayou rapide settlem[t]. handsome planta[tion]s
upper end of the Bayou choaked
this rapids is over a shoal of soft rock, easily cut.
from July to Dec. not water enough on it for loaded boats

River cane settlem[t]. wealthy inhabitants, on the Southern channel of an island 50. mi. long. 3. mi. broad. 60. families

Natchitoches. irregular village, meanly built, except half a dozen houses.

40. families, of which 12 or 15 are merch[ts]. French.
Fort Claiborne 30. f. above now banks.
the lakes furnish plenty of shells for lime, also building-stone, & stone coal.

Salinas 12. miles N. of Natchitoches. water nearly saturated.
a Bayou from Spanish lake. the lake 50. mi. around.
from this lake Bayou Dupont admits boats to within 1 1/2 mi. of Fort Adaize.

one mile above Grand ecore begins an isl[d] 100. mi. long 30. mi. wide
on the S. branch is the Bayou Pierre (stony creek) settlem[t]. settled by France before the[y] ceded Louis[a]. to Spain, & was under the Command[t]. of Natchitoches till 20. y. ago when by an agreem[t] between M. Vogone then Comd[t]. Natchitoches [*meaning* Bayou Pierre] & M. Elibarbe Comd[t]. Natchitoches it was placed under the latter.
40. families. abound with prov[isio]ns.

Campti settlem[t]. a few families. 25. mi. in a straight line above Natchitoches. here begins the great raft, which choaking the river at the points of land prevents navign 100. mi. but boats pass up thro' lake Bistino.

Red river free from all obstruction's from here to mountains
from the mouth of Little river Cane begins to abound and broad rich lowgrounds from 3. to [ ] mi. wide not subject to overflow.

at Long prairie there is a lake, ant[ien][t] settlem[t]. of Caddos where the French had a settlement many years before they ceded Louis[a]. to Spain, they had here a fort, some soldiers, a factory, & a flour mill. a few years ago the mill irons & mill stones were brought down; about 25. years ago the French families moved down, & the Caddos 14 y. ago. the river is forded here.

Riviere la Mine. silver mines 60. miles up it.

River Bahachaha, or Fauxoacheta, or Missouri branch of Red river, heads near head of Arkansa so brackish cannot be drunk. on this & a branch of Arkansa the Panis found the Salt rock. from the mouth of this river to the main branch of the Arkansa 60. or 70. mi.
the country between 33. & 34.° Lat.

Red river here & for 150. mi. up is a mile wide

About 40. y. ago Brevel went with party of Indians up Red river on a hunting voyage & to get horses. kept on S. side. the country generally a prairie, copses of cedar, Cottonwood or Musketo, but not a stick 6. [inches] diam.

then mountainous country, & great deal of rock salt
& silver ore. river now small and ramified.
after cross$^g$. many mountains came to a stream running West.

went on to where streams became large & lands level, soil rich black
loam. here many tribes of Hietans, Appaches, Cansas.
spotted tygers & white bears.
steered nearly Southeast for S$^{ta}$. Fé. passed prairies, then hills, silver
mines & arrived at a town of 100. houses in S$^{ta}$. Fé settlemt.
many such towns for a great extent Southwardly tow$^{ds}$. Mexico.
inhabitants christian Indians & Metiso
rich mines. oar carr$^d$ on mules.
very high mountain between S$^{ta}$. Fé & Red river.
from S$^{ta}$. Fé settlem$^t$ reach$^d$ Panis towns in 18. days he supposed a right
line of 300. miles, all prairie.
Red river boatable a little above Pani old towns. above that for hundreds of miles not a tree large enough to make a canoe.
animals wild horses, buffalo, bears, wolves, elk deer, Foxes, Sangliers
or wild hogs, antelope, white hares, rabbits, spotted tyger, panther,
wild cat.

[Table of distances omitted; almost identical with that printed in W
and N.]

---

## ❧ B6 Thomas Jefferson to John Sibley, Washington, May 27, 1805[7]

The president requests Sibley's help in completing
vocabularies of the Indians west of the Mississippi.

To Doctor John Sibley

Washington, May 27, 1805

Dear Sir,—I have been some time a debtor for your letters of March
20th and September 2d, of the last year. A constant pressure of things
which will not admit delay, prevents my acknowledging with punctuality the letters I receive, although I am not insensible to the value of the
communications, and the favor done me in making them. To these
acknowledgments I propose to add a solicitation of a literary kind, to
which I am led by your position, favorable to this object, and by a per-
suasion that you are disposed to make to science those contributions
which are within your convenience. The question whether the Indians

[7]In *The Writings of Thomas Jefferson* (Washington, D.C: The Thomas Jefferson Memorial Association, 1903), XI: 79–81.

of America have emigrated from another continent, is still undecided. Their vague and imperfect traditions can satisfy no mind on that subject. I have long considered their languages as the only remaining monument of connection with other nations, or the want of it, to which we can now have access. They will likewise show their connections with one another. Very early in life, therefore, I formed a vocabulary of such objects as, being present everywhere, would probably have a name in every language; and my course of life having given me opportunities of obtaining vocabularies of many Indian tribes, I have done so on my original plan, which though far from being perfect, has the valuable advantage of identity, of thus bringing the languages to the same points of comparison. A letter from you to General Dearborn, giving valuable information respecting the Indians west of the Mississippi and south of the Arkansas, presents a much longer list of tribes than I had expected; and the relations in which you stand with them, and the means of intercourse these will furnish, induce me to hope you will avail us of your means of collecting their languages for this purpose. I enclose you a number of my blank vocabularies, to lessen your trouble as much as I can. I observe you mention several tribes which, having an original language of their own, nevertheless have adopted some other, common to other tribes. But it is their original languages I wish to obtain. I am in hopes you will find persons situated among or near most of the tribes, who will take the trouble of filling up a vocabulary. No matter whether the orthography used be English, Spanish, French, or any other, provided it is stated what the orthography is. To save unnecessary trouble, I should observe that I already possess the vocabularies of the Attacapas and the Chetimachas, and no others within the limits before mentioned. I have taken measures for obtaining those north of the Arcansa, and already possess most of the languages on this side the Mississippi. A similar work, but on a much greater scale, has been executed under the auspices of the late empress of Russia, as to the red nations of Asia, which, however, I have never seen. A comparison of our collection with that will probably decide the question of the sameness or difference of origin, although it will not decide which is the mother country, and which the colony. You will receive from General Dearborn some important instructions with respect to the Indians. Nothing must be spared to convince them of the justice and liberality we are determined to use towards them, and to attach them to us indissolubly. Accept my apologies for the trouble I am giving you, with my salutations and assurances of respect.

[Thomas Jefferson]

# ✤ Works Consulted

Abel, Annie H. *A Report from Natchitoches in 1807 by Dr. John Sibley.* In W. Hodge, ed., *Indian Notes and Monographs.* New York: Heye Foundation, 1922.

*American State Papers. Documents, Legislative and Executive . . . Commencing March 3, 1789, and Ending March 3, 1819.* Volume 12. Washington, D.C.: Gales and Seaton, 1832.

Barton, Benjamin. *Element of Botany.* Philadelphia: The Author, 1803.

Bartram, William. *Travels through North and South Carolina.* Philadelphia: James & Johnson, 1791.

Benson, Guy Meriwether, William R. Irwin, and Heather Moore. *Exploring the West from Monticello: A Perspective in Maps from Columbus to Lewis and Clark.* Charlottesville: University of Virginia Library, 1995. Revised edition, Howell Press, 2002.

Brandt, Penny S. "A Letter of John Sibley, Indian Agent." *Louisiana History* 29/4 (1988): 365–387.

Cox, Isaac J. "An Early Explorer of the Louisiana Purchase," *American Philosophical Society Library Bulletin* 1946: 73.

Cutright, Paul Russell. *Lewis and Clark: Pioneering Naturalists.* Urbana and Chicago: University of Illinois Press, 1969. Reprinted Lincoln and London: University of Nebraska Press, 1989.

[*Discoveries.*] *Discoveries made in exploring the Missouri, Red River, and Washita, by Captains Lewis and Clark, Doctor Dibley, and William Dunbar, Esq. with a statistical account of the countries adjacent : with an appendix by Mr. Dunbar.* Natchez [Miss.] Printed by Andrew Marschalk, 1806. Reprinted in facsimile in this volume.

[Dunbar, *Journal* (ed. 1904).] Dunbar, William. "Journal of a Voyage." American Philosophical Society. Call number 917.7 D91. Published in *Documents Relating to the Purchase & Exploration of Louisiana: Printed from the original manuscripts in the Library of the American Philosophical Society and by direction of the Society's Committee on Historical Documents.* Boston & New York: Houghton, Mifflin & Company, 1904.

Dunbar, William. *Journal of an exploring expedition on the red river,*

*December 10, 1804–January 26, 1805.* Mississippi Department of Archives & History Archives and Library Division. Dunbar (William) Papers, call no. z 0114.000 S M.

Dunbar, William. *Journals 1796–1809.* Manuscript journals (two volumes) bound in a single volume with Zebulon Pike's printed journal of his Upper Mississippi exploration. Library of the American Philosophical Society (Philadelphia), call no. 917.7 D91.

Dunbar, William. *Journal,* at Special Collections, Riley-Hickingbotham Library, Ouachita Baptist University, Arkadelphia, Arkansas, call no. 976.703 D899w.

Ellicott, Andrew. *The Journal of Andrew Ellicott.* Philadelphia: Budd & Bartram, 1803. Reprinted Chicago, Quadrangle Books, 1962.

Flores, Dan L. *Jefferson & Southwestern Exploration: The Freeman & Custis Accounts of the Red River Expedition of 1806.* Norman: University of Oklahoma Press, 1984; second printing, 1985. Reprinted June 2002 as *Southern Counterpart to Lewis and Clark: The Freeman and Custis Expedition of 1806.*

Gilman, Carolyn. *Lewis and Clark Across the Great Divide.* Washington and London: Smithsonian Books, with Missouri Historical Society, 2003.

*History of the Expedition Under the Command of Captains Lewis and Clark, to the Sources of the Missouri, Thence Across the Rocky Mountains and Down the River Columbia to the Pacific Ocean. Performed During the Years 1804–5–6. By Order of the Government of the United States.* Nicholas Biddle and Paul Allen, editors. New York: Bradford and Inskeep, 1814.

Holliday, W. J. *Western Americana.* New York: Parke-Bernet Galleries, Inc., 1954.

Hunter, George. *Journal up the Red and Washita Rivers with William Dunbar.* Manuscript official report to the War Department (one volume). Library of the American Philosophical Society (Philadelphia), call no. 917.6/Ex7.

Hunter, George. *Journals, 1796–1809.* Manuscript journals (four volumes). Library of the American Philosophical Society (Philadelphia), call no. Mss. B H912.

Jackson, Donald E. *Letters of the Lewis and Clark Expedition with Related Documents.* Second Edition. Urbana: University of Illinois Press, 1978.

Jackson, Donald E. "Some Books Carried by Lewis and Clark," *Missouri Historical Society Bulletin* 16, no. 1 (October 1959): 3–13.

Jackson, Donald E. *The Journals of Zebulon Montgomery Pike: With Letters and Related Documents.* Two volumes. Norman: University of Oklahoma Press, 1966.

Lester, Hubbard. *The Travels of Capts. Lewis & Clarke.* Philadelphia: Hubbard Lester, 1809.

[*Literature.*] *The Literature of the Lewis and Clark Expedition.* Essays by Stephen Dow Beckham. Bibliography by Doug Erickson, Jeremy Skinner, and Paul Merchant. Portland, Oregon: Lewis & Clark College, 2003.

Mackenzie, Alexander. *Voyages from Montreal.* London: Cadell, Davis, Cobbett and Morgan, 1801. Reprinted Edinburgh and New York, 1802.

McDermott, John Francis. "The Western Journals of Dr. George Hunter 1796–1805," *Transactions of the American Philosophical Society* new series 53: 4 (July 1963).

McMurtrie, Douglas C. *A Bibliography of Mississippi Imprints 1798–1830.* Beauvoir Community: Mississippi Book Farm, 1945.

[*Message.*] *Message from the President of the United States, communicating discoveries made in exploring the Missouri, Red River, and Washita, by Captains Lewis and Clark, Doctor Sibley, and Mr. Dunbar with a statistical account of the countries adjacent* City of Washington: A. and G. Way, printers, 1806.

*Message from the President of the United States, communicating discoveries made in exploring the Missouri, Red River, and Washita, by Captains Lewis and Clark, Doctor Sibley, and Mr. Dunbar with a statistical account of the countries adjacent.* New-York: Printed by Hopkins and Seymour : Sold by G. F. Hopkins, 1806.

Moulton, Gary, ed. *The Journals of the Lewis and Clark Expedition,* 13 volumes. Lincoln: University of Nebraska Press, 1983–2001.

Ronda, James P., *Lewis and Clark among the Indians.* Lincoln: University of Nebraska Press, 1984.

Rowland, Mrs. Dunbar (Eron Rowland). *Life, Letters and Papers of William Dunbar of Elgin, Morayshire, Scotland, and Natchez, Mississippi: Pioneer Scientist of the United States.* Jackson: Press of the Mississippi Historical Society, 1930.

Rush, Benjamin. *Letters,* edited by L. H. Butterfield. Two volumes. Princeton, NJ: Princeton University Press for the American Philosophical Society, 1951.

Shaw, Ralph R., and Richard H. Shoemaker. *American Bibliography: A Preliminary Checklist for 1801–1819.* New York: The Scarecrow Press, 1958–1963.

Sibley, John. "A Letter from Dr. John Sibley, Late of Fayetteville (now of Louisiana) to J. Gales, Printer, in Raleigh; Dec. 13, 1803." Raleigh, NC: J. Gales, 1803. Reprinted in White, David, *News of the Plains and the Rockies,* item A1.

Sibley, John. "Some Account of the Country and Productions near the Red-River, in Louisiana. In an Extract of a Letter from Dr. John Sibley, to Calvin Jones, M.D. dated Natchitoches, July 10, 1804." *Medical Repository* 9 (1806): 425–7.

[Sibley, John]. contributor, *An Account of Louisiana: Being an Abstract of Documents*. Philadelphia: John Conrad & Co, 1803.

Sowerby, E. Millicent. *Catalogue of the Library of Thomas Jefferson*. Five volumes. Washington, D.C.: The Library of Congress, 1955.

Streeter, Thomas W. *Bibliography of Texas 1795–1845*. Cambridge: Harvard University Press, 1960.

Sydnor, Charles S. "The Beginning of Printing in Mississippi." *The Journal of Southern History* 1 (February 1935).

*Transactions of the American Philosophical Society Held at Philadelphia*, volumes 1–6 (1771–1809), various Philadelphia printers, reprinted in facsimile, New York: Kraus Reprint Corporation, 1966.

Tregle, Joseph G. "John Sibley." In *American National Biography*. John A. Garraty and Mark C. Carnes, eds. Oxford and New York: Oxford University Press, 1999.

Thwaites, Reuben Gold, ed. *Original Journals of the Lewis and Clark Expedition 1804–1806, In Seven Volumes and an Atlas*. New York: Dodd, Mead & Company 1905. Reprinted New York: Arno Press, 1969. Includes "Bibliographical Data" by Victor Hugo Paltsits.

Wagner, Henry R., and Charles L. Camp. *The Plains and Rockies: A Critical Bibliography of Exploration, Adventure and Travel in the American West 1800–1865*. Fourth edition, revised by Robert H. Becker. San Francisco: John Howell-Books, 1982.

Webb, George E. "William Dunbar." In *American National Biography*. John A. Garraty and Mark C. Carnes, eds. Oxford and New York: Oxford University Press, 1999.

Welsh, Mary Ann. "Andrew Marschalk, Mississippi's First Printer." Master's project in Library Science, University of Mississippi (August 1957).

Wheat, Carl I. *1540–1861 Mapping the Transmississippi West*. San Francisco: The Institute of Historical Cartography, 1958–1963.

White, David. *News of the Plains and Rockies 1803–1865*. Volume 1. Spokane, WA: The Arthur H. Clark Company, 1996.

White, David. *Plains and Rockies 1800–1865*. Spokane, WA: The Arthur H. Clark Company, 2001. Supplemental volume to the multi-volume set.

# ✂ Index

*Page numbers refer to pages of this edition. Tribes described in Lewis and Clark's "Statistical View" and Sibley's "Historical Sketches" are indexed only to their main entries in those reports. No attempt has been made to index affiliated tribes or languages.*